SCIENTIFIC
UFOLOGY

Other Books by Kevin Randle

PROJECT MOON DUST

CONSPIRACY OF SILENCE

A HISTORY OF UFO CRASHES

With Donald R. Schmitt

THE TRUTH ABOUT THE UFO CRASH AT ROSWELL

UFO CRASH AT ROSWELL

SCIENTIFIC UFOLOGY

How the Application

of Scientific

Methodology Can

Analyze, Illuminate,

and Prove the

Reality of UFOs

Kevin D. Randle, Ph.D.
Captain U.S.A.F.R.

AVON BOOKS ◆ NEW YORK

AVON BOOKS, INC.
1350 Avenue of the Americas
New York, New York 10019

Copyright © 1999 by Kevin D. Randle
Cover photographs: top and bottom photographs courtesy of the United States Air
Force; center photograph courtesy of Kevin D. Randle
Interior design by Kellan Peck
Published by arrangement with the author
Library of Congress Catalog Card Number: 99-94876
ISBN: 0-380-79852-2
www.avonbooks.com

First Avon Books Trade Paperback Printing: September 1999

AVON TRADEMARK REG. U.S. PAT. OFF. AND IN OTHER COUNTRIES, MARCA REGISTRADA,
HECHO EN U.S.A.

Printed in the U.S.A.

OPM   10 9 8 7 6 5 4 3 2 1

Contents

SCIENTIFIC UFOLOGY

1

Science and the UFO

There is a problem with the so-called science of UFOlogy: Those practicing it are anything but scientific in their approach to it. All too often we in the UFO community talk about applying the rigors of scientific methodology to our study, and then we fail to do so. For the most part, we believe in science but all too often reject it when it does not conform to our beliefs about UFOs.

Scientists, on the other hand, reject UFOlogy because of our lack of scientific standards. To the scientific community, we fail to make our case within a proper scientific framework. Our information, according to them, is anecdotal, poorly documented, and without foundation. They claim we have presented no physical evidence for our beliefs in UFOs; in fact, according to scientists, we have no physical evidence with which to make our case.

It seems that we—the UFO community and the scientific community—are at opposite ends of a long spectrum, never to meet. Until or unless something spectacular happens, that is the way the situation will remain—neither side conceding a point to the other.

Of course, this is often the situation in which science and the general public finds itself. Science will make a pronouncement and not be believed simply because it is inconvenient for the public to do so, the pronouncement violates a long-held belief, or it is in conflict with what science said just last week, last month, or last year.

Much of this is the public's fault. We listen to the scientists' words and then interpret them incorrectly. When science suggests a causal relationship between a chemical and cancer, for example, we don't hear how the interpretation of evidence is phrased. We leap to the conclusion that the use of the chemical will cause cancer—not that those who use the chemical are at a higher risk for developing cancer, which isn't exactly the same thing.

Or, in the case of the tobacco companies and cigarettes, we hear the government scientists telling us that smoking causes cancer, while the tobacco scientists are telling us that the evidence for that is not conclusive. Here we have two groups of scientists telling us two things that are mutually exclusive, so both can't be right. One set of scientists has to be wrong. Both are credentialed, both have the same sort of training, and both groups are at opposite ends of the spectrum. How can we, the lay public, understand the situation?

In this case, it is easy. All we have to do is look at who pays the scientists. If they are government scientists and they discover no causal link between cancer and smoking, they'll get paid. If they discover the causal link to cancer, they still get paid. The scientists have no agenda other than learning the truth.

On the other hand, the scientists working for the tobacco companies have an interest in discovering no causal link to cancer. If they find one, they are pressured to cover up or reinterpret the results. We've all seen the scientists on *60 Minutes* telling us about the pressure applied on them by the tobacco companies to hide their results. The scientists have an agenda to convince the public that smoking is not harmful. Given these facts, it is fairly simple to determine which sets of data are most accurate and most likely correct.

But what do we do when the agenda of the scientists isn't as clear-cut? How do we determine whether science is being fair to the question? How does the layperson determine the truth without having to spend years studying the questions for him- or herself? And isn't that what scientists are supposed to do? Aren't they supposed to answer these questions for us accurately, fairly, and with no agenda attached?

Yes, I think so. I think that we all rely on the expertise of others because, in today's world, no single individual can possibly know everything needed to survive. You could spend years learning the law, but that doesn't help if you catch a virus. You can understand the workings of the IRS, but that doesn't help build a personal retirement fund. You can become a master gardener, but that doesn't make you a farmer. The point is that all too often we must leave the answers to those whose expertise can help us learn those answers.

But we have all heard stories of how the experts have been wrong, time and again. We forget that the experts often merely parrot the conventional wisdom of the time and have no expertise beyond what the lay public possesses.

We in the UFO community often point to the fact that the French Academy of sciences, at the beginning of the nineteenth century, rejected the idea that rocks could fall from the sky. Everyone knows that there are no rocks in the sky, and those who suggest otherwise must be deluded, insane, lying, or simply mistaken.

What we rarely talk about is how the French Academy of sciences reversed itself in 1803 when a proper scientific study, along with physical evidence, was offered, proving that rocks could fall from the sky. Jean-Baptiste Biot published his report, and the scientific community in France accepted his study. We in the UFO community could certainly benefit from understanding how Biot accomplished this.

Three weeks after the residents of a Normandy village reported that rocks had fallen from the sky, Biot traveled there from Paris to begin his investigation. I mention this only because it is often weeks, months, or even years after a UFO event has occurred that any sort of investigation begins. Being on the scene of the event is not necessary to proving that the event took place, especially if there is some form of physical evidence left behind.

According to the tale that Biot heard, there were witnesses who had seen a daytime fireball that had been accompanied by a trail, explosions, or detonations, and there was scattered debris.

Some spoke of marks in the trees and on the ground. Others mentioned that small fires started after the rocks fell.

Before going to Normandy, Biot, who had been described as one of the most able of France's natural scientists, talked to geologists in Paris. He studied the rocks collected in various museums, including those that supposedly had fallen from the sky. These "Thunderbolts" collected by the various museums had long been claimed to have fallen from the sky based solely on eyewitness testimony.

Biot also aquainted himself with the geology of the region. He knew there were no volcanoes, no furnances, or the results of smelting in the area. There were no glass-producing factories. He knew what to expect because, coincidentally, a geological survey of the area had been conducted only a few years before the rock fell from the sky.

He also talked to numerous witnesses scattered through four or five small villages. Many of them were independent, meaning that they didn't know one another and didn't talk to one another about the rocks. Their education and socioeconomic levels spanned the whole social spectrum. The witnesses included people who had been trained in the sciences, soldiers, priests, and those who worked the fields and claimed no formal education. Even so, there was agreement among them about what they had seen.

Biot examined the fields for himself. He saw the damaged trees, and he saw where the small fires had burned. He was able to examine some of the rocks that had fallen and compare them to the geology of the area. It was clear that these rocks didn't belong where they had been found because there was nothing like them in the geological survey.

What Biot did—with his examination of the area's geology, search of the physical sites where the fireball had interacted with the environment, and interviews with the witnesses—was establish independent and multiple chains of evidence. Each link in the chain was solid evidence leading to the next link.

The reason this study is important to us in the UFO community is that the falling of rocks from the sky is not an event reproducible on demand. It is a natural event that is rare and outside the control of science. Scientists can observe the results of a meteor fall, but science can't demand that a meteor fall so that they can observe it. At least in 1803 they couldn't.

Although UFOs are not a natural phenomenon, they are outside the control of the UFO community. We must wait for an event and then investigate it. We can attempt to reproduce observations in a laboratory, but that is only if we are investigating a natural phenomenon that we understand. If we are not, then we are required to collect evidence when and where it appears.

From Biot's investigation of meteorites we can learn the proper way to conduct an investigation into UFO sightings. Often we are left with only witness testimony, or with suspected physical evidence, or a combination in which we have good physical evidence and only one or two witnesses, or many witnesses and no physical evidence.

We can also learn the value of experts. Biot wasn't a geologist, but he did consult with some before his trip to Normandy. He wasn't a mineralogist, but he consulted with them before his journey. He prepared himself according to what he knew of the event he was going to investigate. He was ready for what he saw, and he recorded it carefully. Please note that *he prepared himself and he recorded his observations carefully.*

In today's world we don't have to be experts, but we do need to consult with them about the events we are going to investigate. We need to be aware of any natural phenomena that will explain, to everyone's satisfaction, what we are investigating. We must research the scientific literature and find what has been done before we begin our work. There is a large body of UFO-related material in various scientific journals: We must consult these works so that we are familiar with what has gone on earlier and what has been learned earlier.

There are, in the paranormal, occult, or New Age communities, tales that seem inexplicable on the surface. Strange disappearances, for example, dot the literature. Many times these tales are recounted without so much as a telephone call to learn what is new and different. Sometimes that is all that is needed to eliminate a case from the literature.

Take, for example, the tale of Oliver Lerch, a youngster living in South Bend, Indiana, in 1889. According to the various versions of the story, Lerch was sent out to the well for water on Christmas Eve because, as his father reportedly said, "Throats were parched from singing."

Lerch carried a bucket, leaving footprints in the newly fallen snow. Before he reached the well, something grabbed him from above and carried him aloft. He screamed for help, his cries of "They've got me" fading into the cloud-shrouded sky. His footprints stopped short of the well.

A dozen writers have recounted the tale, using it to prove, I suppose, the hostility of the aliens from space, if we assume that it was aliens from space that grabbed young Oliver. Certainly there are no birds large enough to carry off a twelve-year-old boy. There were many witnesses to the tale, including members of the clergy. Police investigated, and the reports of the strange disappearance were written down in the South Bend police files for anyone who wanted to verify the story. At least that was what we were told time and again.

I, for one, wanted to verify it. First I did a literature search, looking for anything that related to this report. I found that the boy was variously identified as Oliver Lerch, Oliver Larch, or Oliver Thomas. He was either twelve or twenty-two. The event took place on Christmas Eve 1889, Christmas Day 1889, Christmas Day 1890, or Christmas Day 1909. He managed to walk through the new snow a distance of 50, 75, or 225 feet before it, or they, captured him. He lived either outside of South Bend, Indiana, or in Wales.

Such a wide variety of information doesn't speak well for the reality of the tale. Small discrepancies, such as the distance he walked before being attacked, are normal and not of overwhelming importance by themselves. The inconsistency of the date isn't all that bad either, until you throw in the 1909 date. The misspellings of the last name don't mean much until you radically alter it. And when you change the location, those with a skeptical eye begin to wonder about the veracity of the tale.

At this point I've done no real investigation; I've merely completed a literature search so that I know something about the case. I have a variety of facts to be checked, and I have the baseline of the story: A young man disappeared without a trace under mysterious circumstances late at night.

Morris K. Jessup, to add a note of authenticity to the tale, reported in *The Case for the UFO* that all the information was written down in the records of the South Bend police for all to see. This was a challenge that I could take. I could call the South Bend Police Department and ask them about the disappearence of Oliver Lerch.

The first thing I learned was that the records of the South Bend police didn't go back into the nineteenth century, as Jessup claimed. There had been a fire, and many of the police documents had been destroyed. The records were fairly complete into the 1920s, but that was about it.

The second thing I did was call the local newspaper. Elaine Stevens of the *South Bend Tribune* was kind enough to search their files for me. She sent a number of articles, all of which seemed to have been generated by the publication of Jessup's book. Francis K. Czyzewski had written a couple of articles about his attempts to verify the report in the 1960s. He wrote that neither he nor the local library could find any evidence that the incident had taken place. There simply was no record of it, either by the South Bend police or the newspapers.

Sarah Lockerbie, also of the *South Bend Tribune*, wrote an article for their Sunday magazine about the disappearance. She spoke to members of the Lerch family who still resided in South Bend, attempting to find a family account of the strange disappearance. When Sherman Lerch, who had lived in the area all his life, told various telephone callers that the story wasn't true, some began to believe that he had something to hide. Maybe the CIA or the Air Force had "gotten" to him.

Because there were a number of original witnesses named in the books claiming something unusual, more records checks could be made. A Methodist pastor, Samuel Mallelieu, was named as having attended the ill-fated Christmas party, but a check with the various churches revealed no one by that name. It was just another of the many dead ends.

To end the story, weather records revealed that both December 1889 and December 1890 were warm, with highs in the fifties and sixties. In other words, there is no evidence that there was freshly fallen snow for young Oliver and his footprints.

The American version of the tale simply did not stand up to any sort of investigation. Discrepancy was piled upon discrepancy. No documentation or corroboration could be found. The story simply wasn't true.

But what about the Welsh version? Could it be that Jessup, among others, had heard and discovered the tale after it had been transplanted to the United States? Maybe the Welsh version was correct and the information had been somehow skewed.

In one of his many books, Brad Steiger wrote about Oliver Thomas and the Welsh version of the story. I spoke to Brad about it. He told me he had since learned that the tale was a hoax. It had never happened, and he had tried to alert people to that fact. Sometimes they just didn't want to listen. And sometimes they decided that those rejecting the tale were government agents with a different agenda.

What we have here is the beginning of a proper scientific investigation. We are given a set of data that do not conform to our view of reality. We have an intriguing story, lots of alleged facts, and what is called supporting corroboration. By the very simple and elementary step of reviewing the literature, we can begin to learn what happened.

From a scientific standpoint, there are a number of steps to follow. Every day, during the weather forecast, we hear what the record highs and lows are for that day. Many of those records come from the late nineteenth century; thus, documents exist that allow us to review one aspect of the story to learn if it is true. In this case, we learn that no snow had fallen, so there could be no footprints, eliminating one of the most dramatic aspects of this case.

We could go on, but we've already seen just where the literature search has taken us. By use of the telephone, newspapers, police department records, libraries, the church, and even the weather station, we have been unable to corroborate a single fact, even though one of those who wrote about the tale claimed that each fact was substantiated by a written record. The conclusion that we must draw—the only conclusion that is possible—is that the Oliver Lerch, Larch, Thomas, of either South Bend or Wales, and who disappeared on one of four dates, did not exist. The story is a hoax.

We have done what science demands: We have attempted to establish a link-by-link chain of evidence concerning this story. When one link broke, wrecking the chain, we shifted to the next until that link broke. When enough of the links broke, when the evidence didn't appear to prove that young Oliver had disappeared in a mysterious fashion, when we found no evidence that young Oliver even existed, we drew the only conclusion possible, though I confess I would have preferred to have the story be true. A little mystery is necessary to keep our lives interesting.

And that is where UFO investigation should be heading—not necessarily into the realm where we want it to go, but into the realm where the evidence takes us. We must begin to establish the multiple chains of evidence link by link until we have enough data to prove a point. We must carefully follow the evidence rather than our beliefs.

For much too long, we have been ignoring the situation. We have rejected logical thought when logical thought would poke holes in our beliefs. As a single, quick example, I heard the following at a UFO conference. The lecturer was telling us that alien beings can pass through solid objects, such as walls, taking their victim of alien abduction with them. This does, of course, fly in the face of logic, but let's grant them, for the sake of argument, the transporter beam of *Star Trek* fame. Let's say they can pass through solid objects, taking their victim with them.

But then he explained how one woman was able to defeat the alien abductors. She wrapped herself in string, tying multiple knots, setting the scissors on the other side of the room so she couldn't get at them. This simple ploy defeated the alien abductors. It seems that they can abduct people through solid objects, but not through string. It just doesn't make logical sense.

And this demonstrates more than anything why science doesn't take our research seriously. It is filled with logical paradoxes that we either fail to notice or ignore completely. Or worse, when those logical paradoxes are pointed out, we react with anger.

And, of course, claiming that those pointing out the problems are government agents doesn't help our cause either.

So, are there any UFO cases that fit the criteria that we have begun to establish here? Certainly. There are very few of them, but they do exist. We can find a number of cases with multiple witnesses, multiple chains of evidence—physical evidence. We can attempt to examine them carefully. We can bring the tools of science to bear on them and see if we can solve them with mundane, everyday explanations or if we find sufficient reason to believe that alien spacecraft are visiting our planet.

Maybe I should point out here that few scientists reject the idea of intelligent alien life on other planets. In fact, I believe that most scientists talk of a universe teeming with life. However, they balk at the idea that the alien creatures have discovered a way of defeating the vastness of space and have reached Earth. Most scientists suggest that the proof for that is lacking.

I disagree. I believe that the evidence has been recovered. It just has not been presented in a proper form for the scientific community. That is the purpose of this book: to present a few of the best cases that have the multiple chains of evidence and see if we can't make the case for the UFO a little more . . . well, scientific.

2

Eyewitness Testimony as a
Form of Evidence

We have all heard about the problems with eyewitness testimony. We all have heard how unreliable human observers are—that they often see what they want to see rather than what is in front of them. Psychology has addressed these problems for years, trying to learn as much as possible about eyewitness testimony and memory.

Many people have written that if you have a dozen witnesses to a traffic accident, you eventually have twelve different eye-witness versions. But that isn't always true. When I taught a class at Kirkwood Community College, we ran an experiment to test the theory. While lecturing, I had an accomplice enter, speak a few words, and then shoot me with blanks. He then ran out the door. Everyone was supposed to write down exactly what they had seen.

As I scanned the papers, I was surprised to find out how accurate the students' observations had been. I thought the reason might be that everyone had been together, in the same room, without distractions from the surrounding environment. We all knew one another, and the point of view was basically the same for all the members of the class.

A week later I asked them to write down what they had seen the week before. No longer did the accounts agree so nicely. The number of shots varied, the dialogue spoken expanded or contracted, and the clothing that had been worn by me or the assassin had changed. The accounts were not in full agreement.

Psychological research has borne this phenomenon out. Studies have shown the problems with trying to remember what happened a year ago, or two, or ten. Even the memories of important events, captured in what is known as "flashbulb" memories, are open to mutation, modification, and distortion. Psychologist Ulric Neisser, who was teaching at Emory University in January 1986 when the space shuttle *Challenger* exploded, realized he had an opportunity to study flashbulb memory. The day after the disaster, Neisser gave the students in his freshman psychology class a questionnaire about the explosion. He then filed the questionnaires for three years, until the students were seniors. At that point he gave them the same questionnaire, but added a single additional question. He wanted to know how reliable they believed their memory of the destruction of the *Challenger* to be.

Here was a chance to learn if those flashbulb memories were accurate, as we believe them to be. We could learn if those sorts of memories were more reliable than those of our everyday activities.

According to the results provided by Neisser and his graduate assistant Nicole Harsh, a quarter of the students didn't have one memory that proved to be accurate. In one case, a student reported that he had been home with his parents when he heard the news. His earlier questionnaire, completed the day after the event, however, revealed that he had been in class at the time.

More important, however, was the reaction of the students to the proof that their memories of the events were inaccurate. None disputed the accuracy of the original statements made in the days after the destruction of the *Challenger*. One student, when confronted with the discrepancy between what she remembered three years later and what she had written only hours after the event, did say, "I still remember everything happening the way I told you. I can't help it." She was defending the memories that were clearly an invention of her own mind.

Because of studies like Neisser's, all retrieved memory, especially that retrieved using hypnotic regression, is coming under more scrutiny. Some states, such as California, now refuse to let a witness who has been hypnotically regressed testify in a trial. There are just too many opportunities for that witness to be led, no matter how careful the questioner is. Any attempt to gain additional information from a witness, no matter how innocent the question is, can render the testimony suspect.

But that doesn't mean that all memories are flawed. It means that we must be aware of the problems that memory can cause. When we interview a single individual about the events surrounding a UFO sighting, we must be alert for the problems that are inherent in memory. When we have more than one witness, we can begin to compare and contrast, and we are able to build an accurate picture.

The key is obviously multiple-witness cases, especially those in which the witnesses are unknown to one another. After a week, or month, or, in the case of UFO research, years, we can rely on the memories of the witnesses if those memories are corroborated by other witnesses, physical evidence, and documentation.

The documentation for a UFO sighting can come from many sources. It might be a newspaper article written at the right time. That will provide information, but we must also be aware that those articles are sometimes inaccurate. Like everything else, we must search for corroboration that the facts as reported are accurate and complete. We do that by comparing and contrasting those articles with the eyewitness testimony and other testimony and evidence.

Documentation can also come in the form of diaries kept by the witnesses. Memories, as written down at the time of the event, are a better source of information than memories reviewed years later. A written record is superior to memory.

The real point is that we must gather all the data, review it, and then decide which makes the most sense in the context of the situation. When we have multiple witnesses telling, essentially, the same story, we can be sure that we are developing an accurate picture of that specific event.

There have been a number of very interesting multiple-witness cases reported over the years. They provide us with a picture of what is happening in the UFO field.

Portland, Oregon
July 4, 1947

A most impressive series of sightings came from Portland, Oregon, where police officers and civilians in widely separated locations watched as a variety of disks flashed through the sky. The first was reported by C. J. Bogne and a carload of witnesses north of Redmond, Oregon, when they saw four disk-shaped objects flash past Mount Jefferson. According to the witnesses, the objects made no noise and performed no maneuvers.

At 1:00 P.M., an Oaks Park employee, Don Metcalfe, saw a lone disk fly overhead. A KOIN news reporter in Portland saw twelve shiny disks as they danced in the sky high above him.

A few minutes after 1:00, Kenneth A. McDowell, a police officer who was near the Portland police station, noticed that the pigeons began fluttering as if frightened. Overhead he saw five large disks east of the city. According to the report he gave to military officers, three disks were flying east and the other two toward the south. All were moving at high speed and appeared to be oscillating. McDowell alerted the police, and they immediately broadcast the information.

After hearing the broadcast, two other police officers, Walter A. Lissy and Robert Ellis, stopped near a park. They saw three disks high overhead, moving at high speed. Neither heard any engine noises, but both did see flashes of brightness that could have been sunlight reflecting from shiny surfaces. According to the police officers, the objects moved erratically and changed their direction of flight. Both men were veterans of the Second World War, and both were civilian pilots.

Also hearing the broadcast was Patrolman Earl Patterson, who stopped to search for the disks. The broadcast suggested that the saucers were "coming out of the sun," meaning they were coming from the direction of the sun. At first Patterson saw nothing, but a few seconds later he saw one object coming out of the west and heading toward the southwest. He said the craft seemed to be aluminum or eggshell white and didn't flash or reflect the light.

Just across the Columbia River, in nearby Vancouver, Washington, sheriff's deputies Sergeant John Sullivan, Clarence

McKay, and Fred Krives also heard the radio broadcast and ran outside. Over Portland, three to five miles away, they saw twenty to thirty disks that looked to them like a flight of geese. They also said they heard a low humming sound.

Not long after that, three harbor patrolmen who also heard the radio report stepped outside. Captain K. A. Prehn, A. T. Austed, and Patrolman K. C. Hoff saw three to six disks traveling at high speed, but they couldn't tell the number because of the bright flashes from them. According to the witnesses, the objects looked like chrome hubcaps and oscillated as they flew. Sometimes the witnesses would see a full disk, then a half-moon shape, and then nothing at all.

They did see a plane in the sky at the time, but all the witnesses said that what they were watching was not an aircraft. Air Force investigators would later wonder if the airplane might have had something to do with the sightings.

Air Force files also report that "A former aircorps [sic] veteran . . . said the object [he saw] was unlike any plane he'd ever seen. He thought it appeared radio-controlled because the disk could change direction at a 90-degree angle without difficulty."

Another witness suggested that he had seen three objects fly east across the Williamette River. The objects did not appear to be very high, but they were traveling very fast. He said that they looked like a metallic disk glinting in the sun. He also said that he and a neighbor saw a single disk later that afternoon.

About 4:00 P.M., more civilians saw the disks. A woman called the police, telling them she'd watched a single object as "shiny as a new dime, flipping around." An unidentified man called to say that he'd seen three disks, one flying to the east and the other two heading north. They were shiny, shaped like flattened saucers, and were traveling at high speed.

About an hour later a man said that he spotted two white or silver objects flying southeast over Portland. Half an hour later he sighted a single disk heading to the northeast.

Finally, in Milwaukie, Oregon, not far from Portland, Sergeant Claude Cross reported three objects flying to the north. All were disk-shaped and were moving at high speed.

In what could be important information, a few of the witnesses reported real objects falling from the sky. Near Eugene, Oregon, a railroad cashier said he saw silvered disks being dropped out of a light airplane flying over the city.

A man in Portland recovered a large piece of paper he had seen fall from a great height. According to the reports, the time that the paper fell coincided with some of the flying saucer sightings.

Naturally, Air Force officers investigated the sightings. As part of the Project Grudge final report, written in 1949, one of the officers reported, "This investigator can offer no definite hypothesis, but in passing would like to note these incidents occurred on the Fourth of July, and that if relatively small pieces of aluminum foil had been dropped from a plane over the area, then any one object would become visible at relatively short distance. Even moderate wind velocities could give the illusion that fluttering, gyrating discs had gone by at great velocities. Various observers would not, of course, in this case have seen the same objects."

The officer also noted, "The above is not to be regarded as a very likely explanation but only as a possibility: the occurrence of these incidents on July 4 may have been more than a coincidence. Some prankster might have tossed such objects out of an airplane as part of an Independence Day celebration."

Ed Ruppelt, former chief of Blue Book, reported on the series of sightings in his book, *The Report on Unidentified Flying Objects*, without commentary about them. Blue Book files label all the sightings as insufficient data for a scientific analysis with the exception of one that they suggested was radar chaff: They were explaining one of the sightings as small bits of aluminum foil having been dropped from an aircraft.

The thing that is most interesting about these sightings is the number of law enforcement officers who reported seeing the objects after the radio broadcast. There is very little likelihood that the police officers would have invented the tales just to climb on the bandwagon. They would not have jeopardized their careers for some kind of practical joke.

Air Force investigation, which took the reports seriously in

1947, failed to find a satisfactory explanation for these sightings. It must be remembered that in this case there was nothing other than witnesses, separated by distance, who claimed to have seen the same thing. The sightings are interesting but certainly not indicative of anything more important.

Levelland, Texas
November 2, 1957

As noted earlier, eyewitness testimony is never going to be sufficient in and of itself to prove the UFOs are extraterrestrial craft. Witnesses, though they don't realize it, allow their perceptions, their beliefs, and their experiences to color their testimony. There is nothing to examine in an eyewitness account except the background of the witness, to see if he or she has a habit of telling tall tales, has trouble distinguishing between real objects and the imagined, and if he or she is a solid citizen not given to flights of fantasy.

If all avenues for explanation have been exhausted in single-witness cases, there is little else that investigators can do. There is no way to learn if the witness was fooled by an unusual meteor late at night, a private plane that filed no flight plan, or a hundred other reasonable explanations that could fit the facts.

But sometimes there is a case with multiple witnesses in widely separated locations who are unknown to one another and who basically tell the same tale. Their timing makes it clear that one witness had neither heard the story of another nor been unduly influenced by media reports. These sorts of cases, made of eyewitness testimony, can expand our knowledge and provide us with valuable clues.

The series of sightings that began around Levelland, Texas, on the night of November 2, 1957, prove this point. Some have claimed that they might have been inspired by the launch and announcement of *Sputnik II,* but no similar outbreak of flying saucer reports accompanied the launch of the first Soviet spacecraft about a month earlier. Besides, the sightings seem to have begun before the Soviets announced the launch—at least, according to the Project Blue Book files.

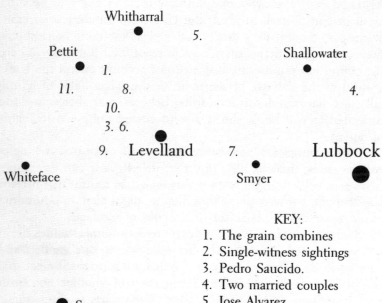

Levelland Sightings
November 2-3, 1957
(Note: Map not to scale)

12.

Amarillo

Whitharral
5.

Pettit
1.

Shallowater

11.   8.
10.
3. 6.
9. Levelland   7.   Lubbock

4.

Whiteface   Smyer

KEY:
1. The grain combines
2. Single-witness sightings
3. Pedro Saucido.
4. Two married couples
5. Jose Alvarez
6. Jim Wheeler
7. Ronald Martin
8. Single witness
9. Truck driver
10. Ray Jones
11. Sheriff Clem
12. Canadian, TX, sighting
Note: *All sightings except No. 11
reflect reports of electromagnetic effects*

Seagraves

2.

Seminole

The first people to see the object were two farmers working fields in the early evening near Pettit, Texas. Both grain combines, each with two engines, used by the men failed as a glowing object passed overhead. When it disappeared, the equipment began to function again.

At 9:30 that evening, a single witness traveling between Seminole and Seagraves, Texas, southwest of Levelland, spotted a light on the highway ahead. As he drove closer, his engine and headlights failed. A few seconds later, the light rose into the sky, and his car began to operate properly again.

The first of the sightings reported directly to Levelland police was made by Pedro Saucido (or Saucedo, depending on the source), who, with Joe Salaz (or Palav, Palaz, Salav, or Salvaz, depending on the source), saw a glowing object sweep across the highway in front of his truck. As it landed near them, the headlights died and the engine failed. Saucido dived out the door and rolled out of the way. Salaz sat terror-stricken, his eyes glued to the object.

The blue-green glow shifted into a red so bright that Salaz could no longer look directly at it. There seemed to be noise coming from inside the craft. It sat on the ground for about three minutes, and then, still glowing bright red, it shot suddenly into the sky.

Saucido crawled from under his truck. Now that the UFO was gone, both the lights and engine began to work again. Afraid that he would run into the object if he continued to Levelland, he drove to another town to call the Levelland police. A deputy sheriff listened to his report but laughed it off as just another flying saucer story, ignoring the obvious distress of the witness.

A few days after the sightings, the Air Force investigator on the case, Staff Sergeant Norman P. Barth of the 1006th Air Intelligence Service Squadron, made a short trip into Levelland to interview Saucido, among others. He wrote a lengthy report, which was forwarded to Blue Book headquarters some time later and provided additional details. Although he interviewed Saucido, that name does not appear in the case report. When the Blue Book files were released to the public in 1976, the Air Force removed the names of the witnesses. However, by reading the statements of the witnesses provided to the press and comparing the details, it is possible to match the reports to the names with some accuracy.

It would seem that Barth gave Saucido a low reliability rating as a witness. Barth wrote, "SOURCE [Saucido] appeared to be [deleted by Air Force officers] He stated his occupation was a barber; however, Sheriff Clem . . . stated that SOURCE was a part-time farm laborer, dishwasher, barber, etc. SOURCE had no concept of direction and was conflicting in his answers."

Saucido provided a written statement for Barth. It said, "To whom it may concern, on the date of November 2, 1957, I was traveling north and west on route 116, driving my truck. At about four miles out of Levelland, I saw a big flame, to my right, front, then I thought it was lightning. But when this object had reach [sic] to my position, it was different, because it put my truck motor out and lights. Then I stop, got out, and took a look, but it was so rapid and quite [sic] some heat, that I had to hit the ground, it also had three colors, yellow, white and it look like a torpedo, about 200 feet long, moving at about 600 to 800 miles an hour."

Saucido didn't provide the third color in this statement. In his interview with Barth, he did say the object was blue and that "the object had a yellow flame coming out of the rear and white smoke surrounding the flame."

Near Shallowater, Texas, two married couples saw a flash of light in the southwestern sky. Their car radio and the headlights dimmed while they watched the light. The couples reported that there were no thunderstorms around them at the time.

About an hour later, just after midnight on November 3, Jim Wheeler saw a red glowing object sitting on the road. As he approached it, his car engine died and his lights went out. The egg-shaped object then lifted off swiftly and silently. As it disappeared, Wheeler's car engine started again and the lights came on. He, too, called the Levelland police.

Almost as soon as the police hung up the telephone from talking with Wheeler, Jose Alvarez called to report that he had seen an egg-shaped object, which had killed his car's engine. And, a few minutes later, Frank Williams walked into the station to report the same sort of thing.

There had now been several reports, spaced over a couple of hours, about a large, egg-shaped craft. Most of the witnesses had talked about the bright red color, said that their engines had died and lights had dimmed as the object approached, and all said that when the object lifted off or disappeared, their cars began to function properly again. Someone estimated the size as 200 feet long, but that seemed to be extreme.

The reaction of law enforcement in Levelland was that someone was playing some sort of an elaborate joke. No one there believed that a glowing red egg was terrorizing the populace. Besides, the weather was poor, with mist and drizzle, and there had been thunderstorms in the vicinity, off and on, all evening.

As the police officers discussed it and tried to laugh it off, Jesse (also identified as James) Long called to report that he had been driving on a country road northwest of Levelland when he'd come upon a landed, bright red craft. His truck engine had died and his lights had gone out. Unlike the others, Long had gotten out of his truck and started to walk toward the object. Before he could get too close, the UFO took off. Long reported that after it was gone, his truck engine had restarted easily.

By this point Levelland sheriff Weir Clem decided that something strange was happening, but he didn't like the idea of chasing lights in the night sky, especially with the weather as bad as it was. Thunderstorms were still in the area, and though they had caused some problems earlier, it was no longer raining in town. There was no excuse for not trying to find the object.

To top it off, Ronald Martin, a college student, was nearing Levelland when he glanced at the dashboard ammeter. Martin told the Air Force investigator, Barth, "I was driving home from Lubbock on state highway 116 at approximately 12:00 P.M. when the ammeter on my car jumped to complete discharge, then it returned to normal and my motor started cutting out like it was out of gas. After it had quit running, my lights went out. I got out of my car and tried in vain to find the trouble. When I found nothing I closed the hood and looked for a passing motorist to obtain help. It was at this time that I saw this object. I got back into my car and tried to start it, but to no avail. After that I did nothing but stare at this object until it disappeared about five minutes later. I then resumed trying to start my car and succeeded with no more trouble than under normal circumstances. I then proceeded home very slowly and told no one of this sighting until my parents returned home from a weekend trip to Hobbs, New Mexico, for fear of public ridicule. They did convince me that I should report this and did so to the sheriff around 1:30 P.M. Sunday November 3rd."

In his interview with Barth, Martin would provide some additional details. He said that the object was oval shaped, and that he thought it was about the size of a baseball held at arm's length. He estimated that the object was about 75 to 100 feet long given the distance it was from him. He said it was white, with a greenish tint, which Martin thought might have been the result of his tinted windshield.

Later, Barth would evaluate Martin's reliability, writing, "SOURCE [Martin] seemed . . . to be very sincere about his sighting. He was appalled at the amount of publicity given him and was anxious to have the sighting resolved. He was unhesitating in his replies; however, during the course of further questioning, he admitted uncertainty in some of his answers. SOURCE can be considered reliable."

About an hour after Martin's sighting, Sheriff Clem decided he would have to investigate. He left the office with deputy Patrick McCullogh and drove the back roads and the highways in the Levelland area. At about 1:30 they saw the glowing UFO in the distance. They couldn't seem to get very close to it.

Barth found Clem to be "fairly reliable." He wrote, "SOURCE impressed the investigator as being of average intelligence. He was eager to cooperate in resolving the sighting and frequently asked the investigator for advice on releases to the press. He was rather pleased with the sudden importance of the county."

In their interview, Clem told Barth that he was out looking for the object that had been reported, and while traveling south on Oklahoma Flat Road at about 20 miles an hour, he saw the streak of light. It had a reddish glow and moved from south to west. Clem thought that it was about 800 feet long and about 400 yards away.

McCullough also provided Barth with a statement. He said he "was driving on the unmarked roadway known as the Oklahoma Flats Highway, and was attempting to search for an unidentified object reported to the Levelland Police Department. When I saw a strange looking flash to be down the roadway approximately a mile to a mile and one half, the flash went from east to west and appeared to be close to the ground. The flash lasted only a fraction of a second, and was red to orange red in color. This flash occured approximately 1:15 A.M. on the morning of November 3, 1957."

About that same time, two highway patrol officers and Constable Lloyd Bollen saw the UFO. They were unable to get very close to it and reported the same sort of thing that Clem had— a red glow in the distance. Thus there were five law enforcement officers who thought they had seen the object, though none got very close to it and none saw much more than a streak of light in the distance.

Also in the vicinity about that time was Ray Jones, the Levelland fire marshal. He was searching for an explanation for the many UFO reports that were being made that night. He saw a streak of light not far from him. His lights dimmed and the engine sputtered until the object was gone.

Barth found another witness, an Air Force tech sergeant who lived in Lubbock and was stationed at Reese Air Force Base. Barth rated the man as "of above-average intelligence and experience. He stated that he was giving his information only to aid in resolving the sighting. SOURCE can be considered unusually reliable."

In his statement, the Source said, "On the night of 2 November 1957, at approximately 2318 [hours], my wife, two children and myself departed my father's home in Sudan, Texas. At about 2330, in the vicinity of Anton, Texas, my wife and I noted occasional lightning and at the same time static on our radio. At approximately 2350 or 2355, I turned south (at Shallowater, Texas) on State Farm Road 1073. In just a few minutes, later this bolt of lightning occured [sic] to our southwest. At the same time, my radio and car lights went out for approximately 1–3 seconds, and then came back on. My wife and I remarked that was certainly a strong bolt of lightning to put out our lights and radio. We didn't think anything about this until we heard the radio report (Sunday night) of this phenomenon, with its location and time factor, certainly coincidence with this flash of lightning that my wife and I observed."

Also part of the Air Force file on Levelland was a report from a man living in Whiteface, Texas. He told Barth, "While driving north about 7 miles north of Sundown, Texas, I saw a light about the size of a basketball about 200 or more feet above the ground traveling from east to west. I stopped by side of road with my wife and we watched the object, a bright red light giving off a glow. It apparently stopped and began swinging north to south about a quarter-mile distance while getting higher slowly and fire or sparks similar to a cutting torch cutting iron scraping out with visible smoke. An object above it seemed to hold up the light on a cable or hose appearing to link between the light and the balloon object above it. It continued swinging north to south 3 or 4 minutes by then at a fast rate of speed it went up into the clouds and disappeared then light went out."

As noted by the Air Force investigators, these sightings received national attention the next day. Newspapers around the country carried the stories of the mystery lights that seemed to stall cars and dim headlights. The Air Force, because of the number of reports, responded with an investigator apparently based at Ent Air Force Base in Colorado Springs, Colorado. This was, of course, Sergeant Barth.

Newspapers in the area reported on the Air Force interest, but they were less than complimentary about the investigation. An Associated Press story, written on November 15, with a dateline of Washington, D.C., reported, "The Air Force has looked into five recent reports . . . and there isn't a flying saucer in the lot."

The local press took that and noted, "*Five* reports out of scores of hundreds received? Was the Air Force perhaps practicing frugality? We might think so, in light of another Washington dispatch (*Science Service*, Nov. 7 [1957]), which said, 'Each major track-down costs about $10,000, including sending out investigating personnel, paying transportation expenses, sending planes aloft to investigate intruders and taking pictures of, perhaps, Venus— plus administrative work.' But on this point there is some instructive evidence."

The article continued, noting, "At Levelland, Texas, the luminous egg-shaped object 200–300 feet long that stopped car motors and radios was identified as: 'a natural electric phenomenon called ball lightning or St. Elmo's fire.' Apparently the technical investigators who conducted this particular $10,000 investigation were not aware that these are *two entirely different* electric phenomena; or that the average diameter of ball lightning is 8 *inches*; or that a good many scientists deny that ball lightning even exists; or that St. Elmo's fire is invariably attached to some solid object. As for the stalled car motors, continued the AF, the same weather that produced St. Elmo's lightning might have—MIGHT have, notice—'soaked the ignition systems of cars.' And what might have dried them out so quickly once the light departed? And *did* anyone's ignition in fact become soaked? Were the witnesses asked this? (One report, said the AF, arose from 'an automobile mechanic's mistake'; no details given.)"

Those details were available in the Blue Book files. In a message that was transmitted to the assistant chief of staff, Intelligence, at headquarters of the Air Force, it was reported, "Investigation proved that a rotor had been changed on the farmer's [Saucido's] truck the previous day. One piece of the old rotor had not been removed and had wedged in between the points causing the electrical system to be now nonoperative. This statement was obtained from the mechanic who had repaired the truck."

Of course, there were other reports of car engines being stalled, including that of Ronald Martin, which had been investigated by the Air Force. The broken-rotor scenario doesn't explain that case.

The local paper continued, reporting, "The investigators said further [note the plural] that they could find only three witnesses who actually saw the big light. The miracle is, they found as many as *three*. For we know, in this case, exactly what the Air Force investigation amounted to. On November 6 the Levelland

Daily Sun News reported, 'Air Force "Mystery" Man Leaves City; Actions, Identity Cloaked in Secrecy.' The anonymous visitor drove an AF vehicle, wore civilian clothes, and 'said he *could not give his name or any identification*' (italics ours [meaning in original]). Around noon on the 6th he spent 30 minutes in Sheriff Weir Clem's office. He returned about 2:30 P.M. for another half hour. About 3 P.M. he headed for Lubbock (30 miles away); came back about 6:30, said to Sheriff Clem, 'Well, I'm gone,' and drove off into the dark, drippy night. Adds the paper, 'There was never any hint as to what he found out or whether he was really a civilian or an Air Force officer.' "

We know, of course, that he was neither a civilian nor an Air Force officer. He was, in fact, Sergeant Barth. The reason he wouldn't identify himself was that to do so would reveal the existence of another Air Force investigation of UFOs that was not part of Project Blue Book. In 1957, and as late as 1985, the existence of this other investigation, originally conducted by the 4602d Air Intelligence Service Squadron, which evolved into the unit to which Barth belonged, was considered secret information.

The newspaper analysis ended with the question "Does the Air Force call this a 'major track-down'? We won't even bother to laugh. Do they say that the activities of the mysterious gentleman's 7-hour day cost $10,000 or anything like it? Then the taxpayers had better start yelling bloody murder, for they are being well bilked. Yet it was on the basis of this feeble parody of an investigation that the Air Force, on November 15, uttered its 'conclusions' about the Levelland object!"

The criticism seemed to be justified. The Air Force investigator did not find, nor did he apparently try to find, some of the witnesses who were in Levelland on November 2, but who had returned to their homes by November 6. It is clear from the file that Barth didn't speak to Jesse Long, of Waco, Texas, who said the object had killed his engine. Nor did he find or interview Jim Wheeler, Jose Alvarez, Ray Jones, or Frank Williams, the farmers near Pettit, the two couples near Shallowater, or the man driving from Seminole to Seagraves, all of whom said the proximity of the object had killed their car engines and dimmed their lights.

In a different unclassified message to the commander of the Air Technical Intelligence Center, it was noted that "Contrary to [Donald E.] Keyhoe's [Director of NICAP] and Washington press reports only three, not nine persons witnessed the incident. Object observed for only few seconds, not lengthy period as implied by press. Mist, rain, thunderstorms and lightning discharges in scene of incident, fact not quoted in newspaper releases."

The message also provided a number of explanations for the sighting. "(1) Burning gas from oil operations in the area reflected off low cloud ceiling existing at time. (2) Downed power line giving off spark display in contact with the ground. (3) Electrical discharge or similar phenomena like St. Elmo's Fire caused by right combination of weather and other conditions. (4) 'Ball lightning' a rare, but nevertheless, possibility in view of lighting [sic] discharges in vicinity."

Barth, near the end of his classified report, concluded by writing, "1. A check with Lowry Flight Service [Lowry AFB, Denver, Colorado], Carswell Flight Service [Carswell AFB, Fort Worth, Texas], Reese AFB Operations [Lubbock, Texas], and Lubbock CAA for any [aircraft] traffic in the area produced a negative reply.

"2. A check for balloon operations showed that Amarillo and Midland, Texas, weather stations released balloons at 1200Z and 2400Z daily. However, these balloons were not likely to be in the area."

Barth went on to propose a number of possible explanations, which were speculative in nature. "The amount of rain in the area, together with the condition of the crops, could have developed a phenomenon similar to St. Elmo's fire. . . . The possibility of burning excess gas from nearby oil operations reflecting off low clouds existed. . . . The possibility of lightning stalling a car and extinguishing the lights existed; however, the possibility decreases as the number of such incidents increases. . . . A check with the oil companies in the area revealed that a limited amount of excess gas from oil operations was being burned. Most of the gas is returned to the ground. . . . A check for downed power lines during the period was made with negative results. . . . The other witnesses reported in newspaper accounts as having observed the object had either disappeared or returned to their homes, leaving no forwarding addresses."

What we see is a great deal of irrelevant material. There were thunderstorms, but they had dissipated by the time the sightings began. Oil refining operations created gas that was burned and might have been reflected by the clouds, though the residents of the area would be familiar with those operations and would probably have no motive to suddenly see strange objects in the reflections. There were no downed power lines that the one Air Force message had postulated. Although the Air Force didn't interview them (and so, to the Air Force, they didn't exist), there were a number of people, all named, who did report that their car engines and lights were affected by the proximity of the UFO. Rather than search for the additional witnesses, the Air Force ignored them.

Contrary to what the Air Force reported internally and suggested to the press were the number of witnesses claimed by Keyhoe. In fact, Keyhoe had underestimated the number. Furthermore, the length of the sightings varied from a few seconds to several minutes. The Air Force was attempting to suggest that the witnesses had seen, and misinterpreted, lightning flashes.

The Air Force did, to their satisfaction, solve the Levelland case. According to the Blue Book files, "After very extensive checks and detailed investigations by the Air Force and with complete collaboration with both Air Force and non-governmental scientists it was concluded that the sighting was due to a very rare phenomena [sic], ball lightning."

It must be noted here that the nongovernmental scientist was Dr. Donald Menzel. In fact, part of a galley proof for one of his books was included in the project file. Menzel wrote, "The evidence, however, leads to an overwhelming probability: the fiery unknown at Levelland *was* ball lightning."

Curtis Peebles also mentioned the Levelland case in *Watch the Skies*. His entire investigation seemed to be founded on the Air Force files. His footnotes refer to the Project Blue Book microfilm, Roll 29 (which, of course, is part of what I used to assemble the information here). There is little or no critical comment about the Air Force investigation in either the book by Menzel or the one by Peebles.

Peebles noted in his book, "The Air Force solutions were made public on November 14 (thirteen days after the flap began). The summaries of the five widely publicized sightings were very brief. The Levelland account was only sixty words long. (The Air Intelligence Information Report was nineteen *pages* long)."

The implication here is that the Air Force had a great deal more information than they released publicly, but the nineteen-page report contains at least two one-page drawings and several pages where only the witness statement is recorded, taking up a third of the page or less. Peebles didn't acknowledge the fact that the Air Force investigator spent only seven hours in Levelland and talked to only three of those who claimed their cars had been stalled.

Peebles also relied on Air Force statements that the object was seen for only seconds and that most eyewitnesses saw only a streak of light. Neither statement is true. Martin said the object was in sight for 4 or 5 minutes. The Air Force investigator didn't find any of the other witnesses except Pedro Saucido. The Air Force was convinced that mass hysteria, the wet conditions, and ball lightning were responsible for the sightings.

What is important in this case is the number of independent witnesses who told of the object in the area and added the dimension of dimmed lights, radio failure, and the stalling of car engines. Many of the claims were made to the sheriff or police before there was any media attention to the sightings. Those suggesting some sort of mass hysteria have a major stumbling block in the way of their argument: How did these witnesses tell the same story within an hour or so of one another?

Menzel and the Air Force make much of the fact that within days of the sighting, hundreds of others were telling tales of low-level flying saucers and their electromagnetic effects. Once the story was out—in the newspapers, on the radio, and on television—then a "mass hysteria" could kick in. But that doesn't explain the sightings in Levelland late on the night of November 2 and very early in the morning of November 3.

One Air Force officer suggested that all the reports they received in November of that year stemmed from the "mass hysteria" that grew out of Levelland. He noted that hundreds of sightings were made after November 2. But a statistical analysis of the sightings reported to Project Blue Book showed this wasn't the case. Instead we see that the number of UFO reports to the Air Force began to grow in the late summer of 1957. That growth peaked on November 6 and then dropped off rapidly.

It could just as easily be suggested that Levelland marked not the beginning of a wave of UFO reports but the middle of it. The increased number of reports to the Air Force after the Levelland sighting might be explained in a simple fashion: People, realizing that the Air Force was gathering the information, now felt an obligation to report what they had seen. The story sparked not a series of sightings but a series of reports.

Conclusions

Eyewitness testimony is only as good as the eyewitness. Its value increases when it is corroborated by other, independent witnesses. During the Oregon sightings in 1947, there were many independent witnesses to something in the sky. They were separated by time and distance, but they were connected by radio and telephone. Many of those reports were sparked by a police radio broadcast that something unusual was in the sky. Police officers and harbor patrolmen went out to look. In many of the cases they were rewarded when they saw something.

Could it be that they were inspired by that first radio call? Could it be that they were inspired by a knowledge of what they were supposed to see? In psychology this is called priming. You expect to see something specific, and when presented with a non-specific stimulus, you see what you expect to see. In other words, those who heard the broadcast went outside with an expectation of seeing something. That expectation could have been enough to cause the men to see disk-shaped objects where there really were none. They would have seen something—possibly a natural phenomenon or the radar chaff postulated by the Air Force—but because they thought they were looking for flying disks they saw, in those twinkling shapes, flying disks.

It could also be that because they were outside, looking into the sky, they saw disks as they flew over. This means, simply, that they saw what was in the sky and accurately reported it. We have no way of knowing, today, which explanation is correct, or even if either is correct. There could be a third possibility that would explain these sightings to our satisfaction.

The Air Force listed most of them as insufficient data for a scientific analysis. We could argue that point, but today, more than fifty years later, there isn't much that we can do. The objects were seen high in the sky, moving from horizon to horizon. They produced no photographic evidence, no interaction with the environment that can be explored, no traces of themselves. We have only the multiple eyewitness testimony that is intriguing but little more.

The Levelland sightings are also multiple eyewitness. There was no physical evidence of the object's passing. It did, however, interact with the environment. It stalled car engines and dimmed the lights. It affected the instruments in the cars and blocked the radio signals. It was eyewitness testimony with a twist.

When reviewing the case, the Air Force would like us to believe that this was an example of mass hysteria. One report that received national attention brought in other reports. But on reviewing the case carefully, we notice that many of the reports of interaction between the object and the electrical systems of the vehicles were made to authorities before there was any media attention. The reports are independent of one another and tend to corroborate one another.

Levelland is one of the few examples of multiple-witness sighting cases in which it can be demonstrated that there was no previous contamination. The new twist—of UFOs stalling cars— had not been well publicized until the Levelland case. If any of the witnesses had heard of it prior to their own experiences that night, it would be surprising.

Yet, even with these perplexing sightings, with the newspapers providing names of witnesses, with both the Levelland police and sheriff involved, the Air Force investigation seemed to be more interested in explaining the reports than investigating them. To the Air Force investigator, if the witness didn't speak to him, that witness didn't exist. That attitude is evident throughout the Air Force file on the case. The final Air Force report said, "Only one observer . . . said an object hovered over or on the ground. One observer said an object moved over his head at a low altitude . . . one observer saw an object hovering and swinging in a pendulum motion [a] considerable distance above the ground. The other observers saw a light streak across the sky or a bolt of lightning."

What we see is an interesting group of sightings that suggests something unusual was observed. There is no evidence of hoax. The conclusion is that something was in that area on that night. It interacted with the environment and seemed to create an electrical field that could, upon close approach, suppress the functioning of regular electrical systems, stalling cars and dimming lights.

This does not mean, however, that what was seen was extraterrestrial in origin. It means that what was seen demands that further research be conducted. If the scientific community requires physical evidence, doesn't the Levelland case, with its multiple and independent eyewitness testimony of an object that has interacted with the environment, demand another look? Isn't this the first of the links in the chain of evidence?

3

Radar Cases as Physical Evidence

Many debunkers and skeptics claim that they don't believe UFOs represent anything solid because they have never been spotted on radar. Our own stealth technology has rendered that argument obsolete. But it should also be noted that the claim is erroneous. There have been many good radar cases involving sightings of UFOs and later visual confirmation of an object, or objects, in the air.

Many people also believe that if we can find a good radar case—that is, one without obvious explanation—then we move closer to proving something about the reality of UFOs. There are good cases involving multiple witnesses, multiple radars, and explanations by officials that are less than plausible. These sorts of cases do supply one aspect of physical evidence about the reality of UFOs, but we must be aware of the pitfalls that dot such a landscape.

To understand radar cases, we must understand something about the functioning of radar. If we know nothing, we can be convinced by facts that have no relevance to what we want to discuss. We must understand the history of radar, as well as its capabilities, if we are to understand and evaluate the radar cases.

Throughout the history of the development of radar, the capabilities of the various sets has been underestimated. During the Second World War, for example, radar operators and specialists in London were surprised and puzzled by a particular radar return that would appear quickly, expand, and then vanish. It happened each morning as the sun began to rise.

To discover that was happening, observers were posted near the scene where the particular blip originated. As dawn broke, hundreds, if not thousands, of birds emerged from nesting and took off in all directions, searching for food. The birds' outward expansion was responsible for the early-morning radar return. No one expected the radars to be sensitive enough to pick up and track the birds.

In September 1951, technicians at Fort Monmouth, New Jersey, were demonstrating their latest radar and how it could automatically track anything up to and including the fastest jet fighters. Using the scope in front of a crowd of visiting dignitaries and generals, a technician tried to lock on to a target about twelve thousand yards away. The target broke the lock, and the embarrassed operator tried to reestablish it, suggesting that the object, whatever it was, had to be flying faster than a jet.

The equipment, the weather, and the operator were all checked, and no one could find an explanation for the radar problems. There were no inversion layers, no unidentified jet traffic in the area, and no outside influences that could account for the experiences of the technician.

The next day at Fort Monmouth headquarters telephoned the radar facility to find out if there was anything on radar south of the base since they were watching something unusual. The officers at headquarters wanted to know how high the object was. The radar suggested it was at 93,000 feet, far above the service ceilings of any aircraft at the time. Rockets that reached those sorts of altitudes were being fired, but none were being fired in New Jersey. It confused those at the radar facility, suggesting that something very unusual had been flying over their base.

More unidentified objects were spotted around Fort Monmouth later that day and the next. Again the automatic tracking of the radars failed because it seemed that the erratically flying craft were faster than modern jets. And finally, a much slower moving object was spotted and tracked for several minutes before it was lost in the distance.

Here were a number of highly credible radar sightings that suggested some unusual objects were being spotted by the technicians. There were also visual sightings of the craft that resulted in additional radar confirmation of their physical reality. These certainly weren't illusions, and no one thought about suggesting a hoax because of the equipment involved, the integrity of the officers making the reports, and the impossibility of creating that sort of an illusion.

But as the Air Force officers assigned to investigate reviewed the accumulated data, they began to find plausible explanations that made sense to them. The object that was faster than a jet wasn't an aircraft at all. The operator had made a mechanical error as he attempted to lock on the target. It was considerably slower than a jet fighter and was identified, based on the time, location, and direction of flight, as a commercial airliner on a routine flight.

The object in the sky that headquarters called about, the object that was flying at an altitude of 93,000 feet, turned out to be a balloon—which headquarters already knew when they called. There had been a discussion about how high it was, and they had asked that the radar be used to determine the altitude. Those who had received the call had overreacted to it, thinking that the officers at headquarters were attempting to identify some sort of UFO.

The last of the Fort Monmouth sightings were identified, again, as a balloon, and as weather-related phenomena. The excitement of the day before—that is, the belief that they had seen some sort of flying saucer—had influenced those who were involved in the second day's activities. They were primed to accept the stories of flying saucers because of the reaction of the others and their belief that the equipment would not make a mistake. They were right: The equipment didn't make a mistake, the operator did.

The point here is that there were good sightings, confirmed by radar. Something was in the sky. But there was also a good explanation for the sightings that was found by proper scientific investigation. It told us something about the capabilities of radar and the way that investigations could be handled. It also demonstrated that just because something was seen on radar, it didn't mean that the object was of extraterrestrial origin.

In fact, what we learn about radar is that just because there is something in the sky, it doesn't mean that what the eyewitnesses are observing is the same object as that located by the radar. There are many cases in which an unidentified blip is located and observers outside are alerted. Looking into the sky, they eventually see something that they believe is related to the blip on the scope. Sometimes this simply isn't the case.

Philip Klass, in *UFOs Explained*, noted that just such a case was reported on September 14, 1972. The West Palm Beach, Florida, airport control tower began to receive telephone calls about a very bright object seen out over the Atlantic Ocean an hour or so before dawn. The controller looked out and saw what he described as a "glowing circular object" that was, according to his estimate, about 2 miles from the tower. To him, it was clearly something very strange.

He then turned his attention to an old surveillance radar that had been reconditioned. After studying the scope, he did find an object that was 10 miles east of the airport. It was larger than the blips of aircraft display on the scope, moving far too slowly to be an airplane. It was flying toward the coast.

The controller made a number of telephone calls and found that the radars at Miami International Airport also showed the object, as did the Air Defense Command radars at Homestead Air Force Base. The controller also talked to the crew of an Eastern Airlines jet, who said that they, too, could see the bright light in the east.

Two F-106 fighters were scrambled into the brightening sky. Although equipped with onboard radars, neither pilot could see the UFO. The controller said that he could still see the object and agreed to help the fighter pilots find it. Vectored by the controller, and after a series of maneuvers including flying over the top of the tower, the pilots identified the light as Venus.

We could take that as a typical Air Force explanation, but the local sheriff, William Heidtman, in response to many calls tried to intercept and identify the light using a county helicopter. He, too, believed that he was attempting to intercept Venus. His identification was independent of the Air Force's, but he did corroborate their conclusion.

There seems to be little question as to what the light in the eastern sky was. Venus, at its brightest, when the conditions are proper, can look more like an oval object flying in our atmosphere than like a planet some thirty million miles away.

The case also demonstrates that when a light is seen in the sky, it is often possible to find "uncollarated" targets on the radarscope. These sorts of cases must be investigated carefully, and it must be remembered that the light in the sky might not be responsible for the image on the radar.

It should also be noted that in this case, though the control tower operator was fooled by Venus, as were hundreds of others, the object was identified. The report was solved by men on the scene who attempted to intercept the object. That identification was corroborated by the local sheriff. While it could be said that the Air Force pilots, because they were Air Force pilots, might have had a hidden agenda, that cannot be said for the sheriff.

This leads us into a discussion of radar itself and its reliability. Roy H. Blackmer, Jr., along with R. J. Allen, R. T. H. Collis, C. Herold, and R. I. Presnell, wrote about the workings of radar in the Condon Committee report. The first point they made was one of the most important. According to them, "At first consideration, radar might appear to offer a positive, non-subjective method of observing UFOs. Radar seems to reduce data to ranges, altitudes, velocities, and such characteristics as radar reflectivity. On closer examination, however, the radar method of looking at an object, although mechanical and electronically precise, is in many aspects substantially less comprehensive than the visual approach. In addition, the very techniques that provide the objective measurements are themselves susceptible to errors and anomalies that can be misleading."

That certainly is true. But it is also true that there are very few cases in which there were only radar contacts and no corresponding visual sightings. To be useful in a scientific arena, both chains of evidence are necessary. And, as demonstrated by Klass, as well as many others, it is necessary to make sure that the object in the sky that has been located by the radar is the same as the one being observed on the ground or by the pilots who are asked to identify it.

The Condon Committee report makes it clear that one of the weak links in the radar cases is the radar operators. The committee wrote, "The radar operator himself is an important part of the radar systems. He must be well trained and familiar with all of the interacting factors affecting the operation and performance of the equipment. When an experienced operator is moved to a new location, an important part of his retraining is learning pertinent factors related to expected anomalies due to local geographical and meteorological factors."

Klass, in his analysis of the West Palm Beach case, pointed out that the radar used in the control tower was a "twenty-year-old ASR-3 that had originally been installed at a larger airport that had since been given a more modern radar, while the old ASR-3 had been reconditioned for use at West Palm Beach." He mentioned nothing about the radar training of the control tower operator, but it seems likely that it was more of an "on the job" training than a complete course in radar operations.

I should point out here that this is often the course taken by writers on UFOs. We *speculate* about a condition rather than *ask* about it. Klass should have found out the level of training of the control tower operator, as should I. In science, we can't simply accept our speculations as fact.

The operator's lack of experience in radar systems, on that specific system, or in the local geological conditions might have led to his false conclusion that the target on the scope was related to the object in the sky. It was a question that should have been asked at the time, though by the time UFO investigators arrived, a viable explanation had been found.

There are, according to the Condon Committee experts, "five possible relationships between radar echoes and targets."

These are:
a) no echo—no target;

b) no echo—when a visual object appears to be in a position to be detected;

c) *echo—unrelated to a target;*

d) *echo—from a target in a position other than that indicated;*

e) *echo—from a target at the indicated location."*

They point out that both the first and last possibility are indicative of the normal operation of the radar. Of the others, they wrote, "Possibility b) becomes of importance where there is an object that is seen visually. Then, from knowledge of the types of targets that are detectable by the radar, some knowledge of the characteristics of the visual object could be obtained."

They continue, "The situations c) where there is an apparent echo but no target are those when the manifestation on the PPI [plan position indicator] is due to a signal that is not a reradiated portion of the transmitted pulse but is from another source."

As far as situation d), according to the Condon Committee report, "First, abnormal bending of the radar beam may take place due to atmospheric conditions. Second, a detectable target may be present beyond the designed range of the radar and be presented on the display as if it were within the designed range of the radar and be presented on the display as if it were within the designed range. . . . Third, stray energy from the antenna may be reflected from an obstacle to a target in a direction quite different from that in which the antenna is pointed. . . . Finally, targets could be detected by radiation in side lobes and would be presented on the display as if they were detected by the main beam."

The last situation, e)—that is, an echo and a target located where it is indicated by the radar—is of primary interest to our discussion. In this case, the primary task is the identification of the target.

The authors noted, "The possible relationships listed above show that radarscope interpretation is not simple. To attempt to identify targets, the operator must know the characteristics of his radar; whether it is operating properly; and the type of targets it is capable of detecting. He must be very aware of the conditions or events by which echoes will be presented on the radar in a position that is different from the true target location (or in the case of interference no target). Finally the operator must acquire collateral information—weather data, transponder, voice communication, visual observations or handover information from another radar—before he can be absolutely sure he has identified an unusual echo."

What all this means is that the evidence developed through a radar case is more complicated than just a blip on the screen and a corresponding light in the sky. The evidence has to be assembled carefully, and the expertise of the operator, or operators, becomes a critical factor. Without an operator who is good at the job, the case is weakened considerably and the conclusions may be skewed.

But when all is said and done, the radar return adds a dimension of reliability to the case. When the target is spotted visually, right where it is supposed to be, it means that we are no longer dealing with illusion or imagination. We are dealing with something that is real and solid.

The Washington Nationals
July 19, 1952

There are very few cases in the history of the UFOlogy where there are many independent witnesses in combination with physical evidence. In a case that would become known as the Washington Nationals, there are independent witnesses, from airline and fighter pilots to radar operators and airport tower personnel. There is also physical evidence in the form of radar tracks that were observed by highly trained and skilled men at Washington National Airport, Andrews Air Force Base, and Bolling Air Force Base. Here was a UFO sighting that demanded proper investigation. All that had to be done was an investigation to determine if there was a natural phenomenon that could explain the sightings.

The Washington Nationals began when, according to the logbook of the CAA (forerunner of the Federal Aeronautics Administration), two radars at the Air Routing and Traffic Control Center (ARTC) in Washington, D.C., picked up eight unidentified targets near Andrews Air Force Base at 11:40 P.M. on the evening of July 19. These were not identified by the radar operators as airplanes because, at times, they were traveling much too fast. First they moved along at only a hundred miles an hour, then they would suddenly accelerate to fantastic speeds. One of the objects was tracked, according to the calculations made at the time, at the center, at over 7,000 miles an hour.

About 20 minutes later, or just after midnight on July 20, the tower personnel at Washington's National Airport reported they had five targets on their radarscopes. Later it would be realized that this made it three individual radars at three separate sites that had solid targets that were not already identified as aircraft. It would mean that the targets reported were not a malfunction of the radar, since all three would not malfunction in the same fashion, providing the same information. The radars were not linked.

One of the controllers at the ARTC finally called for a senior controller, Harry C. Barnes, who in turn called the National Airport control tower. They had unidentified targets on their scopes, as did the controller at Andrews Air Force Base. They had already eliminated a mechanical malfunction as the cause, but with the objects on other scopes in other locations, there was no longer any question of their reality. All the men, including Barnes, were sure they were looking at solid objects based on their years of experience with radar and in air traffic control.

Just after midnight, Airman Second Class (A/2c) Bill Goodman called the Andrews Air Force Base control tower to tell them he was watching a bright orange light about the size of a softball that was gaining and losing altitude as it zipped through the sky.

During this time, Goodman talked to A/1c William B. Brady, who was in the tower. Goodman told Brady that the object was to the immediate south. Brady saw a ball of orange fire. There were discrepancies between the physical description given by Goodman and Brady, but they were relatively small. It could be argued that the discrepancies were the result of the points of view of the two observers.

Joseph DeBoves, who was also on the scene as a civilian control tower operator at Andrews, said that Brady became excited during one of his telephone conversations, yelling, "There one goes." DeBoves believed that Brady was watching nothing more interesting than a meteor.

About 2:00 A.M. on July 20, the radar officer at Andrews Approach Control, Captain Harold C. Way, learned that the ARTC had a target east of Andrews. He went outside and saw a strange light that he didn't believe to be a star. Later, however, he went back out, and this time decided that he was looking at a star.

Bolling Air Force Base became involved briefly about the time Way went outside. The tower operator there said that he saw a "roundish" object drifting low in the sky to the southeast of Bolling. There were no radar confirmations of the sighting, and that was the last of the reports from that base.

The ARTC again told the controllers at Andrews that they still had the targets on their scopes. There is conflicting data because some of the reports suggest that the Andrews radar showed nothing, while other reports claim they did. Now De-Boves and two others in the tower, Monte Banning and John P. Izzo, Jr., swept the sky with binoculars but could see no lights other than the stars.

The sightings lasted throughout the night, and during that time, the crews of several airliners saw the lights right where the radars showed them to be. Tower operators also saw them, and jet fighters were brought in for attempted intercepts. Associated Press stories written hours after the sightings claimed that no intercepts had been attempted that night, but those stories were inaccurate. Documents in the Project Blue Book files, as well as eyewitness testimony, confirm the attempted intercepts.

Typical of the airline sightings were those made by Captain Casey Pierman on Capital Airlines Flight 807. He was on a flight between Washington and Martinsburg, West Virginia, at 1:15 A.M. on July 20, when he and the rest of the crew saw seven objects flash across the sky. Pierman said, "They were like falling stars without trails."

Capital Airline officials said that National Airport radar picked up the objects and asked Pierman to keep an eye on them. Shortly after takeoff, Pierman radioed that he had the objects in sight. He was flying at 180 to 200 miles per hour, and reported the objects were traveling at tremendous speed. Official Air Force records confirm this.

Another Capital Airlines pilot, Captain Howard Dermott, on

Capital Flight 610, reported that a single light followed him from Herndon, Virginia, to within 4 miles of National Airport. Both the ARTC and the National Airport control tower confirmed that an unidentified target followed the aircraft to within 4 miles of landing. At about the same time, an Air Force radar at Andrews AFB was tracking eight additional unknown objects as they flew over the Washington area.

One of the most persuasive sightings came early in the morning when one of the ARTC controllers called the Andrews Air Force Base control tower to tell them that there was a target south of the tower, over the Andrews Radio range station. The tower operators looked to the south where a "huge fiery-orange sphere" was hovering. This again was later explained by the Air Force as a star.

Just before daylight, about 4 A.M., after repeated requests from the ARTC, an F-94 interceptor arrived on the scene. It was too little too late. All the targets were gone. Although the flight crew made a short search of the local area, they found nothing unusual and quickly returned to their base.

Apparently the three radar facilities only once during that night reported a target that was seen by all three facilities. There were, however, a number of times when the ARTC radar and the Washington National tower radars had simultaneous contacts. It also seems that the radars were displaying the same targets that were seen by the crews of the Capital Airlines flights. What it boils down to is that multiple radars and multiple eyewitnesses were seeing objects in the sky over Washington.

With the coming of the sun, the UFOs disappeared from the scopes. Although the men continued to search for them, they found nothing. If the UFOs were weather related, sunrise would not have dramatically affected the situation. The disappearance of the objects at sunrise suggests something other than weather.

But that wasn't the end of the Washington Nationals. There were other sightings, including a good one from New Jersey and one from Massachusetts in which F-94s tried, unsuccessfully, to intercept unidentified lights. According to Project Blue Book files, in both cases the pilots reported radar locks on the objects. Within seconds, however, those locks were broken by the evasive maneuvers of the UFOs.

The second series of sightings began a week later, almost to the hour that the UFOs had first visited Washington National Airport. About 10:30 P.M. the same radar operators who had been on duty the week before again spotted several slow-moving targets on their scopes. This time the controllers carefully marked each of the unidentifieds. When they were all marked, the controllers called the Andrews AFB radar facility. The unidentified targets were on their scope, too, and apparently in the same relative positions.

An hour later, with targets being tracked continually, the controllers called for interceptors. Al Chop, the Pentagon spokesman for the Air Force's UFO project, told me in 1995 that he had been in communication with the main basement command post at the Pentagon. He requested that interceptors be sent. As a civilian, he could only make the request and then wait for the flag officer (general or admiral) in command at the Pentagon to make the official decision.

As happened the week before, there was a delay, but by midnight, two F-94s were on station over Washington. At that point, the reporters who had assembled to observe the situation were asked by Chop to leave the radar room at National Airport because classified radio and intercept procedures would be in operation.

Also present were Major Dewey Fournet, the Pentagon liaison between the UFO project in Dayton and the intelligence community in Washington, and Naval Lieutenant Holcomb, an electronics specialist assigned to the Air Force Directorate of Intelligence. With those men watching, as well as the controllers at various facilities using various radars, the F-94s arrived.

As the interceptors appeared, the UFOs immediately vanished from the scopes. The jets were vectored to the last known position of the UFOs, but even though visibility was unrestricted in the area, the pilots could see nothing. The fighters made a systematic search of the area, but they returned to their base since they could find nothing.

In that 1995 interview Chop told me, "The minute the first two interceptors appeared on our scope all our unknowns disappeared. It was like they just wiped them all off. All our other flights, all the known flights were still on the scope. . . . We watched these two planes leave. When they were out of our range, immediately we got our UFOs back."

Later, Air Force officers would learn that as the fighters appeared over Washington, people in the area of Langley Air Force Base, Virginia, spotted weird lights in the sky. An F-94 in the area on a routine mission was diverted to search for the lights. The pilot saw one and turned toward it, but it disappeared "like somebody turning off a lightbulb."

The pilot continued the intercept and did get a radar lock on the now unlighted and unseen target, but the lock was broken by the object as it sped away. The fighter continued the pursuit, obtaining two more radar locks on the object, but each time the locks were broken.

The scene then shifted back to Washington National. Again the Air Defense Command was alerted, and again fighters were sent. This time the pilots were able to see the objects, vectored toward them by the air traffic controllers. But the fighters couldn't close on the lights. The pilots saw no external details, other than lights where the radar suggested that something should be seen.

After several minutes of failing to close on a target, one was spotted. A fighter piloted by Lieutenant William Patterson turned, kicked in the afterburner, and tried to catch the object. It disappeared before Patterson could see much of anything.

Interviewed by newspaper reporters the next day, Patterson said, "I tried to make contact with the bogies below one thousand feet, but they [the controllers] vectored us around. I saw several bright lights. I was at my maximum speed, but even then I had no closing speed. I ceased chasing them because I saw no chance of overtaking them. I was vectored into new objects. Later I chased a single bright light which I estimated about ten miles away. I lost visual contact with it . . ."

Al Chop remembered this intercept, as did Dewey Fournet. Chop said, "The flight controllers had directed him to them [the unknowns]. We had a little cluster of them. Five or six of them and he suddenly reports that he sees some lights. . . . He said they are very brilliant blue-white lights. He was going to try to close in to get a better look . . . he flew into the area where they were clustered and he reported they were all around him."

Chop said that he, along with the others in the radar room, watched the intercept on the radarscope. They could see on the radar what the pilot was reporting. That tended to confirm the accuracy of the radar.

Patterson had to break off the intercept though there were still lights in the sky and objects on the scope. According to Chop, the pilot radioed that he was running low on fuel. He turned around so that he could head back to his base.

Chop said that the last of the objects disappeared from the scope about the time the sun came up. Ed Ruppelt, chief of Project Blue Book at the time, later quizzed Fournet about the activities that night. According to Ruppelt, both Fournet and Holcomb, the radar expert, were convinced the targets were solid, metallic objects. Fournet told Ruppelt that there were weather-related targets on the scopes but the controllers were ignoring them. Everyone was convinced that the targets were real.

The situation was a repeat of the week before. Headlines around the world, on Tuesday, July 29, told the whole story. In a banner headline that could have come from a science fiction movie, the *Cedar Rapids Gazette* reported, "Saucers Swarm over Capital."

At 4:00 P.M., in Washington, D.C., Major General John A. Samford, chief of Air Intelligence, held a press conference. Of that conference, Ruppelt wrote, "General Samford made an honest attempt to straighten out the Washington National Sightings, but the cards were stacked against him. He had to hedge on many answers to questions from the press because he didn't know the answers. This hedging gave the impression that he was trying to cover up something more than just the fact his people fouled up in not fully investigating the sightings. Then he brought in Captain Roy James from ATIC to handle all the queries about radar. James didn't do any better because he'd just arrived in Washington that morning and didn't know very much more about the sightings than he'd read in the papers. Major Dewey Fournet and Lieutenant Holcomb, who had been at the airport during the sightings, were extremely conspicuous by their absence . . ." As was the Pentagon spokesman on UFOs, Al Chop.

Ruppelt noted that the press accepted Samford's weather-related explanation as the final official solution. But even with the press believing that an official explanation had been found, Ruppelt reported in his 1956 book that the sightings were still carried as unknowns in the Project Blue Book files.

But that wasn't the end of it. Other investigations were made of all the unidentifieds in the Project Blue Book files. The purpose was to determine if explanations for those unidentifieds could be found. Documentation available through the Project Blue Book files provides evidence for the fact that labels and conclusions were changed. For example, in a letter written by Colonel Edward H. Wynn, deputy for Science and Components, in April 1960, he suggested that "Probable causes for sightings based on limited information should be accepted." The explanation of the Washington Nationals shifted slowly from unknowns to temperature inversions.

Ruppelt, however, didn't see it that way. He wrote, "Some people said, 'Weather targets,' but the chances of a weather target's making a 180-degree turn just as an airplane turns into it, giving a radar lock-on, then changing speed to stay just out of the range of the airplane's radar, and then slowing down when the airplane leaves is as close to nil as you can get."

Others argued that the situation was created out of the hysteria in the ARTC, at Washington National, and Andrews Air Force Base. According to some experts, when there is a visual sighting there frequently are "uncollorated" targets on the radarscope. It was suggested that this, coupled with the excitement of the night, produced the frightening results reported by the men at the various radar locations. In other words, with the weather the way it was, pilots seeing lights in the sky would have those sightings confirmed by radar if those pilots had initiated the reports. Of course, in this case, it was the radar operators who started the reporting by asking pilots to search the sky for those "uncollorated" targets.

There were reports that the tower operators at Andrews Air Force Base who had said they had seen a ficry orange sphere over the radio range when told by National Airport radar controllers that an object was there weren't quite as sure of their facts later. They completely changed their story, according to some later investigators, saying they had seen nothing more spectacular than a bright star. They said that they had been excited by all the reports of flying saucers being called to them by the radar operators at other facilities.

Ruppelt reported that no exceptionally bright stars were in the sky in a position to be seen over the radio range. He then wrote, "And I heard from a good source that the tower men had been 'persuaded' a bit." Persuaded by their superiors to suggest that they might have been looking at the nonexistent bright star.

When the University of Colorado assumed the task of investigating UFO sightings in 1967 under a grant from the Air Force, the Washington Nationals were one of the few "classic" sighting reports that demanded further attention. According to the final report by the Condon Committee, "One of the earliest of our field trips (December 1966) was made to Washington, D.C., to interview separately two air traffic control operators who had been involved in the great UFO flap there in the summer of 1952. Fourteen years later, these two men were still quite annoyed at the newspaper publicity they had received, because it had tended to ridicule their reports. Our conclusion from this trip was that these men were telling in 1966 stories that were thoroughly consistent with the main points of their stories in 1952."

The investigation, reported by the University of Colorado scientists, suggested a situation that was different than that reported by Ruppelt and others. The scientists wrote, "There are a tremendous number of reports of UFOs observed on these two nights. In most of the instances visual observers, especially in scrambled aircraft, *were unable to see targets indicated on ground radar, or to make airborne radar contact* [emphasis added]."

This is a strange thing to say, because Michael Wertheimer, who made the preliminary investigation over a day and a half in December 1966 for the Condon Committee, learned the truth. He spoke to Barnes, Andrews AFB tower operator Monte Banning, and other personnel at both National Airport and Andrews. Writing of the sightings on July 20, Tad Foster, of the Condon Committee, noted, "Thus, Pierman, Dermott and Patterson [airline pilots and the interceptor pilot] each observed a visible light, and verbally described its position and/or motion which in turn correlated with the blip on the radar screen."

Joe Zacko, who had been in the tower, also confirmed that he had seen the lights in the sky, as had some of the Air Force personnel, who later changed their stories. In other words, it is clear that there is a body of testimony from a number of different witnesses in different locations who saw lights where the radars showed objects.

The official Condon Committee report also seems to be at odds with what Ruppelt and others, including those who were on the scene in July 1952, reported. Interceptor pilots did see the lights, and onboard radars did lock on to solid objects. In one case, the ARTC radar returns vanished as the interceptors arrived on the scene, and once the fighters left, the objects returned. According to Ruppelt, the objects seemed to respond to the interceptor aircraft. Al Chop reported this to me during the interview I conducted. Weather-related phenomenon would not be adversely affected by the appearance of the fighters.

The University of Colorado report included a number of eyewitness statements, including one from "A USAF Captain [undoubtedly Captain Harold C. Way] at Andrews AFB radar center." The unidentified captain reports, "At about 0200 EST Washington Center advised that their radar had a target five miles east of Andrews Field. Andrews tower reported seeing a light, which changed color, and said it was moving towards Andrews. I went outside as no target appeared on Andrews radar and saw a light as reported by the tower. It was between 10 degrees and 15 degrees above the horizon and seemed to change color, from red to orange to green and red again. It seemed to float, but at times to dip suddenly and appear to lose altitude. It did not have the appearance of any star I have ever observed before. At the time of the observation there was a star due east of my position. Its brilliance was approximately the same as the object and it appeared at about the same angle, 10 degrees to 15 degrees about the horizon. The star did not change color or have any apparent movement. I estimated the object to be between three and four miles east of Andrews Field at approximately two thousand feet. During the next hour very few reports were received from Washington Center. [According to Washington Center's account, however, the 0200 EST object was seen on radar to pass over Andrews and fade out to the southwest of Andrews—G.D.T. (parenthetical statement in original)]. At approximately 0300 EST I again went outside to look at the object. At this time both the star and the object had increased elevation by about 10 degrees. [The azimuth would have also increased about 10 degrees, so that the observed change was apparently equal to the sidereal rate, 15 degrees of right ascension per hour—G.D.T. (parenthetical statement in original)]. The object had ceased to have any apparent movement, but still appeared to be changing color. On the basis of the second observation, I believe the unidentified object was a star."

Of course, we must remember that Ruppelt had said that the Andrews personnel had been pressured into altering their reports. The unidentifieds, on second thought, became stars.

The University of Colorado study concluded, "The atmospheric conditions during the period . . . in the Washington, D.C. area were conducive to anomalous propagation of radar signals. . . . The unidentified radar returns obtained during the incidents were most likely the result of anomalous propagation (AP). . . . The visual objects were, with one or two possible exceptions, identifiable most probably as meteors and scintilling stars."

In Appendix L to the final (Condon) report, Loren W. Crow, a certified consulting meteorologist, wrote, "It is the author's opinion that hot, humid air prevailed on both nights in both Washington and Norfolk. The general weather would have been considered fair weather by the trained observers at the various airports and they may not have reported all the scattered clouds which actually existed. It would have been considered an 'easy shift.' Visibilities remained above six miles at all times. The horizontal movement of scattered clouds, plus formation and dissipation of some few low clouds, both could have been seen at various times by ground observers whose eyes were well adjusted to the darkened sky. Anomalous propagation could have been observed on weather radar units during both nights at both locations. The echoes due to anomalous propagation would have had horizontal motion similar to clouds." Of course, we do have one report of a cloud traveling at 7000 mph, and we have other reports of clouds outrunning the interceptors.

Interestingly, the two Pentagon personnel I interviewed, Major Dewey Fournet and Al Chop, disagreed with the weather-related explanation. Both were sure, based on their observations in the radar room, that the returns showed solid objects. Both were listening to Holcomb, the acknowledged expert in radar. In fact, Chop said that he was unimpressed with the analysis made by a man from over a thousand miles away and fifteen years after the fact.

In 1952, the sightings over Washington National were unidentifieds. Those in the various radar rooms reported that the objects they saw were solid and metallic, not the sort of returns caused by temperature inversions. Pilots were ordered to intercept spotted objects where they were reported to be, and they obtained radar locks, only to have them broken. Airline pilots saw the lights and reported them to radar facilities.

Seventeen years later, as the University of Colorado report was put together, the situation seems to have changed. Now we have only a few radar sightings that have visual counterparts. And we're told that "in most instances visual observers, especially in scrambled aircraft, were unable to see targets indicated on ground radar, or to make airborne radar contact." That isn't the situation reported by Dewey Fournet, who was there. It is not the situation reported by Al Chop, who was there. And it is not the situation as indicated in the UFO project's files.

Bentwaters
August 13, 1956

According to the Project Blue Book files, it began, at 2130Z, or 9:30 P.M. local time, when Tech Sergeant Elmer L. Whenry, a GCA (Ground Controlled Approach) radar operator for the USAF's 1264th AACS Squadron at the RAF Station Bentwaters, England, spotted twelve to fifteen blips on his radarscope. These were not correlated to any of the aircraft known to be in the area at the time.

According to the official files, "This group was picked up approximately 8 miles southwest of RAF Station Bentwaters and were tracked on the radar scope clearly until the objects were approximately 14 miles northeast of Bentwaters. At the latter point on the course of these objects, they faded considerably on the radar scope."

The Blue Book report continues, "At the approximate 40 mile range individual objects . . . appeared to converge into one very large object which appeared to be several times larger than a B-36 aircraft due to the size of the blip on the radar scope. At the time that the individual objects seemed to converge into one large object, the large object appeared to remain stationary for 10 to 15 minutes. The large object them moved N.E. approximately 5 or 6 miles then stopped its movement for 3 to 5 minutes then moved north disappearing off the radar scope."

At about the same time, Airman 2/c (Second Class) John Vaccare, Jr., another radar operator, spotted a single blip 25 to 30 miles southeast. As he watched, the blip seemed to be moving on a 295-degree heading at a very high rate of speed. After about 30 seconds, the blip was 15 to 20 miles from the radar site, where it disappeared. According to the conservative figures, the object was moving at 5000 miles an hour.

At about 10:00 P.M., about 5 minutes after Whenry's first sightings had ended, he saw another blip located about 30 miles east of the station. Although the blip was on screen for only 16 seconds, it moved to a point where it was west of the station and then faded. Calculations by the radar operators suggested that it, whatever it might be, had moved at about 12,000 miles an hour.

From the Bentwaters control tower, others, including Staff Sergeant Lawrence S. Wright, reported a bright light, according to the Air Force file. It was the size of a pinhead held at arm's length and rose slowly from a point about 10 degrees above the horizon. It remained in sight for about an hour, appearing and disappearing. Nearly everyone who has looked at the file and checked the various star charts and maps have concluded that this object was Mars.

As Whenry was tracking the objects on his scope, a flight of two T-33 jets from the 512th Fighter Interceptor Squadron returned to Bentwaters after a routine mission. The two pilots, identified in the Blue Book files only as Metz and Rowe (data available through other, official sources revealed their full names as First Lieutenant Charles V. Metz and First Lieutenant Andrew C. Rowe), were asked to try to find the objects. Although they searched the area for 45 minutes, vectored by the radar operators, they failed to find anything and were unable to confirm the sighting. They broke off and landed about 10:15 P.M.

At 10:55 P.M., another target was spotted, about 30 miles to the east and heading west at only 2000 to 4000 miles an hour. It passed directly overhead and disappeared from the radar screen about 30 miles from the base. This time, however, there was an airborne observation. A C-47 pilot saw the object flash beneath his plane. To him it looked like little more than a blur of light.

The C-47 pilot wasn't the only person to see the light. On the ground, a number of people, looking up, saw the same bright blur. They provided little in the way of useful description of the object.

There were those who believed that this one segment of the case could be identified, just as Mars seems to have explained the Bentwaters control tower sighting. Analysis by UFO debunker Philip Klass led him to speculate that the pilot only saw a meteor, one of the many that can be seen during the Perseid Meteor showers. Atmospheric physicist James McDonald, who also reviewed the case, disagreed, using the ground observations and the pilot's sighting to suggest that the object was between ground level and 4000 feet. Klass failed to give any hint of the ground observations as he wrote the object off. But even if Klass was right about this one sighting, there were others made that same night that were not so easily explained.

The sighting by the pilot and the people on the ground was the last of the events at the Bentwaters base. The action shifted to the west-northwest as Lakenheath Air Force Base radars began to pick up the objects. Ground personnel saw a luminous object approach from a southwesterly direction, stop, then shoot off toward the east. Not much later, two white lights appeared, "joined up with another and both disappeared in formation together." Before they vanished, the objects performed a number of high-speed maneuvers. Most importantly, all of this was seen on two separate radar screens at Lakenheath.

The Blue Book files noted, "Thus two radar sets [that is, Lakenheath GCA and the RATCC radars] and three ground observers report substantially the same thing . . . the fact that radar and ground visual observations were made on its rapid acceleration and abrupt stops certainly lend credulance [*sic*] to the report."

But Klass, in his analysis of the case, finds what he believes to be the fatal flaw here. He seizes on the point that the blip stopped to hover. He wrote, "With the radar operating in the moving-target-indicator (MTI) mode, *only moving targets* should appear on the scope—IF the MTI is functioning properly. In radars of that early vintage, MTI was a relatively new feature and one that often caused problems. For example, the instruction book for the MPN-11A [the designation of that particular radar set design] radar, which also had MTI, specifically warned radar operators and maintenance personnel of the possibility of *spurious signals* being caused by an MTI malfunction. In chapter 5, on page 12, the Technical Order (as the instruction book is called) warned that MTI 'circuits are complex; the stability requirements are severe; the tolerances are close.' And on page 18 of chapter 4, the same manual warns operators of still another potential source of spurious signals that can result from what is called 'extra-time-around signals' [Emphasis in original]."

What Klass is suggesting, without going into a complex and detailed discussion of the workings of radars that are now more than forty years old, is that "this condition can arise during anomalous-propagation weather conditions when echoes from distant fixed targets on the ground far beyond the selected maximum radar operating range defeat the MTI function. Under this condition, the Tech Order warned, 'the signal from this distant fixed target may appear *as a false moving target* . . . ' [Klass's added emphasis]."

Klass is arguing, based on the technical specifications of the radars in use, that the blips during this first sighting are anomalous propagation: In other words, the returns were not of real craft but a "phantom" created by the weather conditions outside and the electronic characteristics of the radars being used.

About midnight one of the operators at Lakenheath called the chief fighter controller at the RAF Station at Neatishead, Norfolk, in England, and reported a strange object buzzing the base. F. H. C. Wimbledon would later say, "I scrambled a Venom night fighter from the Battle Flight through Sector, and my controller in the Interception Control team would consist of one fighter controller, a corporal, a tracker and a height reader. That is, four highly trained personnel in addition to myself could now see the object on our radarscopes."

Blue Book files, which are often confusing, suggest that it took the two-man fighter between 30 and 45 minutes to arrive at Lakenheath. As the aircraft approached, according to the reports, "Pilot advised he had a bright light in sight and would investigate. At 13 miles west, he reported loss of target and white light."

Immediately afterwards the interceptor was directed to another target over Bedford, and the navigator locked on it with his radar. He said it was the "clearest target I have ever seen on radar."

The radar contact was broken, and the Lakenheath controllers reported that the object had passed the Venom fighter and was now behind it—that is, at the six o'clock position, in the lingo of fighter pilots. The pilot acknowledged the message and tried various maneuvers to reverse the situation, so as to get behind the object. Unable to shake the object, the pilot asked for assistance.

But the Venom was now low on fuel, and the pilot decided to return to base. According to the Blue Book documents, "Second Venom was vectored to other radar targets but was unable to make contact." The second aircraft returned to the base, and no other fighters were sent. By 3:30 A.M., all targets were gone.

When the Condon Committee began its investigations in 1967, one of the controllers who had been on duty that night at Bentwaters sent a letter to the committee describing the events. Although it had been about a dozen years, the memory seemed to be well etched because the facts, as related by the letter writer, were borne out in the case file. Naturally there were some discrepancies between what was in the letter and the events as they happened, but nothing of a significant nature.

The controller pointed out that he had not told anyone of the events because he was "pretty sure it is considered (or was) classified, and the only reason I feel free to give you details is because you are an official government agency."

His long letter than described most of the events of that night. He provided a detailed look at the attempted intercept. He made a number of interesting observations in the letter, including information about the intercept. He wrote, "The first movement of the UFO was so swift (circling behind the interceptor), I missed it entirely, but it was seen by other controllers. However, the fact that this had occurred was confirmed by the pilot of the interceptor. The pilot of the interceptor told us he would try to shake the UFO and would try it again. He tried everything—he climbed, dived, circled, etc., but the UFO acted like it was glued right behind him, always the same distance, very close, but we always had two distinct targets. Note: Target resolution on our radar at the range they were from the antenna (about 10 to 30 miles, all in the southerly sectors from Lakenheath) would be between 200 and 600 feet probably. Closer than that we would have got one target from both aircraft and UFO. Most specifications say 500 feet is the minimum but I believe it varies and 200 to 600 feet is closer to the truth . . ."

What all this boils down to is a series of radar observations of objects that displayed characteristics outside the capabilities of aircraft of the day. In at least one of the reports from Bentwaters, the radar sightings coincided with visual observations on the ground and by a pilot in the C-47 (the sighting that Klass had "identified" as a meteor). This should not be confused with the observation of Mars made by tower personnel. That aspect of the case has been resolved to the satisfaction of everyone, whether a believer, or a skeptic, or an Air Force investigator.

On the ground at Lakenheath were witnesses who saw two luminous objects in fast flight. They witnessed the course reversals and the dead stops. The maneuvers rule out meteors, which some have suggested were responsible for the sightings.

In his paper "Science in Default," published in *UFO's A Scientific Debate*, Dr. James McDonald wrote, "The file does, however, include a lengthy dispatch that proposes a series of what I must term wholly irrelevant hypotheses about Perseid meteors with 'ionized gases in their wake which may be traced on radarscopes,' and inversions that 'may cause interference between two radar stations some distance apart.' Such basically irrelevant remarks are all too typical of Bluebook critique over the years."

He also pointed out that "Not only are the radar frequencies here about two orders of magnitude too high to afford even mar-

ginal likelihood of meteor-wake returns, but there is absolutely
no kinematic similarity between the reported UFO movements
and the essentially straight-line hypersonic movement of a meteor,
to cite just a few of the objections to meteor hypotheses."

Two separate radars at Lakenheath, having different radar pa-
rameters, were concurrently observing movements of one or more
unknown targets over an extended period of time. One way of
checking the reliability of a return on one radar is to compare it
to another. If they are operating at different frequencies, then an
inversion layer, if affecting the returns, will be different on the
two sets. Or one will show it and the second will not. It eliminates
the possibility of a spurious target.

The Blue Book files suggest that some of the two-radar
sightings were coincident with the visual observations on the
ground. In other words, not only were the objects seen on multiple radars, but there were also people outside who saw the lights
in the sky.

Attempting to dismiss the case as anomalous propagation,
Klass wrote in his report, "If it were not for the incident involving
the first Venom pilot's reported radar-visual encounter with the
UFO, this case would deserve scant attention because the erratic
behavior of the radar-UFOs is so characteristic of spurious
targets . . ."

Klass then goes on to explain the cockpit configuration of the
Venom fighter, reporting, accurately, that it is set up so that the
pilot sits on the left and the radar operator sits on the right.
Controls for the radar and the screen are situated so that it would
be difficult for the pilot to both fly the plane and work the radar.
He suggests, based on the reported communications between the
pilot and the ground, that there was no radar operator in the
cockpit. This, Klass believes, explains why there seems to be a
radar visual sighting. The pilot, doing double duty, was "over-
whelmed" by the workload and made a simple mistake.

But this is speculation by Klass. He points out. "Never once
did the words 'we' or 'radar operator' appear in the reports; only
the words 'I' and 'pilot.' "

This was a "scrambled" intercept mission. It is unlikely that
the aircraft took off without a full cockpit crew as military regula-

tions prohibit this. In other words, regardless of the speculations by Klass, there would have been a man sitting in the right seat to work the radar. And, if that is the case, then his whole theory is in error and should be rejected.

Furthermore, the single-occupant theory does not explain the other visual sightings at the scene. The case comprises more than a single misidentified blip on the radars. It is a complex case that should have been carefully researched by those who claimed to be interested in finding answers.

The Condon Committee which did investigate the case in a very limited fashion, suggested that they were hampered by receiving the case late. It wasn't until the letter from the controller arrived that they even began to look at it. Only then did they request the Air Force file.

One interesting point is that Klass criticizes some researchers for relying on the twelve-year-old memories of the controller. He prefers to rely on the reports written within days of the sighting. The Condon Committee, however, noted, "One of the interesting aspects of this case is the remarkable accuracy of the account of the witness as given in the letter . . . which was apparently written from memory 12 yr. after the incident. There are a number of minor discrepancies, mostly a matter of figures (the C-47 at 5,000 ft. was evidently actually at 4,000 ft.), and he seems to have confused the identity of location C with B (as noted in his letter); however all of the major details of his account seem to be well confirmed by the Blue Book account."

After their review of the case, the Condon Committee reported, "In conclusion, although conventional or natural explanations certainly cannot be ruled out, the probability of such seems low in this case and the probability that at least *one genuine UFO was involved* seems high."

Let's look at that conclusion again, remembering that Ed Condon, in authoring his report to the Air Force, claimed they found no evidence for UFOs. But the conclusion reached by the scientists of the Condon Committee was ". . . the probability that at least *one genuine UFO was involved* seems high."

Hynek, in a "memorandum for record" found in the Project Blue Book files, wrote about the case, "The Lakenheath case could constitute a source of embarrassment to the Air Force, and should the facts, as so far reported, get into the public domain, it is not necessary to point out what excellent use the several dozen UFO societies and other 'publicity artists' would make of such an incident. It is, therefore, of great importance that further information on the technical aspects of the original observations be obtained, without loss of time from the original observers."

There is no evidence that anyone did any follow-up work, at least in the Blue Book files. Here is a case that, if properly researched, could have given us a great deal of information about UFOs. It contains the elements that the scientific community demands: Not only do we have the reports of the radar operators about what they were seeing on the scopes but we also have visual confirmation by other personnel, including two pilots. Clearly something other than weather-related phenomena was present.

Even the Condon Committee scientists, who, by the time this case arrived, were predisposed to believe that UFOs were nothing more than imagination, misidentification, and illusion, wrote that there was a genuine UFO involved. I should point out here that a genuine UFO does not translate directly into extraterrestrial spacecraft.

Klass, at the end of his report about the case, wrote, "UFOlogical principle #10: Many UFO cases seem puzzling and unexplainable simply because case investigators have failed to devote a sufficiently rigorous effort to the investigation." He added, "This is not really surprising because the vast majority of UFO investigators are persons who want to believe in extraterrestrial spaceships, either consciously or unconsciously. The larger the number of seemingly unexplainable cases, the stronger the apparent support for the extraterrestrial hypothesis."

In this case, however, some of the most persuasive arguments came from the Condon Committee scientists. They didn't want to believe at all; in fact, they hung ridiculous explanations on some of the reports simply to have them labeled as "identified." But they reported that this case was a genuine UFO.

The point is that Project Blue Book and the Air Force had this case in their hands. They were alerted as Air Force Regulation 200-2 demanded, and they had access to all the witnesses. At worst, some of those witnesses would have been civilians assigned to one of the bases involved. Yet there is no evidence in the Blue Book files that Air Force investigators followed up on the reports. There is no evidence that the Air Force cared what the facts were. Instead, someone said meteors might be in the area, and meteors became a source of the visual sightings. Someone suggested that anomalous propagation might be responsible, and anomalous propagation became the source of the radar returns.

In fact, one writer suggested that as the objects approached the radar sites, they seemed to fade and then came back stronger. To him, this meant anomalous propagation because this was a classic symptom of it. Targets often faded and came back stronger under those circumstances.

There is, of course, another equally plausible explanation. Radar sites are designed so that there is little in the way of signal strength directly overhead. The radars are set up to find targets approaching and to display those targets. If the object flies directly overhead, the signal fades and the target fades, only to come back strong on the other side, once the object is out of this "cone of silence."

In other words, if a real, solid object flew over the top of the radar site, the operator could expect it to fade out and then come back. The returns on the scopes did exactly what they should have, not because they were anomalous propagation but because the target had flown over the top of the site.

At Bentwaters-Lakenheath, Air Force investigators took their teletype messages, checked the star charts, and let it go. There are some statements from some of the witnesses, but they take up only a few pages. No other investigation was completed. Nothing else was done—at least that is the evidence available in the Blue Book files.

McDonald, after reviewing the case, wrote, "Doesn't a UFO case like Lakenheath warrant more than a mere shrug of the shoulders from scientists?"

Minot, North Dakota
October 24, 1968

In some cases the physical evidence is extremely dramatic. The Washington Nationals provided dozens of witnesses who saw the objects or lights in the sky, as well as radar tracks from a number of sets at three separate locations. The radar tracks confirmed the visual observations of the various pilots, radar controllers, and tower operators.

In other cases, the physical evidence isn't quite as dramatic, but we do have it. There are cases with ground observations, radar tracks, and—in the case of Minot, North Dakota—even the possibility of interference with radio communications, a classic symptom known as an electromagnetic effect. It provides those multiple chains of evidence that suggest something real is happening.

According to the project record card, the conclusions for the sightings that took place near Minot, North Dakota, on October 24, 1968 are: "Ground-Visual: 1. Probable (Aircraft) (B-52). 2. Probable Astro (Sirius). Radar: Possible (Plasma). Air-Visual: Possible (Plasma)."

In the comments section of the project card, the investigating officer wrote, "The ground visual sightings appear to be of the star Sirius and the B-52 which was flying the area. The B-52 radar contact and the temporary loss of UHF transmission could be attributed to plasma, similar to ball lightning. The air-visual from the B-52 could be the star Vega which was on the horizon at the time, or it could be a light on the ground, or possibly a plasma."

According to the main Project Blue Book file, it seems that the first sighting that night was made about 30 minutes after midnight by Airman Isley. No first names are found in the project case file. He only saw a bright light in the east.

Two hours later, A/1c (Airman First Class) O'Connor sighted a bright light. At the same time, Staff Sergeant Smith reported that he had seen a bright star light. Both Isley and Smith thought the bright lights unusual and were unable to easily identify them.

At 0308 hours (3:08 A.M.) a series of sightings began by maintenance teams around the Minot area. O'Connor, the maintenance team chief, said that all members of the team saw a lighted object that was reddish orange in color. They suggested it was a large object that had flashing green and white lights. According to the Blue Book file, "After they entered N-7 LF [a field site] the object came directly overhead with the sound of jet engines."

The report continued, "SSgt Bond the FSC at Nov Flt stated that the object which looked to him as the sun, came near the handred antenna at Nov-1. It then moved to the right and he sent the SAT out to check and see what it was. The object then moved about one mile away with the Nov SAT following. They came within ½ mile from where it appeared to be landing. When it reached the surface the lights became dimmer and finally went out. After this they could see nothing. SSgt Smith at Oscar-1 saw the object separate into two parts and go in oposite [sic] directions and return and pass under each other. At this time Julelt Flt and Mike Flt Team observed the same things and described it the same way. The approximate grid coordinates of the apparently landing was AA-43. The entire observation period as near as can be determined was about 45 minutes."

At 0324 Staff Sergeant Wagla, A/1c Allis, and A/1c Deer sighted a UFO. A minute later, Staff Sergeant Halko, A/1c Jenkins, and A/1c Richardson sighted the UFO. Ten minutes after that, the crew of a B-52 was brought into the case.

The transcript of the conversations between the tower and the aircraft are available in the Project Blue Book file. The times in the transcript are all in Greenwich Mean Time (Zulu), but I have corrected them for local time in North Dakota so that it will be consistent with the times given for the sightings by ground maintenance and security personnel.

At 0330, the controllers received the information that there was a UFO 24 miles to the northwest. At 0334, JAG-31 (JAG Three One), a B-52 on a calibration check, requested a clearance and was at "Flight Level 200 (2000)."

0334 "MIB (Minot) approach control does JAG 31 have clearance to WT fix at Flight Level 200?"

"JAG 31 roger climb out on a heading of 290 climb and maintain 5000. Stand-by for higher altitude. We're trying to get it from center now."

At 0335, the controller asked, "And JAG 31 on your way out to the WT fix request you look out toward your one o'clock position for the next fifteen or sixteen miles and see if you see any orange glows out there."

"Roger, roger . . . glows 31."

"Someone is seeing flying saucers again."

"Roger I see a . . ." The rest of the transmission from the aircraft is garbled.

At 0352, the controller then radioed, "Three one, the UFO is being picked up by weathers radar also. Should be at our one o'clock position three miles now."

The pilot said, "We have nothing on our airborne radar and I'm in some pretty thick haze right now and unable to see out that way."

At 0358, though the transmissions have nothing to do with the sighting of the UFO, there is a strange event. The pilot requested an instrument-guided approach, and received instructions from the controller about that. The pilot called, and then, apparently, the radio went dead. Although they could hear the instructions from the ground, they could no longer transmit. The controller asked them to "squawk ident," which meant to use the aircraft's transponder which would "paint" the controller's radar with a large, glowing blip.

At 0400, the controller again suggested, "JAG 31, if you hear me squawk ident . . . JAG 31 ident observed. Cleared for the approach attempt. Contact on frequency 271 decimal three and you're cleared for the low approach."

They continued to have radio troubles for another couple of minutes. At 0402, they were again able to communicate easily. The pilot said, "Our UFO was off to our left there when we started penetration."

"Roger. Understand you did see something on your left side."

"We had a radar return at about a mile and a quarter nine o'clock position for about the time we left 200 to about 14 . . ."

They discussed the troubles with the transmissions and then, at 0403, the controller asked, "Affirmative. I was wondering how far out did you see that UFO?"

"He was about one and a half miles off our left wing at 35 miles when we started in and he stayed with us 'til about 10."

"I wonder if that could have been your radio troubles."

"I don't know . . . But that's exactly when they started."

At 0413, as they are working the "low approach," the controller asked, "JAG 31, are you observing any more UFO's?"

"Negative on radar. We can't see anything visually."

"JAG 31, roger. The personnel on from the missile site advise they don't see anything anymore either."

Finally, at 0421, the controller said, "JAG 31, [garbled] requests that somebody from your aircraft stop in at base ops after you land."

"Roger 31. We'll give them a call."

What we have, then, was a group of sightings made by men on the ground, at the missile sites scattered around the Minot Air Force Base. There was a radar sighting on the ground—the "weathers" radar, which was never identified in the Blue Book files. Later, there was a visual sighting from the crew of the B-52, and there was a radar sighting from the aircraft as well. Although the first sightings began just after midnight and the last was made about four in the morning, they were not continuous. There were a number of sightings made by a number of men in widely scattered locations, and they were apparently not in communication with one another.

Project Blue Book was alerted about the sightings that same day. In a memo for the record dated October 24, Lieutenant Marano (again no first name is available in the file) began to receive telephone calls. He learned that both the commander at Minot and Major General Nichols at 15th Air Force headquarters were interested in what had happened. Apparently a lieutenant colonel named Werlich had been appointed the local—meaning Minot—UFO officer. He would conduct the investigation.

The memo for the record explained the incident. "At about 0300 hours local, a B-52 that was about 39 miles northwest of Minot AFB and was making practice penetrations sighted an unidentified blip on their radar. Initially the target traveled approximately 2½ miles in 3 sec or about 3,000 mi/hr. After passing from the right to the left of the plane, it assumed a position off the left wing of the 52. The blip stayed off the left wing for approximately 20 miles at which point it broke off. Scope photographs were taken. When the target was close to the B-52 neither of the two transmitters in the B-52 would operate properly but when it broke off both returned to normal function.

"At about this time a missile maintenance man called in and reported sighting a bright orangish-red object. The object was hovering at about 1000 ft or so, and had a sound similar to a jet engine. The observer had stopped his car, but he then started it up again. As he started to move, the object followed him then accelerated and appeared to stop at about 6–8 miles away. The observer shortly afterward lost sight of it.

"In response to the maintenance man's call the B-52, which had continued its penetration run, was vectored toward the visual which was about 10 miles northwest of the base. The B-52 confirmed having sighted a bright light of some type that appeared to be hovering just over or on the ground."

Now comes one of the most interesting parts, one that seemed to have slipped by the Air Force investigators at Blue Book and which should have alerted them to the unusual aspects of this case. "Fourteen other people in separate locations also reported sighting a similar object. Also, at this approximate time, security alarm for one of the sites was activated. This was an alarm for both the outer and inner ring. When guards arrived at the scene they found that the outer door was open and the combination lock on the inner door had been moved."

With command emphasis on the sighting, and with more than one general officer interested in the case, it was "investigated" by Blue Book. The term *investigated* is misleading because of a comment in one of the memos for the record. On October 30, 1968, Lieutenant Colonel Hector Quintanilla (the chief of Project Blue Book in 1968) had a telephone conversation with Colonel Pullen at SAC Headquarters. Asked if he had "sent anybody up to investigate the sighting," Quintanilla replied, "We did not send anybody up because I only have four people on my staff, myself, an assistant, a secretary and an admin sergeant. I talked to Col Werlich for over thirty minutes and since this didn't appear unusual I didn't send anyone up."

We have a sighting that involved both ground and airborne radars. We have a sighting to corroborate those returns from both the aircraft and people on the ground. In fact, there are people at separate locations who reported seeing the UFO, but according to Quintanilla, there was nothing unusual about the sighting.

On November 1, Colonel Werlich, the Minot officer in charge of the investigation, said that he had already had "the people fill out AF Forms 117," which were the long forms the Air Force used to gather UFO data.

Werlich told Lieutenant Marano at Wright-Patterson, "I monitored them while they filled them out, but I can't see where the navigator can help . . ."

Later, in that same "memo," Lieutenant Marano noted, "The one we are mainly interested in is the one that cannot be identified. The one of radar and the aircraft correlated pretty well."

Using maps, they attempted to identify the low-flying light that could have seen on the ground. According to the report, "There is nothing there that would produce this type of light. The same for O'Conner and Nicely from November 7 [that is, two of the maintenance men from the silo designated N (November) seven] which is near Greno."

Later, in response to a question about the object on the ground, Marano was told, "They were able to see a light source while the 52 got in real close then it disappeared."

The account in the files and the memos for record are somewhat confusing. It seemed that they were suggesting that the men on the ground who had seen the lights and then heard a roar like that of jet engines had seen the B-52. "Almost 80 percent were looking at the B-52. If you would look at an aircraft at 20,000 ft, then you wouldn't see much but I'm an [sic] to place logic in that it was there and what they saw was there. There is enough there that it is worth looking at. Nobody can definitely say that these people definitely saw the aircraft, but within reason they probably saw it."

What this seems to be suggesting is that the officers at Minot think the ground sightings might be of the B-52, but they're not sure. It seems that they realize they are suggesting that the men stationed at Minot are incapable of identifying a huge bomber that is assigned to SAC. How could that many men, some of whom had been around SAC and B-52s for years, suddenly be incapable of recognizing the aircraft—even at night and at altitude? It is an explanation that is ridiculous. Had the men been looking at a B-52, they would have identified it as such.

There is another factor here. Once again we don't have a highly charged environment where everyone has been talking about flying saucers for weeks. We have a number of men who look into the night sky and see something they can't identify. Had it been a B-52, it seems quite reasonable that the men would have identified it as such. Just how clever would they have had to be to find that answer?

Having disposed of the ground visual sightings, after a fashion, the investigators began to attack the radar aspect of the case. But there is an interesting statement in one of the memos for the record that, not surprisingly, is somewhat confusing. Apparently Colonel Werlich, in a telephone communication with Blue Book officers, said, "I only stated one radar in the message because there was only one radar set. The ECM [electric counter measures] equipment hadn't been used. RAPCOM [radar facility] was painting [meaning operating]. IFF [identification friend or foe transponder] was operating in the airplane. It's a fairly good size blip. The object would have been covered by the blip. There is a Sage site [another radar facility] to the south. They do not remember any unidentified paints. The only one that I have is the one on the plane. The unusual part is the B-52 was in the middle of a sentence and the voice just quit transmitting right in the middle of the word . . ."

Werlich seems to be suggesting here that only one radar picked up the UFO, yet he also suggests that if it was close to the bomber, then the IFF equipment, which emits a signal so that the blip on the radar is huge and stands out for easy identification by the radar operator, would have covered the UFO. He also suggests that another site's radar operators don't remember any unidentified blips, which is a fairly weak statement.

Going back through the case file, there is a mention of the weathers radar, but there is no identification of this site. In fact, someone added a penciled question mark above the notation for the weathers radar. If the weathers radar picked up the blip, as suggested in the file, and the B-52's radar had it for a number of minutes (as we know), then two different radar sets had "painted" it.

The other interesting point made during this conversation was that the transmitters on the B-52 shut down. UFOs have often been associated with electromagnetic effects that seem to suppress electrical systems, causing cars to stall, lights to dim, and radios to fade. But this was a selective suppression of the electrical system: Only the transmitters ceased to function. Apparently all other electrical systems on the aircraft continued to operate properly.

Werlich said, "My personal opinion is that it couldn't be a malfunction because they transmitted before and afterwards. The aircraft was not checked out afterwards because the transmission [*sic*] was working."

In a proper investigation, the transmitter should have been checked for a short. The coincidence of the close approach of the UFO might have been just that—a coincidence. But a short would show up again, at some point. There is no indication from the Blue Book record that such is the case. Of course, if it did, there is no reason for Werlich, or anyone else at Minot, to report that to Blue Book.

During the conversation, the Air Force's old standby, a temperature inversion, was mentioned a couple of times. Lieutenant Marano "then explained about the many astronomical bodies that were over the area at the time and when there is quite an inversion they are magnified even greater."

The Air Force investigators were now suggesting that not only couldn't their personnel identify a B-52 when it flew over but now they couldn't identify stars. The ill-trained ground personnel, for some unexplained reason, began to see flying saucers all over the skies above Minot on October 24.

Then on November 1, 1968, in a memo for the record, it is reported, "Talked to Mr. Goff . . . who is quite familiar with airborne radars. Mr. Goff said that from the evidence at this time it would appear to him that the sightings may have been precipitated by some type of ionized air plasma similar to ball lightning. He felt that a plasma could account for the radar blip, loss of transmission and some of the visual sightings . . ."

For a moment or two, this sounded to me like a reasonable

solution to the problem. It then sounded like someone trying to find an explanation for a case where none existed, so I called a friend who teaches physics at a major university. He pointed out that if the phenomenon were true, why isn't it reported more often?

In other words, if plasma was a good explanation for this sighting, then we could expect to see similar things around other aircraft at other times. We could expect to have many reports of intermittent failures of transmitters, airborne radars plagued with plasma images, and reports of glowing plasmas following other aircraft. Yet this simply isn't the case.

During my discussion with the physicist, I kept asking about the glow, and how bright it would be. It began to sound as if we were talking about two different phenomena. He said that plasmas don't glow unless there is another feature. I mentioned the glow around high power lines, and he said that the electricity could excite the plasma to make it glow, but that they didn't glow on their own. In other words, unless there had been another mechanism there causing a glow, those on the ground and in the plane wouldn't have been able to see anything.

The idea of the plasma seemed to have impressed many of the people involved in the case. In a teletype message from Quintanilla to Colonel Pullen at SAC, he wrote, "It is my feelings, after reviewing preliminary information submitted by Monot [obviously Minot], that UFO painted by B-52 on radar and also observed visually by IP [pilot] and personnel on the ground is probably a plasma of the ball-lightning class. Plasmas of this type will paint on radar and also affect some electronic equipment at certain frequencies."

He then made a statement that is contradictory. "Plasmas are not uncommon, however, they are unique and extremely difficult to duplicate in the laboratory."

He finished with, "Also, because of durations, feel strongly that some security guards and maintenance crew were observing some first magnitude celestial bodies which were greatly magnified by the inversion layer and haze which was present at Minot during the time of the UFO observations . . . I consider the UFO reports as fairly routine, except of the plasma observation which is interesting from a scientific point of view. We will study this report in more detail when we receive the raw data from Minot."

Of course, a question springs to mind: Why? You have an answer and you certainly aren't going to change it. Besides, by November 13, Quintanilla had his final solutions. He wrote, "The following conclusions have been reached after a thorough study of the data submitted to the Foreign Technology Division. The ground visual sightings appear to be of the star Sirius and the B-52 which was flying in the area. The B-52 radar contact and the temporary loss of the UHF transmission could be attributed to a plasma similar to ball lightning. The air visual from the B-52 could be the star Vega which was on the horizon at the time, or it could be a light on the ground, or possibly a plasma . . . No further investigation by the Foreign Technology Division is contemplated."

The answers provided in this case are no answers whatsoever. It is a combination of new buzzwords such as plasma, a belief that Air Force personnel, including bomber crews, are unable to recognize stars, and a suggestion that many of these same people can't recognize a B-52 when they see it. Here was a case that deserved more investigation but got none.

The explanations offered are not very good. That was why I called the physicist. I wanted to know what he thought about the plasma idea. He said, "They're reaching here. This just doesn't make good sense."

Conclusions

In examining these cases we have seen evidence that UFO sightings are more than just the imagination of drunken witnesses, poorly educated people, or the delusional. We have seen that radar sets show the objects right where they should be and that the UFOs respond to the threat of military aircraft. Remember, the interceptors sent during the Washington Nationals seemed to chase the UFOs from the sky. This observation was made by the men in the radar rooms who were watching the events and who were certainly qualified to draw these conclusions.

But there is something else here that should bother anyone

who advocates a scientific investigation of the UFO phenomenon—one of the conclusions about the Bentwaters case reached
by the Condon Committee in 1969. The committee was financed
by the Air Force and the committee reported, as they had been
required to do, that they had found no compelling cases that
suggested that anything unusual was happening. According to the
conclusions drawn after their "scientific" study, the Air Force and
science shouldn't waste any more time and money on research
into UFOs—a phenomenon that was probably no more real than
Atlantis or the Easter Bunny.

That would all be fine if it hadn't been for the one statement
written concerning the Bentwaters sightings. Yes, Mars had been
spotted and reported as a UFO. Yes, there had been some explanations of other sightings in the area that seemed not only plausible but likely. And yes, the one conclusion that should have
turned everything upside down was ignored.

The Condon Committee scientists wrote, "In conclusion, although conventional or natural explanations certainly cannot be
ruled out, the probability of such seems low in this case and the
probability that at least *one genuine UFO was involved* seems
high."

Here, in a scientific arena—one in which the scientific community has done the investigating and one in which the desire
for prosaic answers runs high—we are confronted with a statement
suggesting that a genuine UFO was involved at some level. Isn't
this the very sort of evidence that scientists have been demanding
for decades? Isn't this one case sufficient to suggest that a better
scientific study be made?

We all agree that radar-visual cases provide clues about the
nature of the UFO phenomena. But even when there are unob-
jective studies designed to answer questions rather than learn the
truth we see reports that are inexplicable. We see evidence that
something strange is happening and that it is observed by radar.

No, we can no longer say that we do not accept the theory
of alien visitation simply because nothing has been seen on radar.
Yes, we must admit that these sightings do not *prove* there has
been alien visitation. We can only say that the radar cases make
it more difficult to ignore the UFOs and the theories about them.

The Photographic Evidence

There are many forms of physical evidence. Photographs, movie footage, and now videotape are a form of that physical evidence. They provide corroboration of a report and provide us with something that can be analyzed outside the testimony of a witness. Photographs provide something for us to study as we search for the truth.

Examination of photographs often provides clues about the reliability of the observer. There are times when what is visible in a photograph is not consistent with the story told by a witness or witnesses. When these sorts of discrepancies appear, and if they are significant in nature, then a conclusion of hoax can be drawn.

A barber in Ohio claimed to have taken two pictures as a huge UFO hovered over his house. Careful examination revealed that the shadows in the pictures had changed significantly, suggesting that the pictures had been taken hours apart rather than just minutes as the man had claimed. Investigators thus concluded that the tale told by the witness was inaccurate, calling the sighting into question. Most UFO researchers believe that the pictures were a hoax.

Sometimes there is nothing in a picture to give investigators a clue. The label of hoax is applied when a trickster admits his joke. In 1966, Guy B. Marquand, Jr. revealed that a picture he had taken some fifteen years earlier of a domed disk hovering above the mountains near Riverside, California, was a hoax. He said that he was young and was just having some fun.

Sometimes there is just no way to tell what a photograph shows. Carl Hart, Jr. took five pictures of strange lights that had been flying over Lubbock, Texas, in 1951. Although the Air Force, among others, has explained the sightings of the strange lights to their satisfaction, there never has been a good explanation for the pictures, which show formations of lights in the dark night sky.

Dr. Donald Menzel offered a number of solutions for those photographs but none that were adequate. When all else failed, he labeled the pictures a hoax, though there was no evidence that such was the case. In fact, when I spoke to Hart in 1993, he told me that he still doesn't know what he photographed.

And that leads to the real problem with UFO pictures. Though they are a form of physical evidence, they just don't provide sufficient proof that UFOs are extraterrestrial. In November 1972, Stuart Nixon, a NICAP (National Investigations Committee on Aerial Phenomena) director, wrote, "NICAP has never analyzed a structured object picture that is fully consistent with the claim [that] an extraordinary flying device was photographed."

What Nixon was attempting to say in his very candid statement was that all the pictures submitted had some sort of problem. In many cases the problem was minor and could easily be explained by simple memory lapse or misinterpretation of the circumstance. What Nixon and other UFO researchers wanted was a series of pictures that was free of the various questions that always arose.

In fact, the best photographs would be those snapped by independent photographers separated by miles, who were unknown to one another. They would provide the physical evidence, on film, of the extraordinary event and would virtually eliminate any claims of a hoax. So much could be learned that questions about the authenticity of the sighting would be removed.

But there has not been such a case. Skeptics point to the bolide photographed over the Teton Mountains in Wyoming in the 1970s. It was photographed by a number of people and filmed by more. Here was an event that was extremely rare—a meteor so bright that it could be seen during the day. Why were there multiple photographers of that event but nothing in the UFO field of a multiple photographer of a UFO event? To some it suggested that UFOs just didn't exist.

The problem was that the meteor was 40 to 50 miles high and was seen over a huge area. Most UFO sightings involving something other than a point of bright light in the sky are much closer to the ground. The opportunity for a large number of people to see a UFO is not as great as the opportunity to see a high-flying meteor.

What we generally end up with is a single photograph or a set of photographs from a single point of view. We can examine the ground detail and we can interview witnesses, but if a photographer is clever, then a good photograph can be fabricated. At that point the authenticity becomes a question of the reliability of the photographer.

The exception, at least in the 1950s, were the movies that had been taken. It would have been nearly impossible in that era for someone outside of Hollywood, or for someone who didn't have access to very expensive photographic equipment, to fake a convincing UFO movie. Oh, it had been tried. Contactees often had short films that showed UFOs "hovering" above the ground. Often the motion of the craft in the film resembled that of a small object on a thin string as it moved in a circular motion.

"Dr." Daniel Fry, a contactee who lived near the White Sands Missile Range, produced dozens of photographs of the UFOs he saw, and more than a few frames of movie footage. He always maintained that the photographs were real, but when he died, UFO researchers were able to review the movie footage . . . including the outtakes in which the fishing pole or string holding the model could be seen.

That doesn't mean that there haven't been legitimate UFO movies made. A number have been reported over the years. Dr. Robert M. L. Baker, Jr., has analyzed some of these, but he has come away somewhat disappointed. He wrote, "I believe these film clips are rather typical of the anomalistic or UFO motion pictures. Although I am convinced that many of the films indeed demonstrated anomalistic phenomena, they all have the characteristic of rather ill-defined blobs of light, and one can gain from them little insight into the real character of the phenomena. For example, linear distance, speed, and acceleration cannot be determined precisely, nor can size and mass. . . . The films are rather ungratifying subjects for research, because of their low information content (they simply show little dots of light) and because their analysis must often rely, in part, on the soft data of eyewitness reports."

So yes, there are motion pictures that supposedly show UFOs, but the ones considered worth studying are unsatisfactory in some aspects. Yes, there are photographs of structured craft that have been examined, but there are often problems with the eyewitness statements that accompany them.

And, there are those out there who "know" that flying saucers are not extraterrestrial craft, and therefore photographic evidence must have been manufactured by the witnesses. Because of that, they search until they find what they consider the fatal flaw in the movie footage or photographs. Then they label the pictures as hoaxes, or trot out a conventional explanation that explains nothing. They are happy, believing that they have disposed of the troubling evidence. Often, however, the explanation smacks of trickery. The fatal flaw is something that, to others, is innocuous and unimportant. The validity and authenticity of the photograph or the motion picture is often left to the eye of the investigator. And sometimes, just the hint that there is no explanation in a particular case is enough to advance our knowledge.

The Montana Movie
August 15, 1950

One of the major problems in the field of UFOlogy is that there are very few cases where there is both physical evidence and a large number of witnesses. The ideal situation is to have both ends of the spectrum, but, given the nature of the field, it is difficult to find cases that have some kind of physical evidence and a high number of witnesses. Given the nature of eyewitness testimony, it is better to have strong physical evidence.

In August 1950, Nick Mariana, a thirty-eight-year-old Army

Air Forces veteran, sports broadcaster, and manager of a local minor league baseball team, filmed two objects as they flew over Great Falls, Montana. The short film, only about sixteen seconds, would become one of the best, and, therefore, most controversial pieces of physical evidence available.

On a number of occasions, Mariana told both Air Force and private investigators that he had been at the field late on the morning of August 15 to check conditions of the stadium prior to a game. As was his habit, he glanced at the Anaconda Copper Company smokestack to see which way the wind was blowing.

In a statement taken on October 4, 1950, and signed by Captain John P. Brynildsen, it was reported, "Mr. Mariana made these pictures on 15 August 1950 between the hours of 11:25 and 11:30 A.M., at Great Falls, Montana. On the interview he stated that he first sighted the objects while standing in the grandstand of the ball park located at 26th Street and Eleventh Avenue North, Great Falls, Montana, and that he saw two bright disc shaped objects proceeding in a southerly direction at an altitude of approximately ten thousand feet and at a distance of about three-quarters of a mile in a westerly direction, from the observer's viewpoint. Mr. Mariana then stated that he ran downstairs and outside to his car from which he obtained his camera and made the pictures shown in the film. From the time of first sighting to the completion of taking of the pictures, Mr. Mariana estimated consumed approximately twenty seconds. At the time of his taking the pictures, a Miss Virginia Raunig . . . who is employed as his secretary, was a witness."

The film, when reviewed, showed that there were two bright objects in the sky over Great Falls. They appear as only blobs of white light that never are resolved into anything identifiable. Fortunately they are low enough that foreground detail can be seen. The objects fly over the roof of a building and pass behind a water tower before fading from sight. The film would provide scientists, technicians, Air Force officers, and UFO researchers with a bit of evidence that could be measured and investigated.

Interestingly, Mariana, when he first took the film, didn't alert the Air Force. He did, however, alert the local newspapers. Philip Klass, in *UFOs Explained*, wrote, "It seems certain that the Mariana UFO movies are not a staged hoax, aside from the great difficulty of staging them. One typical characteristic of hoax UFO photos is that the incident is almost never reported until the pictures have been developed to see how well they turned out. In Mariana's case, he promptly reported the incident to the local newspaper immediately afterward and at least two weeks before the films were processed."

Even with the publicity the film received in the two Great Falls daily newspapers, as well as the fact that there was an Air Force base located in the town, no one thought to contact the military, nor did anyone from the Air Force seem interested in contacting Mariana. Mariana did show his film to a number of civic organizations, and, at one of them, Clifton Sullivan of the *Great Falls Leader* asked if he could contact the Air Force. Mariana had no objections. Sullivan wrote to the Air Materiel Command at Wright-Patterson Air Force Base.

At that point the Air Force was only mildly interested in the film; that interest might have been sparked by newspaper reports. In October 1950 the UFO project, then known as Grudge, was basically dead. The "squares" were being filled, but the attention focused on flying saucers was fleeting. The Air Force's main objective was to explain the cases and be done with it.

In fact, that attitude is painfully obvious in a series of articles that was carried in the *Dayton Daily News*. In the first article, it was reported that the Air Materiel Command had denied a report that they had confiscated "colored motion pictures of two silver discs." A spokesman said, "We do not have any such films here at Air Materiel Command headquarters."

That was on a Thursday. On Friday it was announced that an intelligence officer from the Great Falls AFB said that Mariana's film was being sent on to Wright-Patterson for analysis.

Four days later, on October 10, the *Dayton Daily News* reported, "Air Materiel Command officials . . . after viewing the color motion pictures taken last August 15 at a Great Falls, Mont., ball park said the film was too dark to distinguish any recognizable objects. . . . The film, which during the past week had become the subject of widespread conjecture, will not be sent on to USAF Intelligence in Washington, but, if he wants it, will be returned to its owner, Nick Mariana, manager of the Great Falls baseball team."

The supposed solution to the case came almost immediately. In a statement by the 15th District Office of Special Investigations at Great Falls to the District Commander, 5th District Office of Special Investigation at Wright-Patterson, it was noted, "A further check of the records of Base Operations, Great Falls Air Force Base, Great Falls, Montana, indicates that an F-94 type aircraft, #2503, and an F-94 type aircraft, #2502, landed Great Falls Air Force Base at 1133 and 1130 hours (Mountain Standard Time) respectively on 15 August 1950. These aircraft were assigned to the 449th Fighter Squadron, Ladd Air Force Base, Alaska. Mr. Mariana stated that almost immediately after taking the motion pictures, two USAF jet type aircraft had flown across the sky east of him, heading in a southerly direction."

In a handwritten note on the letter, some unidentified officer had recorded, "Probably it." That is to say, within hours of learning about the movie footage, without the benefit of an examination of the physical evidence, the Air Force officers at Project Grudge had found a solution.

An investigation was also conducted into the backgrounds of both Mariana and his secretary. Brynildsen learned that Mariana was born in 1912, was a graduate of Montana State University in 1938 and a veteran of the Army Air Forces during the Second World War. He had risen to the rank of corporal and had edited the base newspaper at the Great Falls Air Force Base. He was married in 1941 and had a daughter who was three. He was employed as the manager of the local minor league baseball team and had a syndicated radio show on fourteen stations. According to Brynildsen, "He enjoys an excellent reputation in the local community and is regarded as a reliable, trustworthy and honest individual."

The background of Raunig was not heavily investigated. She was nineteen when the event took place. She told the investigators that she thought the objects had been in sight for only 7 seconds. She couldn't contribute much to the file.

The film was quickly returned to Mariana; that gave rise to one more bit of controversy. According to Mariana, the Air Force had removed the first thirty to thirty-five frames of the film. He said that in those few frames, the shape of the objects, as well as some surface detail, was visible. The film he got back had been altered by the Air Force.

That wasn't the end of Air Force interest, however. In May 1952, Colonel Frank L. Dunn wrote a letter to Mr. Bowen of the Hearst Corporation (the Air Force, before the release of the Project Blue Book files to the general public, attempted to remove the names of all civilians, so there are some gaps in what we know). In the letter he said, "(3) The observer stated the sighting took place between 1125 and 1130 hours, MST, 15 August 1950 and phenomena were in sight for a period of about eight seconds. Mr. Mariana stated that a time of approximately 20 seconds elapsed between his first sighting of the objects and completion of his photography of them. It should be noted that this last time mentioned was obtained from a narrative report of the investigating officer, and is not a direct quotation of statement by Mr. Mariana.

"(4) No reply can be made to your question concerning relative size of objects as they appeared in film compared to film size, since the film was returned to Mr. Mariana and is not available for examination.

"(5) Conclusion as to probable cause of sighting in this case is: Unknown.

"Possible causes considered are: Light reflections on two jet aircraft known to be in the area at the time of the sighting; exhaust of aircraft known to be in area at time of sighting; reflections of sunlight on water tower in vicinity."

Within months, however, the Air Force would find that their interest in the film would increase. During the summer of 1952 thousands of UFOs were seen over the United States. Fifteen hundred would be reported to the Air Force, the majority of them during the summer months. A teletype message was sent from Air Force headquarters in Washington to the Great Falls Air Force Base. It said, "Desire to know if Mr. Nick Mariana is still a resident of Great Falls and, if so, his address and telephone number and present employment. Inquiry must be discreet and preferably without his knowledge. For your info, Mariana obtained about 15 feet of 16 mm Kodachrome movies of 2 unidentified flying objects over Great Falls on 15 Aug 1950. At the time, Mariana resided at [address blacked out] Great Falls and was general manager of the [organization blacked out] as a sports reporter and commentator. His secretary also witnessed sighting and may know his present whereabouts if not residing locally. She is Miss Virginia Raunig then residing [address blacked out] in Great Falls."

Finally, on January 9, 1953, Major Raymond L. Kolman wrote his report on his follow-up investigation, including a longer narrative taken directly from Mariana. Mariana said:

On about the 5th or 15th of August 1950, I, as manager of the Electronics, a local baseball team, walked to the grandstand of the local stadium here in Great Falls, Montana. It was approximately 1130 AM and my purpose was to check the direction of the wind in preparation for the afternoon's game.

Looking toward the smoke stack to see in which direction the wind was blowing the smoke, I saw two saucer shaped, very bright objects completely motionless and in direct line with the smoke stack. I was of the opinion that they were aircraft, but after a few seconds of a still motionless view, I decided they could not be aircraft. I immediately ran to my car, which was parked adjacent to the stadium (approximately 50 Ft.) to get my movie camera. At the same time I shouted for my secretary, and her independent description of these two objects is identical to mine. At the time I thought there might have been a whistling noise, but of that I am not certain. There was no visible exhaust or fire and the objects seemed like two new dimes glistening in the sun. I did not take time to return to the exact spot from where I had originally noticed these objects. I prepared my camera and started taking pictures, from a point immediately adjacent to my car. By this time, approximately five to eight seconds had elapsed since I had run to my car. The two objects were again motionless, but at a point to the left of the smoke stack. It was at this point that I first filmed these two objects. I repeat, they were not covering any distance; that is, they were motionless, but an occasional vibration

seemed to momentarily tilt them, after which they would in-
stantly correct their level plane to its seemingly balanced posi-
tion. The two objects made an abrupt flight in an arc motion
at very high speeds. I approximate the speed to have been over
400 MPH. At all times the altitude was definitely in the 5,000
to 10,000 ft. about the terrain bracket. The end frames of the
movie reel show the objects in line with a high water tower,
which is approximately 130 ft. high. I approximate a 30 degree
angle to have been formed by the level ground and a straight
line from the objects to the spot where I was standing. At the
point above the water tower, the objects hovered motionless for
two or three minutes and then flew out of sight. The clearest
films of the reel were removed by the Air Force when I first
lent them the movies. The only ones which remain in my posses-
sion are those which show the objects at a considerable dis-
tance. I believe the objects were at all times within 2 or 2½
miles of me. Total time that the objects were in view: approxi-
mately 3½ minutes.

The sixth paragraph of Kolman's report though not essential
to understanding the Montana sighting from a scientific point of
view, said, "Shortly after the incident, Bob Considine, a nationally
syndicated newspaper columnist, denounced all who claimed to
have seen 'flying saucers.' Particular reference was made to Mr.
Mariana. This bad publicity resulted in the loss of sponsors on
nine (9) of the fourteen (14) radio stations for Mr. Mariana's
sportcasts. It was nine (9) months before these stations returned
to Mr. Mariana's program and this doubtlessly resulted in considerable financial loss to him. At present, Mr. Mariana is in the
final stages of a lawsuit against Mr. Considine."

This covers the situation around the filming of the objects.
Mariana's memory of the events didn't change much. The timing
of some aspects of it are open to question, as are the estimates
of the distances and speed of the object. The only real problem
was one uncovered some twenty years later. A review of the newspaper records by members of the Condon Committee discovered
that the August 15 date had to be wrong if Mariana was in the

stadium to check on winds for an afternoon game. There were no games from August 9 through August 18.

In studying the above material, my personal bias makes little difference. I am surprised that the Air Force, charged by regulation at the time of the incident with the investigation of UFO sightings, paid almost to attention to the film until required to do so by public opinion. Here was a case that offered physical evidence in the form of movie footage, yet their only, earlier response, was to suggest it was too dark for them to see anything of value. The Air Force investigators returned it within days without much in the way of examination.

It suggests something about the investigation as it existed in the summer of 1950. A number of conclusions about the investigation can be drawn. Obviously the Air Force wasn't interested in wasting manpower and finances on something as ridiculous as flying saucers. After three years, it was clear to the officers at the highest level of the Air Force that no immediate threat to the security of the United States was posed by the flying saucers. Satisifed that no invasion was imminent, the Air Force no longer cared about flying saucers.

A scientific analysis of the sighting, however, could provide us with clues about the flying saucers. Nearly everyone who looked into the case said that there was nothing in Mariana's background to suggest that he would hoax a sighting. Aside from the vast technical problems presented by faking a 16mm movie in 1950, everyone agreed that Mariana was an honest man. Furthermore, the sighting was confirmed by a semi-independent observer—Mariana's secretary.

She is important to the case only because she was present when the film was made. She confirmed that there were objects in the sky and that she didn't know what they were. She estimated that they were in sight, or that she saw them, for only 7 seconds.

This one chain of the evidence—that is, the character of the witnesses—seems to be solid. Air Force investigators noted that Mariana, because of his position as manager of the local baseball team, was quoted in the newspapers on many occasions: He had no need to invent the tale in order to benefit from the spotlight. In fact, even the Air Force investigators noted that Mariana suffered a loss because of his sighting. He had not advocated a point of view, had no contact with the benevolent space brothers, and had not set himself up as one of the experts in the field, yet he was tarred with that brush. Bob Considine had suggested that the movie was a hoax, and Mariana believed that he was being called a liar.

Mariana gained nothing through his sighting. No one ever suggested such a motivation, with the exception of Philip Klass. Klass thought that the publicity of the sighting might have been good for the local baseball team. Klass noted that one of Mariana's friends had said that Mariana was "very public-relations conscious . . . that's the way Nick is . . ."

But given the situation, as well as Mariana's failure to capitalize on the film from a national standpoint, Klass's suggestion seems far-fetched. There is no public relations angle that was exploited by Mariana.

Klass raised one other point that should be addressed. He noted that the sighting took place around high noon over a city of over forty thousand people. Even after the articles appeared in the newspaper, not one witness claiming to have seen the objects photographed by Mariana came forward. Klass believes that there should have been some evidence of others who saw the objects.

In his January 9, 1953, report, Kolman wrote, "It is reported by hearsay that other individuals observed these objects at the same hour on the same day. However, due to the elapsed time since these sightings, no concrete leads can be found to identify other witnesses."

That seems to answer at least part of Klass's criticism. However, from a scientific point of view, that information is useless. The only thing we can do is ignore it. The sighting stands or falls on the testimony of Mariana, Raunig, and the film.

The first look at the film from a scientific standpoint seems to have evolved out of the CIA-sponsored investigation of UFOs known as the Robertson Panel. The panel was a series of meetings held during a single week in January 1953. Although the idea for the panel was an outgrowth of the massive number of sightings reported during the summer of 1952, one of the panel's goals was to view the Montana movie, as well as another film taken in Utah in July 1952. Panel members were going to examine the evidence to determine if there was any reality to the reports of flying saucers.

Dr. Michael Swords, who extensively studied the history of the UFO phenomenon, said about the Robertson Panel, "As soon as they get finished with all the preliminary briefings, the only thing they want to do is look at the films."

After reviewing the film a number of times, the Robertson Panel settled on the aircraft explanation. To them it was a cut-and-dried proposition. In any event, they saw nothing in the film to convince them that UFOs were interplanetary, and of course they saw nothing to suggest that UFOs posed any sort of threat to the security of the United States.

Scientific analysis of the film didn't actually begin until about the mid-1950s. Dr. Robert M. L. Baker, Jr., then with the Douglas Aircraft Company, undertook a complete detailed analysis of the Montana movie. Nearly everyone agrees with the results of his tests: There is no dispute with his analysis of the film. The disagreement appears when we begin to discuss the conclusions.

Using the evidence available on the film, Baker was able to make a number of calculations. For example, using the foreground detail, as well as the speed of the objects as evidenced by their motion, he concluded that if the objects were about a quarter mile from the camera, they were at 320 feet and moving at 18 miles an hour. If they were 10 miles away, they were at 12,800 feet and traveling at 690 miles an hour. To make a more precise determination, Baker would have needed an additional piece of evidence that simply was not available to him. Had there been another witness in another part of Great Falls, then the precise calculation could have been made and we might have been able to answer the question about the identity of the objects on the film.

Baker ran a series of tests using both actual aircraft and scale models. Using a camera similar to the one used by Mariana, he filmed aircraft at varying distances. At 12 miles, a DC-3 seemed to duplicate a portion of the Montana movie. Baker, however, was not impressed with the test results.

Studying the film carefully, Baker determined that the objects were 2 miles from the camera. According to his work, at that range, the F-94s would have been identifiable as aircraft. As the distance from the camera increased, so did the speed, until at 12 miles—the range at which the DC-3 momentarily duplicated the film with reflections from the fuselage—the speed was about three times that possible for that type of aircraft. The details of the plane were only masked for a few seconds, meaning that Mariana should have been able to identify them.

Based on his examination of the film, Baker concluded that the shape of the objects was due to irregular "panning" action by Mariana. A decade later, the Condon Committee investigator on the case, William K. Hartmann, agreed, but he also noted that there was a true and constant ellipticity, or flattening of the objects. In other words, Hartmann thought that the shape might not be completely due to Mariana's panning.

In his analysis, Hartmann continued, "If the 15 August date were correct, the objects were not balloons or airborne debris because they are moving into the wind. They are disappearing to the SW, and Baker's analysis indicates a well determined azimuth heading 171 degrees, while the wind was out of the southwest."

Hartmann continued by ruling out birds because of the disk shape and the "general strangeness to both witnesses . . ." He also eliminated meteors because they were moving too slowly, left no trail, and were not reported anywhere else.

But then Hartmann made a comment that was somewhat surprising, given the nature of the Condon Committee's overall conclusions. In the final report he wrote, "Past investigations have left airplanes as the principal working hypothesis. The data at hand indicate that while it strains credibility to suppose that these were airplanes, the possibility nonetheless cannot be entirely ruled out."

Hartmann also noted, "Assuming that 15 August was the correct date, Air Force investigators found that there were two F-94 jets in the vicinity and that they landed only minutes after the sighting, which could well have put them in circling path around Malmstrom AFB [Great Falls AFB], only three miles ESE of the baseball park. However, Witness I [Mariana] reported seeing two planes coming in for a landing behind him immediately following the filming, thereby accounting for those aircraft."

What we see here is that the scientific evidence available on the film proves that something was in the sky over Great Falls. Unfortunately, the quality of the evidence doesn't allow us to prove that the objects were either of terrestrial manufacture or of extraterrestrial origin. We are left with only the lights on the film.

But other evidence and information might provide us with some additional clues. The exact timing of the event, for example, begins to play an important role in the case. Mariana estimated that the objects were visible for 20 seconds. In Brynildsen's October 6 report, he wrote, "From the time of first sighting to the completion of taking of the pictures, Mr. Mariana estimated consumed approximately twenty seconds."

If that is true, then the aircraft explanation becomes more plausible. Baker's tests, as well as those run by others, suggested that bright reflections from the aircraft fuselage could mask the wings and tail assembly for 20 seconds and therefore could fool both Mariana and Raunig.

But we can make some accurate statements about the timing of this event. The film itself lasts for 16 seconds. We know from Mariana's statements that he had to run to his car for the camera, pick it up, and begin filming. Baker, in his report, noted, "Mr. Mariana estimated that it took him thirty seconds or more after first observing the UFOs to run to his car, set the camera and start filming. His secretary, also at the scene, testifies that the objects remained in view throughout the period between the first sightings and filming."

The tests conducted by Baker showed that reflections from the fuselage would fade considerably as the aircraft moved through the air. After just a few seconds, the brightness would fade and the details of the jets would become visible. Baker's tests seemed to suggest that the aircraft explanation didn't work.

We've now taken a comprehensive look at the available information. We've read the statements provided by both Mariana and Raunig. We've taken a look at the experiments and scientific evaluations conducted by various people under various conditions over the last forty years. Can we draw any sort of positive conclusions?

Well, yes, we can. Remembering first that there is nothing on the film that will directly prove that UFOs—or, rather, these specific UFOs—are of extraterrestrial origin, we can make some definite statements.

First, given the data we have, we know that a number of explanations have been eliminated based on the eyewitness testimony and the evidence on the film. The objects are not balloons, birds, meteors, airborne debris, or meteorological phenomena. Everyone who has examined the films have reached those conclusions.

Second, there is nothing in the background of either witness to suggest hoax, mental illness, delusion, or an inability to identify common objects. Neither gained financially because of the case; and Mariana lost. The testimony of one tends to support the other, and no major discrepancies have been found.

Third, the aircraft explanation is eliminated by two important facts. One, the length of time the objects were in view suggests that fuselage reflections would have decreased to the point where the aircraft would have been visible, and both witnesses, according to their statements, saw the aircraft in a different part of the sky.

As an addendum, it should be noted (though most have ignored it) that Mariana claimed that he saw the objects hovering for a short period of time. That would eliminate the aircraft, simply because they don't hover. I find it surprising that in all that has been written about the Montana movie, I found no references to the craft hovering except in the official Blue Book files.

Mariana also said that he heard a whooshing or whistling sound that accompanied the flight of the objects. If that is an accurate statement, then it could also be postulated that had the objects been jets, the engine noise would have been heard. In fact, in one of the Air Force statements, it was claimed that not only were the jets in the air but they were also using their afterburners, which would have increased their speed and their engine noise. The fact that neither Mariana nor Raunig heard the jet engines is an important point.

Baker also said that he examined the film for evidence of the exhaust from the jets but found nothing. Given today's equipment, it would be interesting to reexamine the film to learn if a disturbance of the air behind the objects is detectable. A disturbance such as that caused by a jet aircraft engine might provide another clue to the identity of the objects.

Fourth, there is a dispute about the date, which many have ignored. It arises because of the home schedule of the baseball team in Great Falls. Mariana was quite clear in his original statements that he was at the ballpark to check the conditions before an afternoon game. But the records show no games on August 15. If August 15 isn't the date, but August 5 is, then new problems arise and old ones are eliminated.

Klass, in his work, suggested no hoax because those perpetrating hoaxes normally wait for the film to be processed before announcing the existence of the pictures. But, according to the newspaper articles, Mariana told the newspaper about the sighting almost as it happened.

But what if the August 5 date is correct? Then there were ten days in which to get the film developed, see what it showed, and then announce it. This would mean that before Mariana said a word about the film, he had already seen it and knew what was on it. There is no indication in the files of anyone attempting to verify the dates the film was processed. That, in and of itself, might have provided a few important clues about the nature of the sighting. At today's late date, there is no way to obtain documentation about the dates for the processing of the film.

Klass does offer an alternative explanation for the Montana movie. He explained that after he began his investigation into the case, he saw a photograph in the January 1969 issue of *Air Progress* magazine that suggested a new explanation to him. The picture showed an F-4K fighter making a low-altitude pass at the Farnborough Air Show. According to Klass, it was enveloped in a glowing blob of white that was about 40 feet in diameter. It looked enough like the blobs of light in the Montana movie that Klass believed he had found the explanation.

Klass wrote, "This prompted me to wonder if this, or some other unusual atmospheric effect, could have produced a similar visual phenomenon at Great Falls—a phenomenon that would be unfamiliar to Mariana and could have obscured the identity of the two F-94s. The official Weather Bureau records for Great Falls for August 15 showed that at 11:27 A.M. the surface temperature was 77°F and the dew-point temperature was 45°F. (Dew-point temperature is the temperature at which the air would have 100 percent humidity.) Thus, August 15 was not an especially humid day in Great Falls. More recently, a similar "localized fog" effect was observed around the fuselage of a USAF B-52 during Boeing flight tests and was photographed by the crew of a nearby 'chase-plane.' The B-52 had been flying at 21,000 feet altitude around 600 mph. Boeing scientists, after investigating the effect, concluded that the temperature of the air was lowered by flowing over the wings, which thereby increased its relative humidity. Under the prevailing atmospheric conditions, this caused water droplets to form in the wake of the airplane, creating a localized fog which reflected the rays of the sun. Just such a condition could explain the Great Falls 'white blobs' and why they remained visible for a time considerably longer than the allowable twenty seconds calculated by Baker for simple reflections off the F-94 fuselages."

But there is a problem with this idea. The two fighters were at a much lower altitude and a much slower speed. That overlooks the fact that the white blob noted by Klass is created by the speed of the air over the wings. In other words, the front of the aircraft would have been visible at some point during the flight. Either Mariana would have recognized the aircraft as such or the film would have revealed, at some point, the shape of the aircraft. Besides, we must remember that Mariana said that he and his secretary did see the jets in a different part of the sky. The phenomenon suggested by Klass is interesting, but it has no relevance to this discussion.

Baker ruled out these sorts of phenomena as well. In the section on motion pictures he wrote for *UFO's A Scientific Debate*, he noted, "After more than a decade of speculation and hypothesis checks, all natural phenomena (birds, balloons, insects, meteors, mirages, and so forth) have been ruled out. (Since the date of the photograph is uncertain, weather bureau reports are not pertinent, but the uniform motion does not seem to be consistent with balloons.) The main possibility is that of airplane reflections or, perhaps, some airplane-related phenomenon such as luminous shock waves. The airplane hypothesis may seem attractive, but it does not really jibe with my analysis or with Hartmann's. In short, planes at the largest distances compatible with their speeds and the angular rate of the images would have been identifiable on the film."

Air Force officers, in a number of statement and reports that appear in the Project Blue Book file, wrote, "The original Air Force conclusion, based on the interrogation of witnesses and the evaluation of data, was that the UFOs were, in all probability, two Air Force F-94 fighter aircraft known to be in the vicinity at the time. . . . Based on the degree of credibility accorded this early ATIC evaluation and the strong corroborative evidence supplied by the recent independent analysis, the Air Force has no compelling reason to alter its original conclusion."

While I disagree with the Air Force that the Mariana film is explained by the aircraft, I must agree that their explanation is not without foundation, given a complete understanding of what is in the file. They were, of course, swayed by the bias against having any sighting labeled as unidentified, as well as a documented policy of providing any explanation for a sighting report.

The Montana movie does not lead us into the extraterrestrial arena. If the objects on the film are not aircraft, then their performance, if they are manufactured objects, was outside the range of our capabilities at the time. That does, of course, suggest an extraterrestrial point of origin, but it doesn't prove it.

In today's environment, this conclusion isn't as important as another, which can be sustained in a scientific arena. The Montana movie is physical evidence of an event that cannot be easily explained in the mundane. From an objective standpoint, all that can be said is that the movie shows something that is not identifiable as either natural phenomena or jet aircraft. If nothing else, the film should appeal to the scientific mind as physical evidence of something outside the bounds of explanation. Science should be curious about this film.

The Tremonton Movie
July 2, 1952

On July 2, 1952, Navy Warrant Officer Delbert C. Newhouse was driving toward a new duty station with his wife and two children. Just after eleven in the morning, 7 miles from Tremonton, Utah, his wife noticed a group of bright objects that she couldn't easily identify. Newhouse, a naval officer and trained photographer, stopped the car to retrieve his 16mm camera from the trunk.

By the time he got the camera out, the objects had moved away from the car. Newhouse said later that when one object broke from the formation, he tracked it so that analysts would have something to work with. He let it fly across the field of view. He did that two or three times. When he turned back, the whole formation was gone. He had exposed about 75 seconds of color film.

The precise details of the story vary, depending on the source. Air Force files, based on the information supplied by others as well as Newhouse, show that Newhouse and his wife saw the objects at close range. It was clear to both of them that the objects were disk shaped, large, and metallic. Neither recognized them as conventional aircraft, so Newhouse decided that he needed to photograph them.

By the time he got the car stopped and the camera out of the trunk, the objects had moved off to long range. In an interview I conducted with him in 1976, Newhouse confirmed he had, in fact, seen the objects at close range. He confirmed they were large, disk shaped, and brightly lighted. He told Dr. Robert M. L. Baker, Jr., who studied the film in 1955, that the objects were "gunmetal-colored objects shaped like two saucers, one inverted on top of the other." Dewey Fournet, onetime Pentagon liaison officer to Project Blue Book, told me that Newhouse had said the same thing to him. Newhouse's descriptions of the objects, then, were consistent.

After filming the objects, Newhouse stored his camera, got back into the car, and drove on to his new duty station. Once there, he had the film processed. He then sent a copy to the Air Force, suggesting they might find it interesting.

The chief of Blue Book in 1952, Captain Edward Ruppelt, reported, "When I received the Tremonton films, I took them right over to the Wright Field photo lab . . . and the photo technicians and I ran them twenty or thirty times . . . the lights in the Tremonton Movie would fade out, then come back in again. This fading immediately suggested airplanes reflecting light, but the roar of a king sized dogfight could have been heard for miles and the Newhouse family heard no sound."

Ruppelt then informed Fournet in Washington about the film. Fournet in turn arranged to have it screened for a number of high-ranking officers, many of whom had ties to the intelligence community. It was then returned to Wright-Patterson AFB to be examined by the Air Force's Photo-Reconnaissance Laboratory.

The Air Force investigation lasted for months, including analysis of the film. They tried everything in their efforts to identify the objects but failed. When coupled to the report and the reliability of the photographer, the Air Force was stuck. They had no explanation.

Ruppelt wrote about the analysis, "After studying the movies for several weeks, the Air Force photo lab at Wright Field gave up. All they had to say was, 'We don't know what they are but they aren't airplanes or balloons, and we don't think they're birds.' "

When the Air Force finished, the Navy asked for the film. A frame-by-frame analysis that took more than a thousand man-hours was made by the U.S. Naval Photographic Interpretation Center in Washington, D.C. They studied the motion of the objects, their relation to one another in the formation, the lighting of the objects, and every other piece of data they could find on the film. In the end, like their Air Force counterparts, they were left with no explanations.

But, unlike their Air Force counterparts, the Navy experts were not restricted in their praise of the film. Their report said that the objects were internally lighted spheres that were not reflecting sunlight. They also estimated the speed at 3,780 miles an hour if the spheres were 5 miles away. At twice the distance, they would have been moving twice as fast, at half the distance, half the speed. If the objects were just under a mile distant, they were traveling at 472 miles an hour.

The Navy experts noted from their studies that "It [the UFOs] appears to be a light source rather than reflected light. No indication of the kind of objects. No bird known to be sufficiently actinic. Could not have been caused by aircraft or balloons. . . . Objects have same apparent shape, color, and general motion. . . . Velocity was computed to the 3780 mph for a shift of 1mm per frame if the object is five miles from the observer."

The Navy, after their frame-by-frame analysis, came to no specific conclusion about the objects in the film. They had no recommendations for continued investigation or for action to be taken.

In fact, according to William Hartmann of the Condon Committee, "The Navy group concluded that the UFOs were intelligently controlled vehicles and that they weren't airplanes or birds. They arrived at this conclusion by making a frame-by-frame study of the motion of the lights and the changes in the lights' intensity. The analysts stopped short of identifying the objects as interplanetary space craft although this implication was evidently present."

Once the Navy was through with the film, it received one more "official" examination. In January 1953, the CIA sponsored a weeklong investigation into UFOs. Dr. H. P. Robertson was selected as chairman of the group, and he invited a number of other respected scientists to join him in the examination of the best of the evidence held by Project Blue Book. Both Ruppelt and Fournet would be at the meeting, but they would not be allowed to attend all the sessions.

Dr. Michael Swords attempted to reconstruct the history of the Robertson Panel, as it would come to be known. Based on what he was able to learn, not only about the mission of the panel, but also of the men who comprised it, he concluded that they were there to explain UFO sightings rather than investigate them. So, when the Robertson Panel reviewed the film, Dr. Luis Alverez said that he believed the objects in the film might be birds. He thought that the motion of the birds seemed to duplicate the motion of the objects on the film. He had found a solution, based not on fact but on his opinion, and that satisfied him.

In an interview conducted in 1995, I asked Fournet about Alverez's belief that he had found a solution for the sighting. Fournet told me, "Dr. Alverez suggested that as a possible solution to that Tremonton movie . . ."

According to Dr. Swords, the morning after the scientists on the panel had seen the Tremonton film and Alverez had made his suggestion, "the Air Force and the CIA mysteriously produced a film of seagulls to show them. And you just wonder, wasn't that convenient? They just happened to have that seagull film handy in the stacks somewhere."

In the years that followed, the suggested explanation of seagulls for the Tremonton movie became the accepted explanation. In their book, Dr. Donald H. Menzel and L. G. Boyd wrote of the Tremonton film, "The pictures are of such poor quality and show so little that even the most enthusiastic home-movie fan today would hesitate to show them to his friends. Only a stimulated imagination could suggest that the moving objects are anything but very badly photographed birds."

Dr. Baker was asked to examine the Tremonton film as he had examined the Montana movie. He reinterviewed the witness, Newhouse, learning that Newhouse had seen the objects close enough to describe them as saucer shaped, and couldn't easily identify them.

Through microscopic examination, Baker determined that contrary to what had been alleged by others, the camera had been in focus. Baker wrote, "According to Al Chop . . . Air Force personnel were convinced that the objects were not airplanes; on the other hand the hypothesis that the camera might have been out of focus and the objects soaring gulls could neither be confirmed nor denied."

However, Baker noted, "Examination under a microscope shows the camera to be well focused as the edges of the images are sharp and clear on many of the properly exposed frames."

Baker, as he had done with the Montana movie, ran a series of experiments, using mock-ups of birds, and filming them from varying distances under varying lighting conditions. He wrote,

"The rectangular flat white cardboards of the aforementioned experiments represented very roughly the configuration of birds. The light reflected by such a surface is probably greater than that from a curved feather surface of a bird. . . . At these distances it is doubted if birds would give the appearance of round dots; also they would have been identifiable by the camera if not visually. However, actual movies of birds in flight would have to be taken to completely confirm this conclusion. The following type of gulls have been known to fly at times over this locality: California Herring Gull (a common summer resident), Ring-Billed Gull and the Fork-Tailed Gull."

It should be noted that wherever Baker mentioned birds or gulls in his report, someone had underlined the passages, as if that person had been searching for evidence to confirm the bird hypothesis and ignoring evidence that refuted it.

Baker wrote, "The motion of the objects is not exactly what one would expect from a flock of soaring birds (not the slightest indication of a decrease in brightness due to periodic turning with the wind or [wing] flapping) and no cumulus clouds are present which might betray the presence of a strong thermal updraft. On the other hand the single object might represent a single soaring bird which broke away in search of a new thermal—quite a common occurrence among gulls."

Baker concluded his report, writing, "The evidence remains rather contradictory and no single hypothesis of a natural phenomenon yet suggested seems to completely account for the UFO involved. The possibility of multiple hypotheses, i.e. that the Utah UFO's are the result of two simultaneous natural phenomena might possibly yield the answer. However, as in the case of the Montana analysis, no definite conclusion could be obtained."

The Condon Committee investigator on the Tremonton film, William K. Hartmann, reexamined the case years after the Robertson Panel. Hartmann reviewed all that had passed before him, noting that Baker had learned from Newhouse that the objects had been seen at close range. According to Hartmann and my review of the Project Blue Book files, the first official mention of the shape of the objects came only during Baker's 1955 interview.

Ruppelt, however, might have an explanation for the failure

to earlier question the shape. He had the opportunity to meet Newhouse some time after he had gotten out of the Air Force. In listening to Newhouse describe the events around the filming of the objects, Ruppelt noticed something interesting. Newhouse, according to Ruppelt, "didn't just *think* the UFO's were disk-shaped; he *knew* that they were; he had plainly seen them."

Ruppelt asked why Newhouse hadn't told that to the intelligence officer who had interviewed him in 1952. Newhouse said that he had. The information had not been forwarded to Project Blue Book because that wasn't one of the questions Ruppelt had told the intelligence officer to ask. Ruppelt wrote, "The question 'What did the UFO's look like?' wasn't one of them because when you have a picture of something you don't normally ask what it looks like. Why the intelligence officer didn't pass this information on to us I'll never know."

This does provide a very good reason for rejecting the seagull explanation for the Tremonton movie: Newhouse saw the objects at close range and was unable to identify them as birds.

Ruppelt also noted that he had spoken to a scientist who believed that the birds hypothesis was accurate. The man claimed that he had seen seagulls soaring on thermals near Berkley and that the motion of the birds resembled the motion of the objects in the film—at least to him. If Newhouse had unconsciously *panned with the action*, then the Navy figures for the speed would be inaccurate.

Hartmann noted this but suggested that the tendency to pan with the action would mean that the speed figures were too low rather than too high. If Newhouse had panned with the action, then the Navy's calculated speed of 3780 mph was not high enough. And, if the objects were moving as fast as had been calculated, birds were effectively ruled out.

Interestingly, Hartmann also takes on debunkers Donald Menzel and Lyle Boyd. In their book *The World of Flying Saucers*, they dismiss the objects as birds and suggest that the film was of very poor quality. Hartmann wrote, "The object may be birds though unresolved because of distances, but the images are small and relatively sharp and lack of a clear identification cannot be ascribed to poor photography."

However, after reviewing all the evidence, the various reports and studies, and interviewing Newhouse himself, Hartmann still concluded, "These observations give *strong evidence that the Tremonton films do show birds* [emphasis in original], as hypothesized above, and I now regard the objects as so indentified [*sic*]."

But Baker, who had made the study in 1955, repeated his conclusions during the symposium on Unidentified Flying Objects sponsored by the American Association for the Advancement of Science, held in Boston on December 26 and 27, 1969. Baker wrote, "A rather appealing explanation is that these objects were birds. On the other hand, this motion is not what one would expect from a flock of birds; there are erratic brightness fluctuations, but there is no indication of periodic decreases in brightness due to turning with the wind or flapping. . . I have never seen bird formations so striking that I would not recognize them as birds, or so unusual that I would film them. The motion pictures I have taken of birds at various distances have no similarity to the Utah film. Thus, to my mind, the bird hypothesis is not very satisfying and I classify the objects as anomalistic observational phenomena."

I would like to point out that I have, on many occasions, had the opportunity to observe formations of various types of birds under various conditions. Keeping the explanation for the Tremonton movie in mind, I watched those birds carefully. Even in distant formations, when it was difficult to see a birdlike shape, the flapping of the wings was clearly visible. This includes formations of birds that had dark feathers, birds seen against a gray sky, a blue sky, near the horizon, and high overhead. It includes birds seen in V-shaped formations and those in clusters, or swarms of birds. I have watched them change direction and swoop toward the ground. And yes, I have watched gulls in Utah. And no, I have seen nothing that resembles the formation of objects filmed by Newhouse.

So a possible answer suggested in 1953 by the Robertson Panel became the final explanation for the films as the years passed. However, in all the analysis that appeared after the Robertson panel, one fact was conveniently left out: Newhouse saw the objects at close range. Fournet told me, ". . . when you look at what Newhouse said when he was interviewed after that . . . when you put all that together, the seagull hypothesis becomes flimsier and flimsier."

The McMinnville Photographs
May 11, 1950

In today's world a photograph or two of a flying saucer are going to be virtually valueless. Anyone with a computer and a good graphics package can take a picture, manipulate it, and create a new negative. All that will be left to those who investigate UFOs will be background checks of the photographer to determine if he or she has a history of practical jokes. Analysis of the negative is not going to produce any sort of evidence that will be useful in determining the authenticity of a picture.

The situation in 1950 was different. Many people were unfamiliar with cameras other than the inexpensive box type. They used black-and-white film and hadn't thought much beyond point and shoot. They were told that if you were inside a building you needed to use a flash, or if it was night you needed to use a flash. These are the people who today, in a stadium full of people, with a brightly lighted show or game on the field, still feel the need to use a flash.

Two photographs were taken in 1950 that have withstood the test of time. They have been examined by the scientific community but were ignored by the Air Force. They are among the best to have been offered as proof that something is happening. They are, of course, physical evidence that there is substance to the UFO phenomenon.

According to the witnesses, Mr. and Mrs. Paul Trent, who lived on a farm near McMinnville, Oregon, they were confronted by a large, slow-moving, disk-shaped object traveling toward them from the northeast. Mrs. Trent was outside, having just fed the rabbits; she was the first to see the object. She called to her husband, who left the house, watched the object, and then ran back in to grab a camera.

Trent then took two pictures of the object as if flew over. As he was taking the pictures, Mrs. Trent noticed that her in-laws were on the back porch of their home about four hundred feet away. She shouted, but they didn't hear her. She then ran into the house to use the phone. Because her mother-in-law went to answer the telephone, she didn't see the object, but her father-in-law did glimpse it as it disappeared into the west.

According to witness statements made many years after the event, Trent said that he took the first picture, wound the film, which in 1950 was a time-consuming process, and took the second. By then, the object, which had been moving slowing, began to accelerate.

The witnesses said that the object was very bright and silvery. Both saw a superstructure on top, which appeared in the photographs. William K. Hartmann reported that the Trents told him that it resembled a "good-sized parachute canopy without the strings, only silvery-bright mixed with bronze." Hartmann noted in his report that the "rather bright, aluminum-like, but not spectacular, reflecting surfaces appears to be confirmed by analysis of the photos. . . . There was no noise, visible exhaust, flames, or smoke."

Although they had what could be the first authentic pictures of an extraterrestrial craft, they didn't develop the film immediately because there were still frames to be used. They did, however, and, according to UFO historian Jerry Clark, discussed the sighting with friends and family. After Trent mentioned the incident to his banker, Frank Wortmann, copies of the photos were put on display in the bank when the pictures were developed.

Reporter Bill Powell saw the pictures in the bank, interviewed the Trents, and convinced them to allow him to publish them. Trent said that he was afraid that they would get in trouble with the government, but Powell convinced him otherwise.

On June 8, about a month after the pictures were taken, Powell's story appeared in the *McMinnville Telephone Register*. He had examined the negatives, found on the floor where the Trents' children were playing with them, and decided there was no evidence of tampering or hoax.

Once the pictures were published, the Trents found themselves the focus of national attention. *Life* borrowed the negatives from Powell and printed them in the June 26 issue. Although the Trents were promised their negatives would be returned, it would be seventeen years before they got them back. During the Colorado study they were loaned by the Trents to Hartmann for his study conducted under the auspices of the Condon Committee.

Hartmann made his own investigation of the tale and examination of the negatives. It was because of the Condon Committee that the negatives were located and returned, eventually to the Trents.

Hartmann, knowing that the photographs were only as good as the reputation of the photographer, noted that a number of local residents had come forward to "attest to the witnesses' veracity. They appear to be sincere, though not highly educated or experienced observers."

Importantly, because of criticism that would be leveled by later investigators, Hartmann wrote, "During the writer's interview with them, they were friendly and quite unconcerned about the sighting."

Hartman, in his evaluation of the case, also wrote, "Two inferences appear to be justified: 1) It is difficult to see any prior motivation for a fabrication of such a story, although after the fact, the witnesses did profit to the extent of a trip to New York; 2) it is unexpected that in this distinctly rural atmosphere, in 1950, one would encounter a fabrication involving sophisticated trick photography (e.g. a carefully retouched print). The witnesses also appear unaffected by the incident, receiving only occasional inquiries."

It could also be noted that a few months later, when Nick Mariana made his brief film of the two objects over Great Falls, there was no economic benefit. He lost sponsorship on many of the radio stations that had used his sportscasts. Even in 1950 there was a feeling that those who saw and reported UFOs were unsophisticated, uneducated, and probably a little off-center in their thinking.

Hartmann ended his analysis of the Trent photographs by writing, "As stated previously, it is unlikely that a sophisticated 'optical fabrication' was performed. The negatives have not been tampered with."

He concluded his section of the report by writing, "This is one of the few UFO reports in which all factors investigated, geometric, psychological, and physical appear to be consistent with the assertion that an extraordinary flying object, silvery, metallic, disk-shaped, tens of meters in diameter, and evidently artificial, flew within sight of two witnesses. It cannot be said that the evidence positively rules out a fabrication, although there are some physical factors such as the accuracy of certain photometric measures of the original negatives which argue against fabrication."

Let's take just a moment and think about this. Many of the scientists who have commented on the UFO phenomenon have asked, repeatedly, Where is the physical evidence? Here is an example of that evidence, examined by a scientist who has suggested, at the very least, that these pictures show a large manufactured craft and there is no indication of a hoax. Shouldn't this evidence, even though there are only two primary witnesses, demand that an impartial and scientific investigation of UFOs be undertaken? Isn't this an example of that physical evidence demanded by science?

It is also interesting to note that the Trents, as well as the reporter, Powell, claimed to have been visited by plainclothes representatives of the Air Force and members of the FBI. Powell told Bruce Maccabee, a physicist for the Navy, that two weeks to a month after the newspaper story, a plainclothes agent of the Air Force showed up at the *Register* office and demanded the pictures. Repeated attempts by Powell to recover the prints went unanswered.

I say that it is interesting because the Air Force file on the McMinnville case is labeled as "information only." In a letter dated March 10, 1965, Lieutenant Colonel John P. Spaulding responded to an inquiry from civilian W. C. Case. He wrote, "The Air Force has no information on photographs of an unidentified flying object taken by Mr. and Mrs. Paul Trent of McMinnville, Oregon. In this regard, it should be noted that all photographs submitted in conjunction with UFO reports have been a misinterpretation of natural or conventional objects. The objects in these photographs have a positive identification."

Is it necessary to point out the contradiction in the letter? The Air Force has no information about the sighting or the photographs, but the photographs have a positive identification.

None of this is, of course, the last word to be heard on the Trent photo case. Philip Klass, in *UFOs Explained,* found a number of reasons to believe the photographs were a hoax. All other possible mundane explanations had been rejected either by the witness testimony or by the photographs themselves. Clearly they did not show balloons, aircraft, meteors, ball lightning, insects, processing flaws, the moon, stars, atmospheric phenomena, astronomical phenomena, paper blowing in the wind, or any of the other misinterpretations that have been used to explain UFO sightings. There were only two possible explanations. Either the pictures were a hoax or they were of a large manufactured craft of unknown origin.

Klass launched his own investigation of the photographs, obtaining prints from the original negatives that he passed along to his colleague Robert Sheaffer. While Sheaffer studied the pictures, Klass began "to probe for 'soft spots' in the Trents' story of events . . ."

Klass reprinted the statement that Mrs. Trent had made to the newspaper in 1950. She'd said, "It was getting along toward evening—about a quarter to eight. We'd been out in the back yard. Both of us saw the object at the same time. The camera! Paul thought it was in the car but I was sure it was in the house. I was right—the Kodak was loaded with film. Paul took the first picture. The object was coming toward us and seemed to be tipped up a bit. It was very bright—almost silvery—and there was no noise or smoke."

Klass then makes an assumption with which I don't agree. He noted that the Trents were aware of the UFO phenomenon and had read enough about it so that they would recognize the importance of the pictures. But, rather than wasting the last three exposures on the film, they waited to finish the roll before having it processed. He was also surprised that after having the film developed they did nothing with the pictures except show them to friends. Klass believed that if they had actually photographed what they believed to be a flying saucer, they would have been more

excited about it, told more people about it, and would have realized the financial potential of having the first authentic pictures
of an alien spacecraft.

It could be argued that if the Trents were familiar with the
UFO literature, they would also know how those reporting UFOs
were treated. It made no difference to some that evidence was
available. They still believed that those seeing UFOs were somehow less than reliable. Within days of Kenneth Arnold's sighting
in June 1947, newspapers were suggesting that those who reported
flying saucers were drunks. One newspaper reported that the "flying disks" had been seen in thirty-eight states, except Kansas,
which was dry. The response to Klass's skepticism could be simply
that the Trents didn't want to be seen as "drunks" or "nuts."

Even after seeing the pictures, the Trents still did nothing
until persuaded to do so by friends. Trent told the reporter that
he was afraid that he would get into trouble with the government.
Klass points out that Trent would have gotten into as much trouble in May as he would have in June. He is suggesting that the
reason for the delay makes no sense. Of course, it could be argued
that Trent's friends talked him into releasing the pictures, something he would not have done on his own.

In his search for "soft spots," Klass does find one point that
is somewhat significant. The Trents are repeaters. That means
they had seen UFOs on more than one occasion. Klass noted
that NICAP, at one time the most respected of the civilian UFO
organizations, warned that one reason to reject photographic evidence was that it came from witnesses who had seen UFOs more
than once. This is, of course, a subjective opinion, and not relevant to the discussion of the Trent photographs.

More important, and of much more relevance, are the findings of Robert Sheaffer. According to Klass, Sheaffer had detected
what he believed to be the fatal flaw in the Trent pictures. Klass
wrote, "Sheaffer's keen eye noted that there were distinct shadows
on the *east* wall of the Trent garage, caused by the overhanging
eaves of the roof. This indicated that the pictures had been taken
in the morning, and not shortly after sunset as the Trents had
claimed. Sheaffer used his training in astronomy and mathematics
to calculate the time of the day when the photos were made,

based on the position of the shadows. He concluded that the pictures had been taken at approximately 7:30 A.M., not 7:45 P.M. Furthermore, his analysis indicated that the photo which the Trents claimed had been taken first had really been shot *several minutes after the other picture, and not a few seconds earlier as the Trents said* [emphasis in the original]."

If this was true, then the Trents had been caught in a lie. If they had lied about one aspect of the case, then the whole thing collapsed. But why lie about the time of day? It would make no difference to researchers if the pictures had been taken in the morning or the evening.

Hartmann, according to what Klass wrote, had also noted the shadows, but he could think of no reason for the Trents to lie about the time. Klass, however, found what he believed to be the reason. He wrote, "Most farmers are out working in the fields around 7:30 A.M., when the photos were actually taken, and Trent's neighbors would think it odd that they too had not seen the giant UFO that the Trents claimed to have seen and photographed. But to claim that the pictures were taken at 7:45 P.M., when most farmers have retired to their houses for dinner, would eliminate most potential witnesses who might dispute the story and photos."

But that really makes no sense. Farmers are in their fields at all hours and it isn't surprising to see them working long after dusk, which is why there are lights on their equipment. More important, more of the general population is outside in the evenings. Even the most cursory examination of sighting reports shows that more are reported between six in the evening and midnight than any other time of day. If the Trents were motivated to move the timing of the sighting, it would be to move it into the morning when there were fewer opportunities for other witnesses.

And if the timing provided by the Trents is accurate, then Sheaffer's suggestion about the ordering of the photographs is reversed. In other words, if the pictures were taken in the evening, then they were taken in the order that the Trents claimed.

It is appropriate to point out that both Klass and Sheaffer have written books explaining away all UFO sightings. Neither Klass nor Sheaffer believes that there have ever been any legitimate

UFO sightings, and that has colored their thinking. If there are no UFOs, then there must be some fact, some bit of information suggesting that the case is explainable or is a hoax.

In fact, if we examine the statements made by the Trents, we do see minor changes in the timing and the events. These are not the result of a hoax but of the problems of human memory. Klass is always quick to point out that memories fail and information is related inaccurately. Here, however, the Trents are expected to remember the exact nature of all the events, including minor and often inconsequential details. These changes are to be expected and are not indicative of a hoax.

The shadows under the eaves, which, Sheaffer believed, indicated that the photographs were taken in the morning, have been written off as random light scattering by other, equally competent researchers. Bruce Maccabee, who has made a number of studies of photographs, found nothing inconsistent with the story told by the Trents and the information available in the photographs.

Hartmann, in his study, had also noticed the shadows under the eaves, but he ignored them. He found nothing to suggest that the Trents were not telling him the truth, and no reason for them to change the time of the sighting. His investigation suggested that the story and the photographs were a consistent, whole package.

The point here, however, is not to determine if the photographs were hoaxes or pictures of a real, large, fabricated object. The point is to determine if there is any physical evidence that UFOs might be real. The Trent photographs provide us with that sort of evidence. We have two main witnesses, the possibility of a third, and we have the photographs, which have been authenticated and claimed not to be a hoax by men with the credentials and the expertise to make those sorts of claims.

It can be noted that the personal bias of some of those men is showing. As noted earlier, both Klass and Sheaffer believe there are no UFOs, and that could color their thinking. But Maccabee is a believer. That could color his thinking. That leaves us with Hartmann, who seemed to be a disinterested third party, even though he worked with the thoroughly skeptical Condon Committee.

But Hartmann has made statements on both sides. In the

Condon Committee report, he suggested that the photographs did show a large fabricated object, and he found no evidence of a hoax. Klass reported that when he confronted Hartmann with the facts of his investigation, Hartmann changed his mind. Klass wrote, "It is a tribute to Hartmann that when Sheaffer and I presented him with the results of our investigations, he promptly revised his earlier views on the Trent pictures. Hartmann seemed especially impressed with Sheaffer's efforts in demonstrating that the pictures had been taken around 7:30 A.M. 'I think Sheaffer's work removes the McMinnville case from consideration as evidence for the existence of disklike artificial craft,' Hartmann said using his favorite euphemism for extraterrestrial spacecraft."

But neither Klass nor Sheaffer could offer a good reason for changing of the time of the sighting. And if the timing was accurate, and the shadows under the eaves were due to random light scattering, then we are back where we began, and we have two interesting photographs which suggest that the UFO phenomenon deserves a closer look.

The Trindade Island Photographs
January 16, 1958

Few photographed events had as many witnesses as those that transpired on January 16, 1958, abroad the *Almirante Saldanha*, which was part of the Hydrography and Navigation Division of the Brazilian navy. The ship had been anchored near Trindade Island for several days. Just after noon, as it was preparing to depart, someone on deck spotted a strange object and pointed it out to the others. It had a flattened, spherical shape with a ring around the center of it. The craft flew over the island, hovered briefly, and then disappeared, traveling to the east.

Almiro Barauna, a photographer, who had been invited on board the ship by the navy to take underwater pictures, was standing on the deck when the object was seen. He would later speak to reporters for the Rio newspaper, *Jornal do Brasil*.

> *Suddenly Mr. Amilar Vieire and Captain Viegas called me, pointing to a certain spot in the sky and yelling about a*

bright object which was approaching the island. At this same moment, when I was still trying to see what it was, Lieutenant Homero, the ship's dentist, came from the bow toward us, running, pointing to the sky and yelling about the object he was watching. Then I was finally able to locate the object by the flash it emitted. It was already close to the island. It glittered at times, perhaps reflecting sunlight, perhaps changing its own light—I don't know. It was coming over the sea, moving toward the point called the Galo Crest. I had lost about thirty seconds looking for the object, but the camera was already in my hands, ready, when I sighted it clearly silhouetted against the clouds. I shot two photos before it disappeared behind Desejado peak. My camera was set at a speed of .125 with an f/8 aperture, and this was the cause of the overexposure error, as I discovered later. The object remained out of sight for a few seconds, behind the peak, reappearing larger in size and flying in the opposite direction. It was lower and closer than before and moving at a higher speed. I shot the third photo. The fourth and fifth shots were lost, partly because of the speed at which the object was moving, and partly because I was being pushed and pulled about in the excitement. It was moving in the direction from which it had come, and it appeared to stop in midair for a brief time. At that moment I shot my last photo, the last on the film. After about ten seconds the object continued to increase its distance from the ship, gradually diminishing in size and finally disappearing into the horizon.

According to a report appearing in Coral and Jim Lorenzens' *Flying Saucers: The Startling Evidence of the Invasion from Outer Space,* Barauna told others that the ship's captain, as well as several other officers, wanted to see if he had gotten any good shots of the object. Barauna developed the film immediately, apparently under the supervision of the various officers, including Commander Carlos A. Bacellar.

Although there was no photographic paper on the ship, they could examine the negatives. Those on the ship confirmed that the negatives showed the same object that had been flying over the island, ruling out the possibility of a hoax.

Within days of arriving back at Rio, Bacellar approached Barauna and asked for copies of the pictures. He took them to the navy and then returned to Barauna's apartment, asking that Barauna describe to Naval authorities the conditions under which he had taken the pictures and the events that led up to them.

According to the Lorenzens, Barauna was asked to appear at the Navy Ministry, where he was questioned by high-ranking officers. Barauna also provided the original negatives to the navy, which were analyzed by the Cruzeiro do Sul Aerophotogrammetric Service. Again, according to the Lorenzens, Barauna was told that the negatives were genuine and that no evidence of trick or hoax had been found.

Barauna was asked to return to the Navy Ministry some time later. Running a number of tests, officers determined that the craft had been flying between 600 and 700 miles an hour, was about 120 feet in diameter, and about 24 feet thick.

Rio de Janeiro's newspapers carried a number of stories about the photographs and the situation around them. *Ultima Hora* reported on February 21 that there were at least one hundred witnesses to the sighting. Barauna told another reporter that "At the end of the meeting, the chief intelligence officer said he was convinced my photos were authentic. He showed me another photo taken by a Navy telegrapher sergeant, also at Trindade."

On February 22, a Brazilian Air Force captain, J. T. Viegas, confirmed Barauna's story. He also confirmed that the photographs were taken to Navy headquarters for review, along with a report and photographs sent from the United States.

Commander Paul Moreira da Silva of the Hydrography and Navigation Service issued a statement on February 22. He said, "The object sighted in the skies of Trindade was not a weather balloon, nor an American guided missile. I cannot yet give my conclusions, for the data are being analyzed in a secret evaluation at the Navy Ministry. I can tell, however, that the object was not a meteorological balloon."

Dr. Olavo Fontes, APRO's Brazilian representative, began to collect the various newspaper statements given by witnesses. Fontes had been told of the sighting by a friend in the Navy who had once been skeptical of UFO reports. Now convinced of their reality, he wanted to assist Fontes.

Fontes visited the Navy Ministry. Everything he learned there convinced him that no hoax was being perpetrated. In fact, Fontes was shown the four pictures taken by Barauna, and a fifth, taken by another photographer days before Barauna photographed the object.

Within days, a Brazilian congressional investigation was launched. The details were published in all the Rio de Janeiro newspapers:

> *The Navy Ministry is requested to answer or explain the following items of the inquiry presented by Representative Sergio Magalhaes on February 27, 1958, and approved by this House: (1) Whether it is true that the crew of the Almirante Saldanha witnessed the sighting of a strange object over the Island of Trindade; (2) Considering that the official statement released from the Navy Ministry's officer recognizes that the photos of the strange object were taken "in the presence of members from the crew of the Almirante Saldanha," it is asked whether an investigation was made and whether the reports from the Navy officers and sailors involved were recorded; (3) In the hypothesis of a negative answer the Navy Minister is requested to explain the reasons on which he has based his inclination to attribute no importance to the fact; (4) If it is correct that the photos were developed in the presence of officers from the Almirante Saldanha and that the picture showed the image of the strange object since the first examination; and (5) If the negatives were submitted to a careful examination to detect any photographic trick contrived before the sighting; (6) Why the information was kept secret by Navy authorities for about a month; (7) Whether it is correct that other similar phenomena were observed by Navy officers; (8) Whether it is correct that the commanding officer of the Navy tow ship Tridente witnessed the appearance of the strange object called a "flying saucer."*

> *The appearance of these strange aerial objects known as "flying saucers" has attracted the world's interest and curiosity*

for more than ten years. For the first time, however, the phe-
nomenon is witnessed by a large number of members from a
military organization, and the photos of the object receive the
official seal through a statement released to the press by the
Navy Minister's office. Yet, as the problem affects the national
security, more information is necessary to clarify the facts. There
is some controversy in the information divulged through the
press, but the Navy apparently has no intention of releasing
the complete report to stop the confusion and inform the public.
Furthermore, in spite of the Navy Minister's office declaring
(officially) that a large number of people from the Almirante
Saldanha *crew had sighted the strange object photographed*
over the Island of Trindade, there was no request for the witness'
reports or any other measures, as the chief of the Navy high
staff admitted when interviewed by the press.

Two months later, the newspapers reported on the official,
and secret, Navy answer to the House of Representatives. The
report noted that the investigation hadn't started with the Barauna
photographs, but some weeks earlier when the UFOs began appearing over the island. The analysis of the Barauna photographs
concluded, "Personal reports and photographic evidence of certain value indicate the existence of unidentified aerial objects."
Jerry Clark, in his massive encyclopedia about the UFO phenomenon, provided a slightly different version of the quote:
". . . existence of personal reports and of photographic evidence,
of certain value considering the circumstances involved, permit
the admission that there are indications of the existence of unidentified aerial objects." The two versions say basically the
same thing.

But this would not be the last word. Donald Menzel soon
labeled the case a hoax. Menzel wrote Dick Hall, then with the
National Investigations Committee on Aerial Phenomena (NICAP),
that he had reached a conclusion about the sightings over Trindade.
Menzel wrote, "I have in my possession one well-authenticated case
of a saturn-like object, whose nature is known and clearly distinguishable in his particular instance. A plane, flying in a humid
but apparently super-cooled atmosphere, became completely en-

veloped in fog, so about all one could see was a division where the stream lines were flowing up and down respectively over and under the wings. The cabin made a saturn-like spot in the center, and the wings closely resembled the appearance of the Brazilian photographs." The speed and maneuvering, according to Menzel, was the result of an illusion created by the sun shining on the highly reflective fog. This is, of course, the same explanation that Klass would offer to explain the Montana movie.

Menzel, apparently unsatisfied with that explanation, came up with another one a few years later. In the book *The World of Flying Saucers*, coauthored with Lyle Boyd, Menzel wrote that the case was a hoax. He said that Barauna had used a double exposure to fake the photographs and then worked with an accomplice to create a sensation, as well as a believable story. He claimed that when reporters interviewed the officers and crew of the ship, no one said they had actually seen the object—despite the fact that Hall had sent Menzel a copy of a March 1958 article from the Brazilian magazine *O Cruzeiro*, in which several of the witnesses were named. The Lorenzens, in their book, provided additional names of those involved in the case.

Menzel, who always criticized the UFO community for playing fast and loose with the facts, reprinted the Brazilian press release. According to Jerry Clark, ". . . when the original and Menzel's version are compared, some significant discrepancies become apparent."

The original read, "Evidently, this Ministry cannot make any statement about the object sighted over the island of Trindade, for the photographs do not constitute enough evidence for the purpose." Menzel wrote, "*Clearly*, this Ministry cannot make any statement about the *reality of the* object, for the photos do not constitute enough evidence for *such* a purpose [Changes in italic]."

Clark noted, "Whereas the first statement acknowledges an object and a sighting, the second [by Menzel] implies that their reality is open to questions—hardly the Brazilian Navy's intention."

To be fair, it must be noted that Menzel quoted, exactly, the statement as it appeared in the Blue Book files. There was nothing to indicate where that version originated, if the version quoted by others was a draft of the final copy, or if someone had mistranslated the statement for one or the other American sources.

Menzel, along with coauthor Ernest H. Taves, attacked again in *The UFO Enigma*. They reported that "A hoax notorious in UFO annals was launched in February 1958, when a professional photographer aboard the Brazilian training ship, the *Almirante Saldanha*, took a series of photographs of an alleged UFO flying over the island of Trindade, in the South Atlantic Ocean east of Brazil. Acclaimed by the flying-saucer clan as the most convincing UFO pictures yet available, the photographs were published internationally. The apparent endorsement by the Brazilian Navy and later by the Brazilian government itself quickly collapsed when it was established that the photographer was well known for his trick photography and that no one else, except a friend (and presumed accomplice), had seen the disk flying overhead. It also came to light that the same photographer had, a short time before, attempted to sell a number of fabricated photographs of UFOs."

Menzel and Taves then offered a way for the photographer to have faked the pictures. He could have taken pictures of a model against a black background and then reloaded the camera with the same film. Once on the ship, he could photograph the landscape of the island, producing his very convincing fakes. Of course they offer no evidence that such is the case—only that it could have been done.

But, once again, others simply didn't agree with this assessment. There were, literally, dozens of witnesses, making this one of the few photographic cases in which there were multiple witnesses. The stories told by those witnesses seemed to corroborate one another. And, according to the reports, the film was developed in the presence of ship's officers.

Menzel had studied the photographs and changed his explanation about them from a rather rare weather-related phenomenon to one of hoax. It was not the first time that he had done this. After Carl Hart, Jr. had photographed the strange lights seen over Lubbock, Texas, Menzel had suggested a temperature inversion, creating an illusion of lights in the sky. Later, without justification, he suggested that the pictures were faked.

Menzel's idea about the Trindade Island pictures might have been the result of U.S. Navy interest in them. They refused to make any public comment, but in 1963, Major Carl R. Hart (not to be confused with Carl Hart, Jr. of Lubbock) did quote from an Office of Naval Intelligence report. He wrote, "This gentleman [Barauna] has a long history of photographic trick shots . . . [H] e prepared a purposely humorous article, published in a magazine, entitled 'A Flying Saucer Hunted Me at Home,' using trick photography." But the article had been written as a debunking piece to show how other UFO photographs, especially those taken in Brazil in 1957, could have been created.

The official Project Blue Book file is very thin, considering the nature of the photographs. However, given their disregard of other photographic cases, it is somewhat surprising to find that they did have a file on this case, especially when they ignored solid cases in the United States.

The attitude of various American officials can be seen in a document prepared and forwarded by Captain M. Sunderland. He wrote, "The whole thing is a fake publicity stunt put on by a crooked photographer and the Brazilian Navy fell for it. This seems like the most likely considering Brazilians' love for sensationalism and gossip, their well known propensity for never letting the truth stand in the way of a good story and general bureaucratic inefficiency."

It would seem that the Brazilian Navy fell for the "hoax" only because there were a number of officers and sailors who corroborated the tale told by the photographer. This is not to mention several sightings that preceded the one on January 16 and the existence of another picture taken about two weeks earlier by a different photographer. All of that combined to suggest that the photographer, no matter how clever, could not have faked the sighting in the presence of others.

The statement made about the nature of Brazilian society is more than a little insulting. It is a way of dismissing the photographs as trivial without having to explain them intelligently. But that sort of thinking on Sunderland's part wasn't confined to Brazilians. The final statement in his report was, "It is the reporting officer's private opinion that a flying saucer sighting would be unlikely at the very barren island of Trindade, as everyone knows Martians are extremely comfort loving creatures."

The problem with this case, as with so many others, is that no follow-up investigations have been made. Here is a series of photographs, apparently taken in the presence of dozens of witnesses who saw the object in the sky. There are multiple chains of evidence, independent of one another. Yet no follow-up has been done.

Dr. Mark Rodeghier of the Center for UFO Studies said that Dr. J. Allen Hynek, at one time the scientific consultant to Project Blue Book, had gone to Brazil in the early 1970s and talked with Barauna and some of the other witnesses, but no photometric examination of the photographs has been attempted. He did confirm, if nothing else, that the case had multiple witnesses. Here was an opportunity to advance the case for the UFO, or, at the very least, provide a form of physical evidence proving that something was happening and something was being observed. But the climate of the times, the distances involved, and our own attitudes toward both UFOs and South America have colored our thinking.

The Heflin Photographs
August 3, 1965

The pictures taken by Rex Heflin on August 3, 1965 were labeled a hoax by the Air Force almost immediately after they were taken. The Air Force based this conclusion on a preliminary examination of copies that had been printed in the newspaper. They believed that the pictures were of a small model, about 3 feet in diameter, that had been suspended about 20 feet above the ground. Although they would engage in another, more lengthy investigation, they would not alter their original assessment when that research was completed. The case is carried as a hoax in the Blue Book files.

The story of Heflin's photographs appeared in the Blue Book flies in great detail. In Attachment 2 of the official report, it was stated:

> At approximately 1130 hours PDT on 3 August 1965, Mr. Rex E Heflin was driving SSW on Myford Road to check out

a matter (not identified) pertaining to his job for the Orange County Road Department. After checking the item he turned his vehicle (Ford "van bus") around and began to head NNE, still on Myford Road. He was still traveling at only a few MPH (three to ten) when he first observed something out of the corner of his eye, out of the left side window of the vehicle. At first he assumed that it was a helicopter until the object was almost directly in front of his vehicle. Because of the unusual shape of the object, Mr. Heflin quickly stopped the vehicle and grabbed the Polaroid camera which was on the front seat (SOP for traffic investigators), and took one picture of the object through the windshield. (NOTE: Marine Corps investigators determined that the object was at a bearing of 10 degrees magnetic at the time the photograph was taken.) The UFO continued an ESE course at slow speed. Mr. Heflin was able to take two additional photographs of the UFO through the right door window of his vehicle. (NOTE: Marine Corps investigators estimate that the bearing of the UFO in picture nr 2 was about 90 degrees magnetic, and that the bearing of the UFO in picture nr 3 was about 70 degrees magnetic.) This would indicate that picture nr 3 was taken after the UFO had changed course to NE heading.

Mr. Heflin's comment to the Investigating Officer varied somewhat from those given to the Marine Corps investigator. However, it is believed that the undersigned conducted a more thorough investigation and that Mr. Heflin's comments which are noted below are essentially correct. Mr. Heflin stated that he had attempted to use his two-way radio once or twice just before he sighted the UFO and could neither transmit nor receive any signal although the radio panel lights indicated that the radio was operational. Detailed questioning indicated that this definitely occurred before the UFO sighting and not during the UFO sighting. Mr. Heflin stated that after the UFO had disappeared that he attempted to use his radio and found that it was working normally. He also started that he had not had any other radio malfunctions in the preceding weeks.

Just after taking the third picture of the UFO, Mr. Heflin heard a vehicle approaching from the rear. Concerned that he might have parked in an awkward position, he turned around to see if there was enough road clearance for the vehicle to pass him. Noting that he was on the shoulder of the road, he immediately turned again to look at the UFO but found that it had "disappeared into the haze."

The Investigating Officer has noted some skepticism on the part of several individuals as to whether or not Mr. Heflin could have observed the UFO, stopped his vehicle and taken three photographs—all in a 15 to 25 second time period. A check was made with people who are familiar with this particular model camera, and it was determined that an experienced man could easily take three photographs within a 12-second time period.

At the end of the working day, Mr. Heflin returned to his office in the Road Department building and showed his photographs to several co-workers. They were subsequently filed in a desk drawer. After a few days (and after several duplicate photographs, conversations, comments, and general bull sessions), a friend of Mr. Heflin who is a former employee of the Road Department convinced Mr. Heflin that they should try to sell the photographs to LIFE Magazine. The friend was unidentified, however Mr. Heflin's supervisor, Mr. Kimmel, substantiated this bit of the story. The friend called the LIFE Magazine office in Chicago and was informed that they were interested. Subsequently, the friend mailed the pictures to the Los Angeles office and presumably the photographs were forwarded to the main office in New York (or Chicago?).

About two weeks later the photographs were returned from New York(?) directly to Mr. Heflin without written comment. At about the same time the Los Angeles office telephoned Mr. Heflin to say that the main office had declined to utilize the pictures "because it was too controversial at the time." Time passed and apparently more copies of the pictures were made and handed out to various friends and friends of friends, until most of Santa Ana was saturated with the UFO pictures.

One of these pictures was obtained by a druggist who then apparently showed it to a friend, a customer who worked for the Santa Ana Register. On or about 18 September, Frank

Hall of the Santa Ana Register contacted Mr. Heflin, borrowed the three original prints, returned the originals to Mr. Heflin and wrote an article which was published with the UFO picture (Nr 1) in the Santa Ana Register on 20 September 1965. Two of the three photographs were released by the Register on 20 or 21 September to UPI. One or both of these pictures and accompanying articles were published by various newspapers on 21 September 1965.

There are some other facts that need to be explained. Heflin apparently loaned the original prints to anyone who asked for copies of them. First he gave them to the Marine officer who investigated the case, without asking for a receipt. The prints were quickly returned. Then a man claiming to be with the North American Air Defense Command (NORAD) contacted him by telephone. He visited later, showed credentials that seemed authentic, and was given the originals, again without receipt.

Although his actions might seem odd (and have been questioned by some), Heflin made them clear. He had provided the original photographs to the Marines and gotten them back. He had provided the original photographs to the newspaper and had gotten them back. If the NORAD officer had returned the pictures, Heflin would have provided them to the Blue Book investigators without a receipt. Heflin believed all the investigators and reporters when they said they would return his pictures.

The Air Force tried to find out who the NORAD officer was, but they had no luck. Others noted that NORAD wouldn't be investigating UFOs and certainly wouldn't have taken the originals without making arrangements to return them. Air Force investigators suggested that because NORAD would not be routinely investigating UFO sightings, and because there was no evidence that such an investigation by NORAD had taken place, Heflin's story must be a hoax.

But Heflin's chronology and reports aren't the only part of the case in dispute. Air Force records suggest that the Air Force only became interested in the case after the public release of the photographs. Yet, in the Project Blue Book files, there is a report of the photo analysis of the pictures dated August 14, suggesting an Air Force investigation within two weeks of the event.

The Condon Committee asked the Air Force about it and was told that the report's date was a typographical error. Certain Air Force officers had noticed the date earlier and had questioned it. No one explained why the date hadn't been corrected or why a notation hadn't been attached to the report. In reality, the incorrect date is probably not important.

With that question answered to their satisfaction, the Condon Committee investigators began to pick apart Heflin's story based on exactly that same sort of error. For example, Hartmann noted in his original report for the Condon Committee that Heflin had spoken about his NORAD visitor as a single man. According to a September 25, 1965, report filed with NICAP, Heflin had said that "a man with a briefcase later called . . . and said he was . . . and that he would like to see . . . [Heflin] agreed to loan the pictures to him providing he would . . ."

Colorado investigators interviewed Heflin on January 15, 1968. They asked, "Why is it that you are now clear on there having been two NORAD visitors, while on the very next day the Air Force man came away with the idea that a man came up and flashed his card . . . ?"

According to Hartmann in the Condon Committee report, "He [Heflin] immediately replied in effect that only one man showed his card. He repeated that there were two men, in their early thirties, but that one stood back while the other did most of the talking. Since two independent reports from the next three days clearly indicate one visitor, while the witness has since insisted there were two, the 'NORAD episode' is still regarded as open to serious question."

But this isn't a very important question. It can easily be explained as a simple mistake by Heflin. Human memory is a very complex thing, and there are changes and mutations in memory each time it is accessed. The importance attached to the number of men who appeared at Heflin's home is the same as the importance attached to the date of the Air Force photo analysis. It is a mistake that is insignificant.

Analysis of the photographs should have taken primary importance in the investigation, but it was Heflin's testimony that was scrutinized in detail. There were, however, some analyses of the pictures that could have been significant.

First is the misdated Air Force report, numbered 65-48. In paragraph 2, labeled Analysis, it was reported, "Although it is not possible to disprove the size of the object from the camera information submitted and distances to the object quoted in the report by Mr. Rex E. Heflin, we feel that the following is the true case. The camera was probably focused on a set distance and not on infinity, as the terrain background was blurred on all three photographs. The center white stripe on the road and the object appeared to have the same sharp image. Therefore, it is felt that the object was on the same plane as the center white stripe or closer to the camera and could not possibly be the size quoted in the report. Using the width of the road as a factor, it was estimated the size of the object to be approximately one to three feet in diameter and approximately fifteen to twenty feet above the ground."

The Air Force investigators also reported, "A test was conducted by the FTD Photo Analyst and Photo Processing personnel with the results showed on the attached photos. The photographs were taken with a Polaroid Camera, Model 110A using 200 ASA film. . . . The object seen in the photographs was a 9" in diameter vaporizing tray, tossed in the air approximately 8 to 12 feet high at a distance from the camera of approximately 15 to 20 feet. The result of the test shows surprising similarities between the object on the test photography and the object on Mr. Heflin's photography."

On the other side of the coin, however, was the photographic analysis conducted by Ralph Rankow, a NICAP member, who said that his preliminary findings supported the authenticity of the pictures.

In all fairness it must be noted that no one expected the Air Force to conclude anything other than the fact that the pictures were some kind of fake. And no one expected NICAP to conclude anything other than the fact that the pictures were authentic. The political agendas of the two organizations are apparent in their analyses of Heflin's pictures.

Can such a conflict be resolved? Other factors might provide some clues for us. Marine investigators, as well as those for the Condon Committee, for example, attempted to learn if any of the radars at the El Toro Marine Base, not far from where Heflin took the pictures, revealed anything that could be decisive.

In a "Narrative Report and Assessment," Captain Charles F. Reichmuth wrote, "No interception or identification action was taken on the date of the sighting, however, a check made by the Marine Corps investigators indicated that no UFO was observed on the Marine Corps Air Facility radar at the time of the reported UFO observation."

In 1965, that assessment might have had some significance. Stealth technology has rendered the radar arguments moot. However, according to the Condon Committee, "The 'Facility' referred to by the Air Force investigator is a relatively small base within direct sight of the Myford Road site, but contains only a sporadically used training radar installation. Marine officials interviewed 15 January 1968, were unable to determine whether radar was in service 3 August 1965."

That seemed to eliminate the radar argument, at least as applied to that specific facility, but Condon Committee investigators thought the report might refer to the surveillance radars that were used in Air Traffic control at El Toro. They learned that even if the UFO had appeared on those radars, the operators would have ignored it unless it posed a threat to traffic at the base. According to the Condon Committee report, "We were informed that no action would be normally taken unless it [the UFO] approached or endangered commercial or military aircraft, in which case only the larger aircraft, not the 'light aircraft,' would be contacted."

In other words, the radar data was a wash. It proved nothing other than the fact that the object was not noted on either of the Marine radars. And that is the key. It hadn't been noted, but that didn't mean that it hadn't appeared, a fine point that was mentioned by the Condon investigators.

There was also a controversy surrounding the fourth of the Heflin photographs. When he returned to the office on August 3, he showed the three pictures of the UFO to his coworkers. He allowed friends to have the pictures copied. He showed those

The Very Large Array radio astronomy facility about fifty miles west of Socorro.

The Chamber of Commerce in Socorro, New Mexico, near the scene of Lonnie Zamora's 1964 sighting.

Photos by Kevin D. Randle

The city limits of Levelland, Texas. It is obvious that Levelland got its name because of the flat terrain.

Photo by Kevin D. Randle

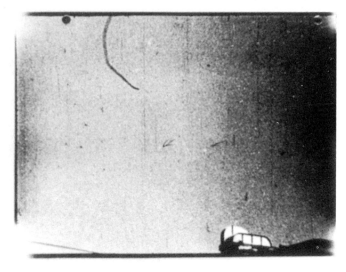

The twin objects filmed by Nick Mariana in August 1950 over Great Falls, Montana.

Photo courtesy of USAF

One of the four photographs taken by Rex Heflin in August 1965. Analysis by the Air Force and Ground Saucer Watch suggested a hoax, while analysis by others such as NICAP suggested the photos were authentic.

The Air Force, in an attempt to prove Heflin's photographs were a hoax, created this picture by throwing a small object into the air and then photographing it.

Photos courtesy of USAF

Archnemesis Phil Klass, self-described smartest, most handsome, funloving, and kind UFO researcher.
Photo courtesy of Philip Klass

Guy B. Marquand, Jr., created this UFO photograph as a young man. It is an admitted hoax, yet it turns up periodically as proof that we are being visited.
Photo courtesy of USAF

Photograph of the Saturn-shaped object taken from the deck of the
Brazilian research vessel *Almirante Saldanha* in 1958.

Photo courtesy of APRO

An enlargement of what some consider to be among the best of the
photographs of a UFO.

Photo courtesy of APRO

The last of the photographs taken by Almiro Barauna as the object disappeared.

Photo courtesy of APRO

Investigated by the University of Colorado UFO study, this photograph by Paul Trent was found to be authentic.

Photo courtesy of APRO

pictures to investigators and discussed them with reporters. Hundreds were aware that he had taken three pictures of the disk-shaped UFO.

What no one knew at the time was that Heflin had taken a fourth picture of a smoke ring that was allegedly left by the UFO. It was taken from farther down the road and could be an important clue as to the authenticity of the case.

The documentation available, as well as that from the Air Force file, the NICAP investigation, and the *Santa Ana Register*, makes no mention of this fourth picture. The Condon Committee investigators wrote, "During the early NICAP interview the presence of a fourth photo was not recorded, although the ring was apparently mentioned. During the Air Force interview, the witness not only did not mention the smoke ring or fourth photo, but gave a somewhat different description of the disappearance of the UFO."

The Air Force report noted, "Just after taking the third picture of the UFO, Mr. Heflin heard a vehicle approaching from the rear. Concerned that he might have parked in an awkward position, he turned around to see if there was enough road clearance for the vehicle to pass him. Noting that he was on the shoulder of the road, he immediately turned again to look at the UFO but found that it had 'disappeared into the haze.' "

When questioned about this, Heflin said that he had been advised by a NICAP investigator to withhold some of the information from the Air Force. An attempt by Condon Committee investigators to clear up the problem resulted in Heflin's denying that he had invented any of the testimony. Everything he had said was true, but that didn't explain why there was only a single reference to the truck diverting his attention. The NICAP investigator thought that this one aspect of the tale might be a falsehood.

The problem with that thinking is that once you have caught the witness in a deliberate lie it calls all other testimony of that witness into question. If he would lie about one aspect, why not others, and how do you know the difference?

The lie seemed to be designed to explain how the photograph of the smoke ring was taken. It was designed to explain an apparent discrepancy in the time line. The appearance of the truck—

which diverted his attention—covered the point easily. But if it was true, why didn't he mention it again, after telling the Air Force about it?

This is not the place to begin an essay on human memory. It is known that our memories of events begin to deteriorate quickly. Details that are important one day are forgotten the next. All the latest studies of memory suggest that many details are forgotten within twenty-four hours of an event. If an event has no real significance, almost all memory of it will be gone a week later.

This problem with memory could easily explain the shifting nature of UFO reports. If the witness has not memorized the events to create a hoax, then we must expect some discrepancies to appear. However, the disappearance of a vehicle that caused a break in the observation of a UFO seems to be an extreme example of this sort of thing.

At any rate, these changes in the story were enough for the skeptics and debunkers to dismiss the Heflin tale as a hoax. These "internal inconsistencies" proved that Heflin had invented the story for the publicity and excitement.

Those who wished to dismiss the Heflin story also directed attention to the clouds that appeared in the fourth picture. According to weather records from five different reporting facilities, there were no clouds in the sky on August 3. If true, that would suggest that picture number four was not made at the same time as the others, throwing off the chronology. It would also document a lie told by Heflin.

There were others who have analyzed the pictures to the point where it is nearly impossible to figure out which analysis is accurate. William Spaudling of the now defunct Ground Saucer Watch concluded in the 1970s that the Heflin photographs were faked. He claimed that his "enhancement" of the photographs revealed a line that apparently began at the top of the saucer and disappeared from the frame in the truck window. That seemed to be the end of the Heflin photos. They were a hoax.

Robert Nathan, another UFO researcher, claimed that in his enhancements of the Heflin photographs, he never found any lines. He worked with better equipment than Spaudling. Bruce

Maccabee, a physicist for the Navy and a photo expert himself, sided with Spaudling. On December 29, 1997, Maccabee wrote, "I therefore had to conclude that the 'line' above the UFO really was there (in spite of Nathan's protestations)."

Nearly twenty years after the Condon Committee report was issued, Heflin would tell reporter Robert J. Kirkpatrick that he had "lost considerable credence in the scientific community when [I] saw the weight they placed on a review of the weather data supplied by five agencies in the area. Anyone familiar with the weather in Orange and Los Angeles counties knows what extreme variations exist in weather conditions from one locality to another and how quickly conditions can change."

Heflin, however, claimed that there was an additional witness. He told Kirkpatrick that a private pilot who had been flying from the Fullerton, California, airport also reported the UFO. He never came forward to corroborate the sighting.

Heflin also told Kirkpatrick, "In fact, a member of another field crew said he saw the same UFO. But he died in a traffic accident before any investigators could interview him."

These sorts of witnesses are of no value now because we have no record of their statements or who they are. A man who died before he corroborated the story, who left no legacy of his report, does nothing to validate the Heflin case. There is no way to learn if he actually saw the UFO, if he suggested he had because he wanted some of the spotlight, or if this was just an attempt to show that others had, in fact, seen something.

The Condon Committee investigators drew no real conclusion in the Heflin case. They wrote, "From the point of view of the Colorado study the principal question of concern is: *does a case have probative value in establishing the reality of unusual aircraft?* In a case like this, where both the observer and the photographs *clearly* allege an extraordinary vehicle, a second question is, of course, automatically implied: Does the case represent a fabrication or was the object a true unknown? . . . We are concerned only with establishing evidence as to whether or not there exist extraordinary flying objects.

"In that context, this case is equivocal."

In the conclusion section, it was noted that "The strongest

arguments against the case are the clouds in photo four and the inconsistent early records regarding the 'NORAD' visitors. The photos themselves contain no geometric or physical data that permit a determination of distance or size *independent* of the testimony. Thus the witness' claims are the essential ingredients in the case. The case must remain inconclusive."

That wouldn't be the end of it, of course. The *Orange County Register* published an article by Amy Wilson on July 22, 1997. According to the article, Ed Riddle, a technical writer in Menlo Park, said that he had first seen Heflin's pictures when a man brought them into the lunchroom several days before anything was published in the newspaper. Riddle said that the man said that a friend or neighbor had "rigged up a toy train wheel and some monofilament fishing line, hung them out his truck window, shot them and would maybe, just take them to the paper for some fun."

According to Riddle, in 1965, he called the newspaper to let them know that the pictures were a joke. But his tale was met with "gruff talk about how if a man didn't have any proof, they didn't want to hear about it."

Wilson also reported that a second caller had told them that Heflin lost his job because of the controversy over the pictures. That wasn't true either. Heflin worked for the highway department for thirty years. In fact, he retired in 1978 as chief of the Traffic Investigation Division after a disabling injury. Clearly Heflin's career was not adversely affected by the UFO photographs.

It is interesting to note that after so many years, the original copies of Heflin's photographs were returned to him. Everyone had been working from copies of the copies, some of which were many generations removed from the originals. Now that the originals have been located, it is time to take another look at them to see what can be learned from them. That might allow us to figure out this case.

There is probably one final comment that should be made. Many inside the UFO community worry about how much money is made by those who claim to have seen something strange. Heflin's pictures have been used in dozens of magazine articles and books about UFOs. When he took the pictures in 1965, he didn't bother to have them copyrighted. Anyone could use them without having to pay for the privilege. Heflin never received any money for the use of his pictures.

The Photographic Conclusions

The existence of good motion picture footage or a series of still photographs is never going to be sufficient to prove that flying saucers are of extraterrestrial origin. They are, however, evidence that something extraordinary is happening.

The skeptical community, the Air Force, and the studies sponsored by the Air Force have all worked hard to eliminate the photographic physical evidence from the record by suggesting either mundane explanations or calling the evidence faked. Often they have done this with no evidence to back up their pronouncements. They haven't cared that their conclusions are not scientific or that they have little to do with the facts. They have only cared that they could slap some label on a case and then ignore it.

But the evidence we have just reviewed has ruled out those explanations. The Montana movie, according to the experts, shows two jet fighters in the sky above Great Falls. Never mind that the witnesses saw the jets in a different part of the sky. If the eyewitness testimony is inconvenient, ignore that testimony.

Never mind that the film, combined with the time the objects were seen, is too long for the objects to be obscured by sunlight reflections as suggested. Never mind that the witness said that he saw an oval shape behind the bright lights he filmed.

We ignore that because it doesn't fit with what we want to believe. All of us have seen an aircraft reflecting sunlight in such a way as to obscure its true shape. Yes, it looked oval. But within seconds it turned and revealed its true shape. Or, as it continued to fly, it revealed its true shape. Or, as we continued to move, it revealed its true shape. Within seconds that happened. But Mariana had the objects in sight for nearly a minute, and the true shape was never revealed.

Delbert Newhouse saw the objects he filmed as they flew over his car. He saw a distinct saucer shape and reported as much to the Air Force when they finally asked a question about the objects' shape. But the Robertson Panel, and later the Condon Committee, rejected the eyewitness testimony to conclude that the objects on the film were soaring seagulls.

The movies have been rendered inconclusive by the desire to find a mundane explanation for them. Label them and they are no longer proof of anything other than our desire to delude ourselves.

The still photographs have fared no better. Those taken by the Trents in McMinnville were labeled by the Condon Committee as solid evidence with no suggestion of a hoax. But that just isn't enough. Now shadows under the eaves suggest to debunkers that the pictures weren't taken when the Trents said. No evidence of a hoax was offered other than the debunker belief that the Trents lied about the time the pictures were taken. If they lied about that, to the debunker thinking, then the case was a hoax.

Checking the pictures, those same debunkers have said they were not taken in the order described by the Trents. Of course, if the Trents had taken the pictures at the time they said, the evidence on the pictures would be consistent with their story. What should have been done, by those who had access to the original negatives, was to check the frame numbers. The negatives should have been numbered. But no one ever looked to confirm the order in which the pictures were taken. To me, this seems to be an elemental step that was avoided by skeptic and believer alike.

The Trindade Island photographs also seem to show a flying saucer. The story told by the photographer is supported by dozens of other witnesses. But Donald Menzel, as he would do time and again, rejected those claims with no evidence. As mentioned earlier, he wrote, "The apparent endorsement by the Brazilian Navy collapsed when it was established that the photographer was well known for his trick photography and that no one else, except a friend had seen the disk flying overhead."

He offered no proof of this. He cited no sources for this. He just made the pronouncement, which, if true, would destroy the credibility of the pictures. But he had no proof it was true.

Finally we have the series of pictures taken by Rex Heflin.

Again the hoax label has been applied, but the evidence of a hoax by Heflin seems to be lacking. Some measurements done by the Air Force suggested a three-foot model. Other measurements, completed by believers, suggested an object twenty feet in diameter.

But the point is that the hoax label had been applied. When all else fails, label the evidence as a hoax and let it go at that. No evidence that it is a hoax is required. The assertion is enough to ruin the credibility of the pictures.

We have seen five examples of evidence of something unusual flying through our atmosphere. Five examples that are not easily explained. Five examples of a structured craft that is of unearthly design and capability. In the scientific arena, it would seem that these examples would be enough to pique the curiosity. It would seem that scientists would want to determine if the evidence has been faked, if it is a natural phenomenon that we don't understand, or if it is evidence of alien visitation.

Instead we have scientists who work overtime to prove that we are gullible and unable to think for ourselves. These movies and photos would seem to be enough to start the investigation. Instead, they have been ignored.

5

Direct Physical Evidence of UFO Sightings

It was the University of Colorado study directed by Dr. Edward Condon that defined for us the concept of direct physical evidence. Roy Craig, of the Condon Committee, wrote, "Several types of physical effects have been presented as evidence that an object of unusual nature had been present at a given location. Such effects consist of: (1) markings on the ground, vegetation, or objects with which an UFO, as something from an UFO, reportedly made direct or indirect physical contact; (2) material residue allegedly deposited from or by an UFO; (3) articles or portions of articles manufactured by intelligent beings, but reportedly not produced by known cultures. A fourth known conceivable type of physical evidence, consisting of non-earthly or captured 'flying saucer,' would be most impressive evidence. The existence of this type of evidence has been suggested by some reporters, such as Moseley (1967), who reported the claim that a captured flying saucer was held at a military base in Ohio, and Allen (1959), who presented a photograph of a tiny humanoid creature and four adult Earth residents, claiming the creature was a crewman of a saucer which crashed near Mexico City in 1950. During the course of this study, however, no indication was found that this fourth type of evidence had ever existed."

In fact we have looked at evidence of crashed flying saucers, including evidence from a tale that has emerged from Roswell,

New Mexico. There is no indication, however, that those on the Condon Committee were aware of the events at Roswell, so their rejection of the fourth type of physical evidence is based not on knowledge but on ignorance.

It could also be argued that, at present, the Roswell case is built entirely of eyewitness testimony. Many solid and credible people have claimed firsthand knowledge of the crash. However, we are examining the physical evidence aspects of the UFO phenomenon; the Roswell case, in its current state, falls outside that category.

But there have been cases of UFO crashes that did come to the attention of the Condon Committee, and of which the physical evidence did exist. All of them, with one exception, fall outside the "current" nature of our investigation. The Condon Committee decided to avoid, for the most part, cases that predated the formation of their project. However, the case of the UFO crash at Shag Harbour began in October 1967, while the project was in operation. In fact, there is a brief study of it in the final version of the Condon Committee report.

The committee's investigation consisted of telephoning several sources in the Shag Harbour area. They reported they were first alerted to the case by Jim Lorenzen of APRO, demonstrating that their system for gathering reports as they were made was lacking in coverage. Based solely on their telephone investigation, the project scientists decided that there was nothing to be accomplished by further work. They believed there was no reason for one of their investigators to travel all the way to Canada.

In the short (under two pages) report, Dr. Norman E. Levine wrote, "He [Jim Lorenzen] stated that the original report had come from two teen-agers, and that the Navy was searching for wreckage. No aircraft were reported missing in the area . . . A corporal of the RCMP stated that the first report had come from five young people, 15–20 yr. old, who while driving near the shore had seen three or four yellow lights in a horizontal pattern comparable in size to a 'fair-sized' aircraft . . . They observed the light while they drove on about .25 mi., then reported the incident to the RCMP detachment." This statement makes no mention of Constable Ron Pond's report of the observations he made or any of the observations made by other adult observers. We are left with the impression that the sighting is based on the reports of a number of young people, the majority of whom are teenagers.

In the report, Levine did write:

> Two officers [O'Brien and Pond] and the corporal had arrived about 15 min. later, in time to see the light on the water. It persisted about five minutes longer. Ten minutes after it went out, the two officers were at the site in a rowboat; a Coast Guard boat and six fishing boats were on the scene. They found only patches of foam 30–40 yd. wide that the fishermen thought was not normal tide foam . . .
>
> The site of the presumed impact was in between an island and the mainland, about 200–300 yd. offshore. Apparently no one actually saw anything enter the water (though I must point out that a number saw the object descend to the water, which is, essentially, the same thing). However two young women driving on the island reported that a horizontal pattern of three yellow lights had tilted and descended, and then a yellow light had appeared on the water . . . The RCMP corporal stated that the light on the water was not on any boat, that Air Search and Rescue had no reports of missing aircraft in the area, and an RCAF radar station nearby reported no Canadian or U.S. air operations in the area at the time, nor any unusual radar object . . . A search by Navy divers during the days immediately following the sighting disclosed nothing relevant.
>
> Five days later the Naval Maritime Command advised the project [that is the Condon Committee] that the search had been terminated. The watch officer read a report from the RCMP indicating that at the time in question a 60 ft. object had been seen to explode upon impact with the water . . . A captain of a fishing boat that had been about 16 mi. from the site of the earlier reports, reported to the project that he and his crew had seen three stationary bright red flashing lights on the water, from sundown until about 11:00 p.m. The ship's radar showed four objects forming a six mile square; the three lights were associated with one of these objects [so now we see

that Levine is contradicting himself with radar reports and people seeing the object descend]. At about 11:00 p.m., one of the lights went straight up. The captain had judged that the radar objects were naval vessels and the ascending light a helicopter; he had attached no significance to these observations until he had heard on the radio of the sightings; he then reported the foregoing observations . . . However, since the position he reported for the objects was about 175 n. mi. from the original site, the two situations do not appear to be related.

No further investigation by the project was considered justifiable, particularly in view of the immediate and thorough search [that had failed to find anything which would suggest that the Condon Committee should be very interested in the case] that had been carried out by the RCMP and the Maritime Command.

But there was a story there. Canadians Chris Styles and Don Ledger decided to pursue the case because, to them, it deserved more than the glance that had been given it by the Condon researchers and other UFO investigators. According to them, the events began on the night of October 4, 1967, near the small fishing village of Shag Harbour, Nova Scotia. A UFO—by some estimates as large as 60 feet in diameter—seemed to descend to the surface of the water about a half a mile from shore. There were four bright lights on it that flashed in sequence.

As it hit the water, there seemed to be a bright flash and explosion. Several witnesses, thinking that some sort of aircraft might have crashed, called the Royal Canadian Mounted Police at Barrington Passage. Although some talked in terms of an aircraft accident and others mentioned only the bright lights, no one suggested a UFO.

It wasn't long before three officers were at the shoreline. Corporal Victor Werbicki was the officer in charge. Constable Ron O'Brien and Constable Ron Pond were there to assist him. Pond had seen the lights from his cruiser. Later, as the object dived toward the water, he saw a shape behind them. In other words, Pond reported, not only the lights themselves but the fact that those lights were on a solid object.

Standing on the shore with the Mounties were a number of other witnesses. All of them could see a pale yellow light that floated about a half mile from shore. Through binoculars, they could see that whatever floated on the surface was creating a foaming, yellow wake as it moved. Because of the location of the object, Coast Guard cutters and local fishing boats were summoned. But the object, whatever it was, disappeared before any of the boats arrived. Those on the fishing boats did see the dense yellow foam, but it had dispersed before Coast Guard Cutter #101 arrived. At three in the morning the search was suspended, but it was set to resume at dawn.

A preliminary report was prepared by the Rescue Coordination Center at Halifax for transmittal to Canadian Forces Headquarters in Ottawa. It merely pointed out that something had crashed into the water of Shag Harbour. As the message was headed up the chain of command, that something was described as "no known object." According to Styles, the "Air Desk," which he described as the equivalent to Project Blue Book in the United States, was alerted; they ordered the Maritime Command to dispatch a mobile unit.

According to the information available, the HCMS *Granby* was dispatched to Shag Harbour. They apparently searched the area until last light on Sunday, October 8, using divers. When they failed to find anything, the search was called off. Media interest in the case faded at that time.

The point, however, is that here was a case that promised not only the physical evidence that the Condon Committee wanted but also the sort of "crashed" saucer debris that would be conclusive. Their response, as noted, was to make a telephone call and then, persuaded that only "teenagers" had seen the lights, give up.

The Condon scientists did study the Ubatuba, Brazil, case from September 1957. In September of that year a magazine writer received a letter from an unidentified man who claimed he had seen a spacecraft explode over the water near Ubatuba. Pieces rained into the ocean and along the beach. The man had picked up some of them and sent just a few small pieces to the writer.

He, in turn, alerted Olavo Fontes, who tracked the research for APRO. According to Fontes, the Brazilian government analyzed the largest of the fragments, determining that it was made of one hundred percent magnesium. To Fontes and the leadership of APRO, this suggested proof of extraterrestrial visitation.

Two of the fragments were sent on to APRO Headquarters for further analysis. These were eventually loaned to the Condon Committee for nondestructive analysis. They concluded, "Although the Brazil fragment proved not to be pure, as claimed, the possibility remained that the material was unique. The high content of SR was particularly interesting, since SR is not an expected impurity in magnesium made by usual production methods, and Dr. Busk knew of no one who intentionally added strontium to commercial magnesium. . . . Since only a few grams of the Ubatuba magnesium are known to exist, and these could have been produced by common earthly technology known prior to 1957, the existence and composition of these samples themselves reveal no information about the sample's origin."

The controversy over the purity could not be resolved because the first sample had been destroyed in the testing process. The pieces tested by the Condon scientists may not have had the same composition as the first sample, something the scientists should have realized.

But all the points are moot. The original witness, or witnesses as claimed by Coral Lorenzen, were never found. No one came forward to claim authorship of the original letter. Without that link, the chain of evidence was broken right at the beach. An anonymous source had claimed to have seen the UFO explode, but no one could prove that it had happened. As proof, the fragments just weren't sufficient.

The Condon Committee concluded their review of the physical evidence with, "This project has found no physical evidence which, in itself, clearly indicates the existence in the atmosphere of vehicles of extraordinary nature. Belief in the existence of such vehicles, if such belief is held, must rest on other arguments."

Socorro, New Mexico
April 24, 1964

The implication by the Condon Committee, the Air Force, and many in the scientific community is that no direct physical evidence of UFOs exists. But there are many good physical evidence cases that suggest that some sort of craft not only interacted with the environment but actually might have landed. There are a number of cases in which a craft was seen about the time that the physical evidence was left. There are fewer cases in which occupants of the craft were seen, and fewer still that the Air Force investigated, produced no solid explanation for, and labeled as unidentified. One of the few that has met all these descriptions is the landing that took place on April 24, 1964, just outside of Socorro, New Mexico. It was a case that would gain national attention, be featured on front pages of newspapers around the country and on national television news broadcasts. And it would become so important that, according to the Air Force files, even President Johnson was interested in the investigation.

According to one of the official reports to appear in the Project Blue Book files, Lonnie Zamora, a police officer in Socorro, was chasing a speeder in the early evening when he heard a loud roar and saw a flash of light in the sky to the southwest. Believing that a dynamite shed in the area had exploded, he broke off the pursuit of the speeder, altering his course to take him by the shed.

Zamora would later tell investigators that the flame was bluish and orange. That would lead some of the scientists to believe that the flame was chemical in nature. He suggested the flame was descending slowly and was narrow, almost funnel shaped.

He turned onto a gravel road, driving slowly to the west. He was searching for the dynamite shack, not sure exactly where it was located. In a gully to the south of the road, he spotted an object that he thought, at first, was an overturned car. He stopped for a moment, one or two seconds, and from that point, he saw "two people in white coveralls, quite close to the object."

According to the statement that Zamora supplied to Air Force investigators, one of the people seemed to stop and look straight at him. Zamora believed that the person was startled to see him so close to the craft. Zamora wanted to help them, still not sure exactly what he was seeing.

The object, he still believed, was an overturned car. He realized that it was made of shining metal such as aluminum, white and smooth, but not shiny like chrome. The object was egg or oval shaped.

He used the radio to alert the sheriff's office that he would be getting out of the car. He stopped again and, while still using the radio, began to get out of his car. As he started walking down to where the object was resting, he heard a roar that was not like that of a jet. It was a low-frequency noise that rose until it was a very loud sound. As the roaring increased, Zamora saw another flame under the object, which began to rise straight up. Again he thought the flame was blue and orange but he saw no smoke, though there was dust in the air.

As soon as he saw the flame, Zamora turned to run. He ran into the rear bumper of his car and fell. He lost his glasses. He scrambled to his feet and ran for another fifty feet when he fell again. He rolled to his stomach and covered himself as best he could, fearing that the object would explode. After a few seconds, the roar faded.

When it was silent again, Zamora looked up in time to see the object in the sky, moving away from him. It was moving toward the dynamite shed at about fifteen feet, just barely making it over the roof.

Zamora ran back to the car and radioed the station. He told the radio operator to look out the window to see if he could see the object. Unfortunately, he couldn't see anything outside because of the direction of the window and the angle from which he was trying to see it.

The first of the New Mexico State Police officers to arrive was Sergeant Sam Chavez. Although Chavez was not involved in the sighting and saw neither the craft nor the aliens, he did see the markings left behind before anyone had a chance to walk over the scene. One bush was burning, and some clumps of grass were burned. Four holes, apparently from landing gear, were pressed into the soft earth.

During the next several days, the official Air Force investigation was started. Air Force officers examined the landing site, interviewed the witnesses, and took photographs. Colonel Eric T. de Jonckherre wrote a report that was forwarded to Project Blue Book.

According to the documentation available in the Blue Book files, Technical Sergeant David N. Moody, of the Project Blue Book staff, stationed at Wright-Patterson AFB in Dayton, Ohio, was brought into the investigation. In his report he wrote, "At 0530, Sunday, 26 April 1964, I received a call from Captain Hector Quintanilla requesting that the Socorro sighting be investigated immediately. . . . This action was dictated by a call from the Command Post at 330, a call from the Emergency Action Group at 430 and another call from the Command Post just prior to my notification of the event. The contacts for data already collected were Lt. Col. King . . . and Captain R T Holder. . . ."

Moody's report included the details of Zamora's sighting and then added information about Chavez's activities after the craft had taken off. Moody wrote, "From the ensuing activity monitored on the radio Sgt Chavez immediately made an effort to reach patrolman Zamora and arrived about 3 minutes after the object under observation by Lonnie Zamora had disappeared. Sgt Chavez then went to the area where the craft or thing was supposedly sighted and found four fresh indentations in the ground and several charred or burned bushes. Smoke appeared to come from the bush and he assumed that it was burning, however no coals were visible and the charred portions of the bush were cold to the touch. Sgt Chavez contacted the FBI, who in turn contacted White Sands and Agent Barnes and Lt. [sic] R T Holder of the latter organization . . . Sgt Chavez secured the area and made an investigation of the ground surrounding the scene to 800 yds. He determined that the only tire marks were those of Patrolman Zamora's vehicle and the State Police car and found no prints or track activity of any kind other than that noted in the FBI report. Further he stated that the marks were definitely 'fresh,' and the dirt showed evidence of "dew" or moisture. . . . At no time did he observe the craft or object described by Patrolman Zamora. . . . had the object been visible he would not have been in a position to see it."

Moody also noted that everyone who had interviewed Zamora was impressed with his sincerity. They were all of the belief that "if a hoax has been perpetrated Lonnie Zamora is definitely not a part of it."

At the end of his report Moody made two comments that are interesting to those of us who began to investigate years later. First, he wrote, "No conclusion as to cause could be reached by myself or Major Conner [who accompanied Moody to Socorro]."

He also wrote, "Coral Lorenzen and husband were in Socorro at the time and had interviewed both Lonnie Zamora and Sgt Chavez, and also Capt Holder prior to the arrival of Major Conner and myself."

Air Force consultant Dr. J. Allen Hynek made a one-day investigation of the case. On April 28, he flew to Albuquerque and met with Major Conner of Kirtland Air Force Base. Though he had problems getting to Socorro, he finally made it and had a chance to talk to Sergeant Chavez about the case. Chavez told Hynek that Zamora "was getting disgusted with the whole thing and with the general misrepresentation he was the victim of."

Hynek met with a representative of the FAA who happened to be in Socorro as part of an investigation. The man, whose name Hynek failed to learn, said that he thought it strange that the FAA's radars had not detected the object. According to Hynek, "He felt that MTI radars can pick up cars on the road, that this object should certainly have been picked up by the radar equipment."

Hynek was impressed with the sincerity displayed by Zamora, and the physical evidence in the form of landing gear markings. He said that he found no evidence that Zamora was capable of creating such an elaborate hoax. In his report to the Air Force, he wrote, "From all of the above and from my personal observations, I would conclude the following: That Zamora, although not overly bright or articulate, is basically sincere, honest and reliable. He would not be capable of contriving a complex hoax, nor would his temperament indicate that he would have the slightest interest in such. . . . His fright was genuine, and his feeling that he had seen something truly unusual is attested by the fact that he asked whether he should speak to the priest first before saying anything about it."

As for the physical evidence, Hynek was unable to see much

of it because, as he noted in his report, "By the time that I got to see the area, it had been so badly trampled over that I could make no assessment of the burned areas. There appear to be a fair amount of charred particles mixed with the dirt, and some charred cardboard was also found. . . . In [sic] conclude, therefore, that Zamora saw a tangible, physical object, under good daylight illumination, and from fairly close range (at the closest, almost as little as 100 feet)."

Importantly, Hynek wrote, "Although Zamora was the only witness [found and interviewed by the Air Force or Hynek] to the actual sighting, nine people in all saw the markings. Altogether nine people saw the markings within hours of the sighting and before the hourds [sic] of curiosity seekers descended upon the place the following day."

It is important to remember that, according to Hynek, one of those nine people was Art Burns of the FBI. Burns, as well as the others, were of the opinion that the tracks were fresh. The fact that the FBI was involved at all was covered up by the participants of the investigation at the insistence of the FBI. In public, they were referred to as local law enforcement officials who happened to be on the scene.

Hynek also interviewed those at the Socorro newspaper, the *El Defensor Chieftain*. Hynek wrote. "He [the editor of the newspaper] had gone into this thing quite thoroughly . . . His story, published on Tuesday, April 28, 1964, is an excellent summary . . . It includes one point not mentioned previously: 'At least one other person—an unidentified tourist traveling north on US 85—saw the UFO just before it landed in a gulley. Opel Grinder, manager of Whitting brothers' Service Station on 85 North, said the man stopped at the station and remarked that aircrafts [sic] flew low around here. Grinder replied that there were many helocopters [sic] in this vicinity, and the tourist said, "It was a funny looking helocopter, if that's what it was." The man said further that the object had flown over his car. It actually was headed straight for the gully where it landed moments later. The tourist also commented that he had seen a police car heading up the hill. This was apparently Zamora's car.'"

Hynek, in his report, mentioned another aspect that would

become important later. He wrote, "I also questioned, while in Socorro, my old friend, Dr Jack Whotmen, President of the New Mexico School of Mines, who said he knew of no geophysical or other types of experiments going on in the area at the time. He, as the rest of the townspeople, *were puzzled by the event* [emphasis added], but the general underground slull of opinion was that it would turn out to be some device which the government still had under raps [*sic*]."

Several months later, on March 12 and 13, 1965, Hynek returned for another short investigation. He visited Zamora, Chavez, and the editor of the Socorro newspaper. In his final report, Hynek wrote, "The more articulate Sergeant Chavez still firmly believes Zamora's story . . . although I made a distinct attempt to find a chink in Zamora's armor, I simply couldn't find anyone, with the possible exception of a Mr. Philips, who has a house fairly near the site of the original sighting, who did anything but completely uphold Zamora's character."

Hynek's new investigation responded to a long letter that had been sent to him by Dr. Donald Menzel, suggesting a possible explanation for the sighting. On February 19, 1965, Menzel wrote to Hynek, making a number of suggestions about the Socorro sighting.

First, Menzel suggested that some of the clues had not been properly addressed simply because this was a UFO investigation and not a criminal investigation. For example, Menzel noted that Zamora had seen two people in white coveralls who could have been large kids or small adults. He wrote, "The costume sounds like that often worn by filling-station attendants or garage mechanics."

Later in his letter, he wrote, "The white coveralls might, perhaps, be a clue to the culprits. Do they work in a filling station? Was, by any chance, this Whitting Brothers Service Station? Is Opal [*sic*] Grinder possibly an accomplice? Does Opal have high school assistants? Does Zamora's record of arrests, over the previous five or six months, include more than one arrest of the same person? Were any of these persons employed by the service station?"

Menzel also wondered if Zamora couldn't have been the victim of a hoax. In a rather elaborate scenario, Menzel suggested that "he [Zamora] might have antagonized some of the local teenagers, who devised a hoax to get even. . . . In other words, we see as the most likely possibility that someone planned this whole business to 'get' Zamora. . . . In addition to the simple chemical phenomena, some fireworks elevated on a small balloon could have easily produced what Zamora reported. . . . If you accept this idea just as a working postulate, one can see how easy it would have been to explain the whole phenomenon. Any bright youngsters, possibly juniors or seniors in high school, could dream up this plan. Perhaps they are in a local UFO club."

Menzel then detailed his hoax: The teenagers baited Zamora with a speeding car to lead him out into the desert. Using two or three hydrogen-filled balloons and a "flare producing device," they would wait for Zamora and use the balloons to carry the flare aloft where it would explode the balloons in a burst of fire and flame. Menzel wrote, "They must have definitely tried to simulate an explosion, since the proximity of the dynamite shack could hardly have been a coincidence."

He also suggested that the boys "manufactured a fake UFO. To get it off with small balloons means that it is pretty light. They take a big piece of aluminum foil, cut it in the form of an ellipse with two legs appended . . ."

Menzel acknowledged that his theory was far-fetched but hoped that Hynek would investigate the possibilities. Menzel had decided that some sort of hoax had been perpetrated because there seemed to be no alternative explanation except something that was truly out of the ordinary.

Hynek's full report continued for eight pages but did not once suggest how the sighting could have been faked or why it would have been. He did, however, discover that Zamora didn't see the flame from the highway before he spotted the object in the gully. Hynek wrote, "He denies ever having said anything about a flame at that time, only at the time when he saw it rise from the ground. . . . I will have to agree with Menzel that this part of Zamora's evidence is very mixed up and suggests some embroidery of the original sighting either by Zamora or by Captain Holder when excitement was running high."

Addressing the hoax theory, Hynek wrote, "None of the people I talked with gave any credence to the hoax hypothesis, generally considering it to have been far above the capabilities, motivations and provocation of the hoaxers. . . . No paraphernalia of a hoax was ever found. . . . Finally, it was [Dr. Lincoln] LaPaz's feeling that had it been a hoax, it surely would have leaked by now. . . . I do not believe that the Socorro high school students could have kept a secret this long. Furthermore, it would seem that any youngsters that hated Zamora sufficiently to have gone to all this trouble to perpetrate a hoax would now be very envious of the glory he is getting in a movie and all the publicity he has received and would certainly burst his bubble right now. Finally, there is the matter of the tourist who reported a strange object to Opel Grinder. This could not very well have been part of the hoax since the tourist was a complete stranger . . ."

Hynek even explored the possibility that the hoax had been designed by members of a local UFO club. He found no evidence that such a club existed in Socorro. It was just another of Menzel's inventions—he would postulate facts into existence to claim a hoax when no evidence of that hoax was ever found.

Hynek mentioned that he interviewed Felix Philips, who lived close to the landing site but did not hear anything strange, even with the windows and French doors of his house wide open. Philips was apparently the one person Hynek interviewed who believed that some sort of hoax had been perpetrated in the case.

Hynek wrote that he was not concerned with this seeming discrepancy because "the wind was blowing down the gully" and the Philips house is in the opposite direction. "This, of course, can make a tremendous difference in the ability to hear."

In his search for an answer, Hynek never found any indication of any secret government projects that would explain the case. Documents available in the Project Blue Book files suggest that Air Force investigators had the clearances necessary to learn if something from White Sands, or any of the other facilities nearby, had left the range to land momentarily at Socorro. They didn't even have to know the name of the project or the experiment being conducted—all they needed was a note that whatever had landed belonged to someone at White Sands, and the investigation could have been quietly abandoned.

In the mid-1990s, Air Force officers investigating the Roswell UFO crash suggested that the lunar lander, in testing in 1964, might explain the Socorro landing. But again, no documentation was found to place any testing of the lander close to Socorro at the proper time. Hynek suggested, in 1964, that if such an explanation was going to be offered, they have the proper documentation to back up the claim.

Hynek's final conclusion was that he could not identify what had landed in Socorro. He didn't like Philips' claim of a hoax, or Menzel's suggestions that it was a hoax, because "there are just too many bits of evidence that militate against this hypothesis."

Philip Klass, who entered the UFO community some time after the Socorro sighting, made his own investigation. He wrote in *UFOs Explained*, "My investigation led me to disagree sharply with Hynek's statement that the Socorro case was 'one of the soundest, best substantiated reports.' Contrary to Hynek's observation, I found many 'contradictions or omissions.'"

Klass, interviewing the same witness interviewed by Hynek, as well as others to whom Hynek never spoke, goes in a different direction. He talked to several "scientist-professors" (whom he didn't identify) at the New Mexico Institute of Mining and Technology in Socorro. Klass was surprised that, with a single exception, none of the scientists were interested in the Socorro UFO event. He wrote, "If the story was true, the most exciting scientific event of all time—a visit from an extraterrestrial spacecraft—had occurred almost within sight of the institute. How could these scientists be so uninterested?"

Then he shifted gears, because one of the scientists told him to "nose around a bit." Klass asked for more information and was told that Socorro had no industry other than the institute. Tourists passed through on the main highways (one of which is now Interstate 25 leading from Albuquerque to El Paso, Texas), but they never stopped except to buy gas and to eat. Before the Air Force offered their Project Mogul explanation in 1994 for the Roswell crash, I had driven through Socorro a number of times, stopping only to eat or buy gas.

Klass quoted from the local newspaper. "One of the best ways a community can boost its economy is to attract new industry. *Today, the fastest, most effective way to attract new industry is by first attracting tourists.* The reason is that industrialists, in selecting plant locations, are seeking for their employees the same kind of 'community atmosphere' that appeals to tourists [emphasis added by Klass]." He had found his answer.

But Hynek had also talked to people at the institute—including the institute's president, who was an old friend of Hynek's. If there was anything to the idea that this was a hoax that could, somehow, bring attention to the town, then here was the man who should have been aware of it. Instead, the president of the institute told Hynek that he, along with everyone else, was puzzled by the events.

Klass rejected the idea of the missing witness, labeling it as false because "the sequence of events really contradicts rather than supports Zamora's account. Recall that while Zamora said he was still chasing the speeding motorist, he reported seeing a flame which indicated that the UFO was then in the process of landing atop the mesa—some two thousand feet west of highway #85. Not until some time later—I would estimate nearly a minute, from having personally retraced Zamora's path—could the police car have been seen driving up the mesa. So the 'missing witness' could not possibly have seen a UFO fly over the highway and at the same time have seen Zamora driving up the mesa until some time later when he reportedly saw evidence of the 'landing' far to the west."

Overlooking for the moment the fact that we are dealing with secondhand testimony and the fact that no one has interviewed the "missing witness," we must also remember that the Zamora account has been described by Hynek as very mixed up and suggests some "embroidery of the original sighting either by Zamora or by Captain Holder when excitement was running high."

But there is another fact that appears in the Blue Book file that apparently was not followed. On April 26, 1968, some four years after the sighting, a man from Dubuque, Iowa, wrote that his mother had sent him a clipping that the "missing witness" was from Dubuque. According to the letter, the man had been

traveling through New Mexico when he saw the UFO that Zamora reported.

It smacked of one of those "remembered" facts that couldn't
be verified. In this case, however, it turned out to be true. According to the Dubuque *Telegraph-Herald* on April 29, 1964,
"Two Dubuquers Spot Flying Saucer."

The article reported that Paul Kies and Larry Kratzer had
been vacationing in New Mexico when, driving along Highway
60 a mile east of Socorro, "something shiny" took off.

Kratzer told the reporters, "We saw some brown dust, then
black smoke—like rubber burning—then a fire. The smoke hid
the shiny craft as it flew away."

The newspaper reported that they had seen the object on
Saturday, but that seems to be a mistake. The newspaper also
reported, "The object was spotted about 5:45 p.m. by other persons too. A sergeant with the New Mexico State Police said that
he saw the object on the ground." Clearly this is a reference to
Zamora of the local police.

This was a lead provided to the Air Force in 1968, but they
never bothered to follow up on it. Here was an opportunity to
corroborate the Zamora tale by adding two additional eyewitnesses. Here was an opportunity to add to our knowledge, but
the Air Force ignored the lead.

A year after the Socorro landing, on April 24, 1965, an article
in the *El Paso Times* written by Jake Booher, Jr. reported that the
town officials were quick to realize the significance of the UFO
landing. Although Booher reported that Zamora wanted to forget
the sighting, the town's seven thousand residents didn't. They
were going to turn the landing site into the tourist attraction that
would also attract industry.

Klass wrote, "The place where the UFO reportedly landed
was especially convenient—almost midway between the two highways that bring tourists through Socorro—so it was relatively easy
and inexpensive for city officials to provide an improved road that
connected the site to the two highways."

In the next paragraph, Klass exposed what for him was the
real story. The land next to the landing site was worthless. But,
if the site was developed as a tourist attraction, the worthless land

would suddenly become valuable. It could become the site of hot-dog stands, souvenir shops, and maybe even a motel or two. This property, according to Klass, ". . . by a curious coincidence . . . was owned by Mayor Bursum, officer Zamora's boss."

In what would become the third hoax scenario, the Socorro sighting, according to Klass, was the result of the mayor's attempting to create a tourist attraction in Socorro. Of course, the tourist attractions were never developed, and the cars still flash by Socorro unless someone is hungry or needs gas. If someone stops, it is to find directions to the Very Large Array, a radio telescope on the Plains of San Agustin some fifty miles to the west, along Highway 60.

Delphos, Kansas
November 2, 1971

Once again we have a physical evidence case that has been judged as highly credible by a panel of reputable scientists and which has but a single witness to the craft's landing. And once again the case would be called into question by debunkers who suggested a profit motive for inventing the tale of a flying saucer.

According to various sources, it was about 7:00 P.M. when Ronald Johnson, sixteen at the time, was called in to dinner. He was about finished with his chores and said that he would be in when he was done. Erma and Durel Johnson ate dinner and then called again for their son. This time Erma received no response.

Later Ronald told his parents that after his mother called him the first time, he heard a rumbling sound in the distance. He saw, about 75 feet away in a small grove of trees near a shed, a brightly lighted object that was covered with red, blue, and orange. He thought the craft was about 9 feet in diameter and 10 feet high, with a slight dome on top and a bulge around the middle. The bottom appeared to be flat. Ronald Johnson said that it looked like a mushroom.

According to him, the light was extremely bright and hurt his eyes. He would later say that for a moment, as the object began to wail with a high-pitched hum like that of a jet engine, he was momentarily blinded. He could hear the object as it apparently took off toward the south.

A few minutes later his sight came back and he could see the object in the sky. He ran into the house to tell his parents, though they refused to believe him at first. Finally the three of them went back out, and they could see the object, as large as a full moon, hovering. It was as bright as, and the same color as, an arc-welder's torch. Finally it moved off into the distance, eventually disappearing.

Now they walked over to the site where the UFO had been hovering. On the ground they saw a glowing ring. According to them, parts of one of the old trees was glowing. Both of the adults reached down to touch the soil, but it wasn't warm, as they had expected. Both reported that their fingers became numb. When Erma Johnson tried to wipe the soil from her fingers, the part of her leg she touched also went numb.

Durel Johnson walked back to the house for a camera and then returned to photograph the ring. He then called Willard Critchfield, editor of the local newspaper.

Critchfield, however, wasn't interested. The *Delphos Republican* was a weekly, and Critchfield was trying to get it ready to be printed for delivery. Johnson and his son drove into town the next day and spoke to reporter Thaddia Smith. She decided the story warranted a visit to the farm and, with her husband, accompanied the Johnsons back.

Smith later reported that "Upon arriving . . . I knew instantly that something had left evidence that it had been there. . . . The circle was very distinct. . . . The soil was dried and crusted. The circle or ring was approximately eight feet across, the center of the ring and outside area were still muddy from recent rains. The area of the ring that was dried was about a foot across and very light in color."

Smith also called Sheriff Ralph Enlow, who, with Kansas Highway Patrol Trooper Kenneth Yager and Undersheriff Harlan Enlow, drove to the Johnson farm. The sheriff, in his official report, wrote, "Mr. Johnson took us out . . . where we observed a ring shaped somewhat like a doughnut with a hole in the middle. The ring was completely dry. . . . There were limbs broken from a tree and a dead tree broken off, there. There was a slight discoloration on the trees."

Enlow's official report also noted that "on 11-03-71 Mr. Lester Ernsbarger . . . in Minneapolis [Kansas] advised Deputy Sheriff Leonard Simpson that at approx. 7:30 p.m. 11–02–71 he had observed a bright light descending in the sky in the Delphos area."

About a month later, Hynek read a newspaper clipping about the sighting and called Ted Phillips, a UFO investigator who specialized in physical trace cases. On December 4, Phillips talked to the sheriff and was given a soil sample. Phillips then went to the farm to speak to the Johnsons.

With the Johnsons, Phillips examined the ring which was still in evidence. They scraped the snow away from it and tried to pour water on it, but the ring remained dry, shedding the water. Because there had been rain and snow in the area in the month before Phillips visited, he found that to be significant.

On January 11, 1972, Phillips made another visit to the Johnson farm. He discussed the possibility of a hoax with both the *Delphos Republican* reporter Thaddia Smith and with Sheriff Enlow. Both believed there was no possibility of a hoax, saying that the Johnson family was respected and that they were truthful, conscientious and trustworthy.

In March 1972, the *National Enquirer* began offering a fifty thousand dollar prize to anyone who could produce evidence, or submitted a report, that proved that an extraterrestrial craft had visited Earth. Later still, they announced they would pay five thousand dollars to the best case submitted each year if no one qualified for the larger award. Remember that date. It was March 1972.

Judging of the cases would be done by a "blue ribbon" panel of UFO experts that included Hynek, Dr. Robert Creegan (a professor of philosophy at the State University of New York at Albany), and Dr. James A. Harder (a civil engineer from the University of California at Berkeley). Jim Lorenzen, the international director of APRO, at the time the nation's second-largest UFO group, was named as a consultant.

In May 1973, the *National Enquirer* announced that they had found no single case that qualified for the "grand" prize, but the panel had unanimously selected the Delphos physical trace case for the five thousand dollar award. The newspaper also reported that "Dr. Hynek emphasized that the panel had carefully investigated the possibility of a hoax, but are [sic] completely satisfied that the sighting was real."

That attracted the interest of Philip Klass, who was delighted to learn that there was a selection process to "rate" UFO sightings. He believed that if he could attract these, showing a reasonable and prosaic explanation for them, then the reality of the whole of the UFO phenomenon could be challenged. Because of that, Klass launched his own investigation, which included a trip to Kansas.

First, he mentioned that the Johnsons did not react the way he believes people who had witnessed a UFO should react. He thought that the temporary blindness experienced by Ronald should have called for a visit to the doctor. The numbness of fingers the older Johnsons experienced when they touched the soil should have induced a trip to the doctor. To Klass, the fact that they did not seek medical treatment for any of these problems suggested that they were spinning tales. Why waste good money, money that is in short supply, for a doctor's visit when they knew that there was nothing wrong because there had been no UFO? At least that was Klass's logic.

The explanation could be much simpler. The numbness of the fingers was not debilitating. When the symptoms didn't worsen, it might be that the Johnsons figured it would just go away, as had their son's brief blindness. Maybe they didn't want to waste the doctor's time with something they considered trivial. Whatever the reason, Klass's logic fails here because there are alternatives to his line of thought that make just as much sense.

Klass was also bothered by the reaction of the newspaper editor. Critchfield, learning that there had been a UFO landing in a nearby town, decided to finish the task of completing the morning's edition rather than rushing to the scene. Here was news that, if true, should have commanded the undivided attention of not only the local editor but also the news media around the country.

But this tale of a saucer landing was not the first to have been reported. For two decades there had been similar claims, and there were newspapers that refused to even listen to such tales. When I mentioned to a reporter that I had documents that could prove that the Condon Committee investigation was a setup, she told me that her editors didn't care. They didn't believe there was alien visitation and were satisfied with the negative results published by Condon.

So Klass's criticism about the newspaper editor, put into the context of the time, is weak. We had already seen the treatment of the Zamora sighting, when a police officer had seen the landed craft. Who was going to believe a couple of Kansas farmers telling of a landed craft?

Klass also attacked the Ernsbarger sighting. He mentioned that while some UFO investigators had concluded that Ernsbarger was independent corroboration of the sighting, he didn't believe it. According to the timetable, Ernsbarger claimed the craft was descending at 7:30 P.M.; Klass said that other testimony put the UFO at that moment in the grove of trees or ascending. It was, therefore, not corroboration.

In a perfect world, Klass would be right. But in this world, or rather the world of 1971, the clocks in one house might not agree with the clocks in another. The difference could be enough to account for the discrepancy. That's not to mention the fact that 7:30 could mean 7:20 or 7:40 and that the timing wasn't that critical.

Klass does better when he suggests that the ring found by the Johnsons probably wasn't glowing. He noticed that the ground was a grayish-white. If there had been bright moonlight, it could have been reflected by the ring, giving the impression that the ring "glowed" when, in fact, it did not. Klass learned that at that time there should have been a full moon in the sky. He didn't bother to learn if there had been any clouds that might have obscured the moon, but even with that, his explanation for the glow of the ring makes sense.

He also does very well when he points out that Johnson told him that all his mail was being censored by the Delphos post office. Johnson told Klass that the censorship was obvious and deliberate. Klass checked with the post office and was told that no censorship was being practiced.

It could be argued that the local postmaster would deny tampering with the Johnsons' mail if it was being censored. However, it does stretch credulity to the point of breaking. I have no doubt that Johnson's mail was not being searched by the post office. And I have no doubt that Johnson, for whatever reason, believed it was.

Is this allegation, however, enough for me to reject the rest of the story? No. Klass does point out that Johnson was now receiving mail from around the world. I have seen enough of this sort of mail to understand what was happening. With no way of separating the lunatic fringe from the serious, it is quite simple to be drawn into their conspiracies and beliefs. They write of governments silencing witnesses, destroying evidence, and lying to each other and their own populations. It wouldn't have taken much for Johnson to have gotten swept up into that paranoia, afraid that he was being monitored for reporting the UFO. Much of his mail must have been about those sorts of conspiracies.

Contrary to what Klass has written, there are cases in which those reporting UFOs have found their lives turned upside down. Just a few years earlier, in 1968, a police officer who reported chasing a UFO from eastern Ohio into western Pennsylvania lost his job. It made no difference that there were many other witnesses, including police officers, who saw the craft. It made no difference that the officer did not claim it was men from Mars. What made the difference was that he reported the sighting and his name was mentioned in the local newspapers. Because of that, and the ridicule directed toward him by fellow officers and defense attorneys, he was no longer effective as a police officer.

This would seem to be an incentive to keep the tale of a flying saucer to oneself, rather than quickly spreading the word. But it would also be incentive for a newspaper editor to finish his or her work before chasing another tale of a flying saucer. The actions of the participants can be understood in the context of what was happening around them and the fact that many didn't want to waste their time on what they believed to be fantasy.

The context of the situation can also explain Durel Johnson's fascination with the monetary aspects of the case. Klass reported that Johnson was a little excited about the prospect of "winning" the *National Enquirer* award. Klass noted that Johnson, who had rented the farm, had learned that the owner was about to sell it; Johnson eventually found a loan, but Klass worried that Johnson would never be able to pay off his mortgage.

Enter the *National Enquirer* and their award for the best UFO case. If Johnson could win the prize, then he could afford his farm. Even if he didn't win the major prize, the five thousand would help. But this couldn't have been a motive for inventing the tale: The *National Enquirer* "contest" had not been announced until *after* the Johnson family had made their report. The fact that Johnson knew of the award and the prize money is irrelevant.

Klass suggested that Johnson believed others were profiting from his sighting. Johnson was aware that Stanton Friedman, a former nuclear physicist and now a UFO lecturer, had visited nearby Concordia College. According to the information Johnson had, Friedman had received about a thousand dollars for the lecture. That was a nice piece of change for standing in front of an audience for a few minutes.

Johnson also seemed to believe that Ted Phillips was making money from his sighting. Johnson wanted to make money and told Klass, "If I don't get anything out of *this circle*—I mean if I don't get something out of the *National Enquirer* . . . Ted Phillips is going to be sued [emphasis in original]."

And Johnson was annoyed that the president of the Delphos Bank had collected a small fee from a newspaper for telling them of Johnson's UFO sighting.

Klass had found the motive for the claim: Money. Johnson was obsessed with the money. The tale, apparently, was invented with money in mind, though there is no evidence that anyone had thought of that until others arrived and seemed to be making money. But money as a motive couldn't be the reason, because the monetary reward didn't exist at the time the sighting was reported.

The final and possibly only real problem for the debunkers was the mysterious circle left by the UFO. Samples had been taken by many. Laboratories around the country had analyzed the soil in an attempt to learn if there was anything unusual about it. Johnson and others had reported the glow, and a year after the sighting, nothing grew on the ring. That suggested something unusual.

Klass tried to find out if any sort of structure had ever stood on the site. Aerial photographs are taken by the Department of Agriculture periodically to learn how much land is under cultivation. Such photographs had been taken in 1965 and 1971. Klass tracked down these photographs, had blowups made, and found . . . nothing.

There had been no outbuilding or silo on the site. He did note that the number of trees seemed to have decreased between 1965 and 1971, but that certainly had nothing to do with a UFO sighting.

Next he speculated that some sort of feeder had been on the site, based on a test that suggested a high level of zinc in the soil. Such a feeder wouldn't have been visible from the air. Klass noted that animals, excited by feeding, often urinate. If that was true, there should have been organic material in the soil. Klass learned that such was the case. In fact, he discovered a high salt content in the soil, which would be expected if urine was the source of the organic material. The high salt would explain why nothing grew on the ring.

For Klass, the final straw was the fact that when Clancy D. Tull, a UFO investigator, asked the Johnsons to take lie detector tests, they declined. Further, when Tull suggested hypnotic regression for Ronald Johnson, they also refused. This to Klass suggested a hoax.

In *UFO's Explained,* Klass wrote, "And so my efforts to positively 'nail down' the source of the whitish ring and the curious composition of the solid underneath have been frustrated. In this respect the Delphos case is not 100 percent explained. But I would hope that the other evidence turned up by my investigation is sufficient to cause you to question the conclusions of the *National Enquirer's* panel of experts."

But Dr. Michael Swords, writing in the *Journal of UFO Studies* published by the Center for UFO Studies, disagreed with

Klass's belief that the case was basically solved. After reviewing in great technical detail the various tests conducted by several laboratories, including those at the Department of Agriculture, NASA, Oak Ridge, and various universities, Swords drew a number of conclusions. For example, he wrote, "There seems to be no question that the surface soil *was* [emphasis in original] hydrophobic [in other words, did not absorb the water], luminescent [meaning it did have a dim glow], and anesthetic [could cause the numbness experienced by several witnesses], but to what this can be attributed is still unknown."

Klass used a single report and questioned the testimony of the witnesses. Swords used many reports and did not use the testimony of any of the witnesses. He was only interested in the results of the lab tests.

Klass suggested that his examination of the soil in the ring had revealed no evidence of high heat, and he rejected the idea that the ring could have been caused by the UFO. But heat is not the only form of radiation that exists. Texas A & M University, in the report of their analysis, wrote, "Microwaves in the 1,000–10,000 megahertz at power densities about 100 watt seconds per centimeter squared, can cause plant symptoms similar to burning and can definitely cause dehydration. . . . Microwaves can cause breaking of trees and tree branches if the water contained therein changes to steam rapidly. . . . From your descriptions, the 'ring' of soil was not only dried, but changed in structure. Changes in soil structure such as you describe would require the application of large amounts of energy. . . . In summary, some of the effects you describe could be attributed to exposure to relatively high power densities of microwaves; others could not. All the biological effects described could conceivably be caused by energy in some portion of the electromagnetic spectrum, but no one area could account for all the effects described."

The University of Nottingham reported, "Because the yellow compound oxidizes rapidly to give a blue-fluorescing product, this could potentially explain the 'glowing' soil reported. Soil extracts show amounts of material which fluoresce blue-white when viewed in 360nm light. Ring soil fluoresces more brightly than control soil."

To be fair, the same study reported, "Yes, I believe the soil samples which you collected near Delphos, Kansas, are from a 'fairy ring' [mushrooms that grow in a circular pattern]. The white material in the soil is fungal mycelium of a basidiomycete or mushroom. Microscopic examination of the soil plainly shows the filaments of the fungal mycelia and the presence of clamp connections typical of the basidiomycete."

Others who studied this aspect of the soil samples apparently did not agree. Swords, in the commentary, wrote, "Several researchers noted odd substances associated with the soil: 1. a 'waxy' or polymeric organic compound near or on the surface; 2. an apparently chemiluminescent organic compound partial isolated by Dr. Erol Faruk of Nottingham and measured by Battelle [Memorial Institute]; 3. an organic polymer vaguely mimicking fungal filaments, but not constituted of proper fungal filaments, possibly having some soluble elements, and described by [Hubert] Lechevalier as 'the interesting material.' "

Unlike Klass, Swords wrote, "What we are left with are questions. The case is not solved. The chemical peculiarities *may* have been explainable by mundane biology plus exotic energy environments, or by exotic chemistry and physics. No honest scientist can claim to know. If one credits the primary witness as presenting a subjectively honest account, one can still not offhandedly assume any specific causal agency. We must remember that the report in his case primarily hangs on the words of one young witness who was affected physiologically by *whatever* occurred."

We could continue with the scientific discussions of what was observed at Delphos. Lechevalier wrote to Swords, telling him, "It is possible that there was a fungal ring at Delphos, but the only thing that I can say is that the cottony masses that I saw were not fungal hyphae."

It should be noted here that not one of the scientists who examined the soil samples postulated a galvanized livestock watering container. That was Klass's speculation, based solely on the elevated levels of zinc reported in the soil samples by a single agency. No one else attached particular significance to this one finding, and no one else suggested it was the result of the oxidization of a galvanized device of any sort.

Swords wasn't alone in his conclusion that there was no evidence of a hoax. Erol A. Faruk wrote, "I . . . drew conclusions from the results which supported the idea that a genuine observation of a hovering, illuminated object had occurred as described by the witnesses. . . . Not only did this analysis strongly indicate that a simple hoax was not credible, but also that a model could be postulated which supported the sighting report in all its salient aspects."

In other words, the physical evidence found at the site, and investigated by so many different laboratories, suggested that the sighting happened as reported. There were no inconsistencies in the report or the physical evidence.

There are some interesting aspects to Faruk's report. He wrote, "I believe the U.S. Department of Agriculture's identification of mycelia from a basidiomycete or mushroom is probably quite accurate." This also tends to eliminate Klass's theory.

Faruk also wrote, "The obvious question to ask is whether this outward growth continued after the discovery of the ring. According to the principal investigator, Ted Phillips, it did not. Periodic reinspection over six years showed no evidence of growth of the ring or any change in its shape. Moreover, in private correspondence Phillips also revealed that soil samples removed from the ring the day after the event exhibited none of the filamentary material, while those taken a week or so later did. These observations strongly indicate that the mycelia are incidental to the ring's cause . . ."

What we find in the Delphos case is a report of a landing of an unconventional craft witnessed by a single individual. When the craft took off, other witnesses were available, including one who was unrelated to the Johnsons. They reported their sighting as quickly as they could, and they reported physical evidence associated with it.

Investigation by Klass found what to Klass were important discrepancies in the tale. However, analysis of the soil and impartial investigation suggest that the discrepancies are just the sort of thing that you would expect in this sort of case. The discussion, with Klass, about the financially motivated reports of UFO sightings, while interesting, have no real bearing on the case. Klass's discussion of a galvanized animal watering trough, again, is interesting and, again, irrelevant. No evidence has been offered for his explanation. If we are not required to find evidence to support a theory, then we can offer all sorts of theories.

Finally, analysis of the various soil samples produced nothing that could be considered conclusive. Again, there were interesting irregularities in the soil, all of which could be explained in the mundane, though no satisfactory explanation was offered.

Swords might have said it best when he wrote about this case, "I find myself in a deja-vu experience with former Project Blue Book director Ed Ruppelt, who—no matter how hard he tried—could never get a case beyond the conclusion 'unknown.' "

It meant, simply, that no explanation in the mundane had been offered, but the evidence, as it existed, failed to be conclusive. It did not prove that something from another world had visited Delphos, Kansas. It only meant that there had been nothing found to label the case as solved.

Conclusions

There have been more than 4,500 landing trace cases reported since the first of the flying saucer sightings in 1947. In many of them there is only the evidence left behind. No one saw the craft that left the circular markings, the burned area in crops or grass, or the depressions in the ground. In some cases an object was seen in the area, but no one can link that craft in the sky to the evidence on the ground. And in a few of the cases, such as those discussed here, the craft was seen on the ground and the evidence was found when the object disappeared.

Even if we eliminate all those sightings in which no craft was seen, we are still left with a large residue of good cases. Here we examined only two of the many. No solid explanation for either has been offered. Skeptical suggestions that the Zamora sighting was a hoax based first on the belief that teenagers were getting back at Zamora, and later that Zamora and the Socorro mayor had concocted the story to boost tourism, are without merit. No evidence for either explanation was offered.

Yet, because the allegation has been hurled, there are those who believed that Socorro was "solved." But what about the two men who happened onto the sighting and who corroborate what Zamora saw? No longer are we left with a single witness to this spectacular sighting, but now we have three such witnesses, separated by time and distance. The two men from Dubuque could not have been party to a hoax, no matter who was responsible. They eliminate the Klass theory completely.

The hoax solution, regardless of the beliefs of the skeptics, has not been proved. Merely suggesting the idea of a hoax is sufficient to tarnish a case. But when we look at the facts, we find no evidence of a hoax.

The same can be said for the Delphos case. Klass believes there was a financial motive for inventing the tale, and he makes much of Johnson's speaking about money and his mortgage. But the facts show that no one was talking about financial reward for a UFO sighting when the case was first reported.

And even Klass admitted, "And so my efforts to positively 'nail down' the source of the whitish ring and the curious composition of the solid underneath have been frustrated. In this respect the Delphos case is not 100 percent explained." His efforts to label the case a hoax had failed, yet the stain remains.

So once again we are left without the solid proof that some UFO sightings translate into alien visitation. But we do have, once again, the physical evidence that something is happening out there. It is something that demands further research. We need to look at the direct physical evidence of visitation to determine if we should continue to explore the subject. If nothing else, the evidence suggests that we should.

6

The Psychology of UFO
Sightings

There are questions about the UFO phenomenon that can be answered scientifically. There are observations, scientific fact, and common knowledge that can suggest answers and provide clues. Sometimes, however, the proper scientific framework does not exist and we must establish it. Sometimes the skeptics and the debunkers make a claim and it is accepted as fact even without the proper scientific framework. Sometimes we just have to look at the case, or cases, apply scientific principles, and allow the chips to fall where they may.

Alabama and Georgia
July 24, 1948

It was on July 24, 1948, that Captain Clarence S. Chiles and copilot John B. Whitted, while flying at about 5000 feet, saw what they first believed to be "one of the Army's new jet jobs." In seconds, the craft had approached. Both men realized that it wasn't a jet but a cigar-shaped object with no wings, a double row of square windows, and an exhaust flame shooting from the rear.

The object had seemed to be slightly above them, then it descended and flashed by on the right. After passing them, it seemed to begin a climb, and disappeared in the distance.

Because it was about 2:45 A.M., most of the passengers in

Chiles's plane were asleep. Only one, Clarence L. McKelvie, from Columbus, Ohio, was awake and looking out the window. He saw nothing except a "strange, eerie streak." It was quite intense, according to McKelvie, but he saw no detail on the light. He did tell Air Force investigators that he thought the light was moving on a straight line and was at an altitude slightly higher than the aircraft.

Chiles tried to find out if anything had been flying that night that could account for the sighting. He contacted the Eastern Airlines radio operator in Columbus, Georgia, who learned that nothing experimental or jet powered had been airborne.

Questioned within hours of the sighting, Chiles, in a statement given to Air Force investigators, said, "The fuselage appeared to be about three times the circumference of a B-29 fuselage. The windows were very large and seemed square. They were white with light which seemed to be caused by some type of combustion. I estimate we watched the object for at least five seconds and not more than ten seconds. We heard no noise nor did we feel any turbulence from the object. It seemed to be at about 5500 feet."

Chiles, in a later statement dated August 3, 1948, wrote, "It was clear there were no wings present, that it was powered by some jet or other type of power shooting flame from the rear some fifty feet . . . Underneath the ship there was a blue glow of light."

Within hours of the sighting, Chiles and Whitted were on radio station WCON in Atlanta, Georgia. They were also interviewed by William Key, a newspaper reporter. At some point during the interviews, someone suggested they had been startled by a meteor, but both men rejected the idea. They had seen many meteors during their night flights, both as military pilots and later as airline pilots, and were aware of what meteors looked like and how they performed.

There are some other points to be made here. In a newspaper article written by Albert Riley, the pilots were quoted as saying, "Its prop-wash or jet-wash rocked our DC-3." That fact would seem to rule out the meteor theory proposed by some.

In another newspaper article that is part of the Air Force's

Project Blue Book files, Chiles was again quoted as having said he felt there was a prop wash. ". . . [B]oth reported they could feel the UFO's backwash rock their DC-3."

The Air Force was, of course, charged with the investigation of these sorts of reports, and they searched for other, similar sightings made that night. They gathered evidence from every airline they could find that might have had aircraft in the air in a position to be misidentified as the cigar-shaped object, or that were in a position to have spotted the same object. They queried all branches of the military service, searching for other pilots who might have seen the UFO but who had failed to report it earlier. They tried to find additional witnesses, either on the ground, or in the air, to corroborate the tale told by Chiles and Whitted.

Interestingly, they were successful in their searches. About fifteen minutes before Chiles and Whitted had their sighting, there was another report from the Blackstone, Virginia, area. According to the Blue Book files, "Object #2 was observed by Feldary, Mansfield and Kingsley at 0230 hours 24 July 1948, while airborne, between Blackstone, Virginia, and Greensboro, North Carolina. This sighting is considered separately [from the Chiles-Whitted sighting] since the descriptions of speed as 'meteoric' or 'terrific' the manner of travel described as an arc or horizontal, and the fact that it 'faded like a meteor' seem to indicate that the object seen was not the one observed in Incident 1 [that is, the Chiles-Whitted report]."

Other sightings in the Chiles-Whitted folder are from events that took place two nights later. They were included because the descriptions of the objects seem to match some of those given by Chiles and Whitted.

The search for additional information turned up a report from Robins Air Force Base, Georgia. Walter Massey, a 23-year-old ground maintenance crewman, said that he saw a cigar-shaped object fly directly overhead. Massey was interviewed on August 10, 1948, by Lieutenant Colonel Cropper, the acting district commander, 6th District Office of Special Investigations (that is, AFOSI).

He learned that Massey was "standing fire guard on a C-47 [the military version of a DC-3], directly across from Operations," and he had to "take down the takeoff time which was between 0140 and 0150." Because of that, we have a good idea of the exact time of his sighting.

Massey told Cropper, "It was coming out of the north. I was facing the north and actually didn't see it until it was overhead, but it came out of the north and was in my view for about twenty seconds. The last I saw of it the object was taking a southwest course."

He continued, saying, "The first thing I saw was a stream of fire and I was undecided as to what it could be, but as it got overhead, it was a fairly clear outline and appeared to be a cylindrical shaped object with a long stream of fire coming out of the tail end. I am sure it would not be a jet since I have observed P-84s in flight at night on two occasions."

Massey thought the object was about 3000 feet high, but said that at night he couldn't be sure. He also said that he thought, at first, it was a "shooting star or meteor, but a shooting star falls perpendicular. This object was on a straight and level plane."

Of course, we know that meteors can seem to fly at all sorts of angles, and given the location of the observer and the meteor, it can seem that the flight is, more or less, straight and level. Massey was asked how the object differed from a meteor; he pointed out that what he saw was long and cylindrical in shape. In other words, he was describing an object that trailed a glow.

Interestingly, Colonel Cropper asked, "Did it give you the impression that there were windows or holes and did the decks appear to be divided into sections?"

Massey answered, "I am not sure. It would be hard to tell if there were windows and a divided deck could not be recognized from the ground."

That was a very good answer on Massey's part. Clearly he wasn't taking his cues from Colonel Cropper, who then asked him, "Did you read the newspaper account of the two civilian pilots who saw this strange object about the same time, and did the paper's description seem to refer to the object you saw?"

Massey responded to that question by saying, "I read the write-up about the rate of speed. I don't see how they could tell if it had square windows or round windows but the description seemed to fit my impression."

When asked specific questions about the object, Massey said, "It looked like it was about the size of a B-29 . . . It was too large for a jet. It seemed to be a dark color and constructed of an unknown metallic type."

When questioned about seeing anything like this at any other time, Massey said, "During the Battle of the Bulge, a sergeant and myself were on guard duty and saw something that resembled this object in question. We later found that we had witnessed the launching of a German V-2 rocket. It carried a stream of fire that more or less resembled this object. This object looked like rocket propulsion rather than jet propulsion, but the speed and size was much greater."

Because of the similarities in the description of the craft, the locations, and the timing, Air Force investigators linked the two cases. They wondered, rightly, if the various witnesses could have seen the same object. They also wondered why it had taken the craft an hour to fly the 200 miles between the two locations. If it was moving at the 700 miles an hour estimated by Chiles, then it should have gotten to the Montgomery area faster than it did.

But Massey's wasn't the only report to match the one made by Chiles and Whitted. Investigators also found a report dated July 20 from The Hague, Netherlands. Witnesses claimed to have seen a fast-moving object through broken clouds. They reported a double row of windows and rocketlike shape. Although this object was seen four days before Chiles and Whitted made their report, the description seemed to be a fairly close match.

In fact, Captain Robert R. Sneider, one of the project officers, wrote that there were four separate incidents, "one having occurred on 24 July 1948 and the others on 26 July 1948. A preponderance of the evidence is available to establish that in almost all cases an unidentified object was seen within stated times and dates over an extended area, pursuing a general Southerly course. Descriptions as to size, shape, color and movements are fairly consistent."

Incident #1, according to the files was, of course, the Chiles and Whitted sighting. Incident #2 was an object seen by pilots between Blackstone, Virginia, and Greensboro, North Carolina. Incident #3 was seen on July 26, late in the evening. It was a brilliant blue-white but was not a meteor according to the file because it was seen to maneuver.

Dr. J. Allen Hynek, the consultant to the Air Force project, noted for the record that meteors could seem to fly straight and level, and, under the proper circumstances, could even seem to climb. However, these objects did not maneuver violently, and to him, as well as project officers, that ruled out an astronomical explanation for the case.

Incident #4 involved a number of witnesses in Georgia who claimed to have seen a green, glowing, football-shaped object that had a silvery tail. According to the Air Force report, "The last observer stated that the speed was '10,000 to 20,000 mph' and that 'it appeared to be ¼ the size of a full moon', and that 'it was a multi-colored, brilliant light trailing burning fragments'. The terrific speed together with the descriptions of a multi-colored light trailing burning fragments seems to establish the object as a meteor."

The Air Force report concluded that "The only incident which possesses absolute intelligence significance is Incident #1. It is obvious that this object was not a meteor."

Sneider, on November 12, 1948, wrote, "The flying anomaly observed, remains unidentified as to origin, construction and power source."

But eventually there was another explanation offered. Hynek, in his attempts to explain the case, suggested that Massey might have been mistaken. Maybe he saw the object at the same time as Chiles and Whitted. If that was the case, then, according to Hynek, "the object must have been an extraordinary meteor." The glowing ion trail might have produced the "subjective impression of a ship with lighted windows." Hynek thought that psychological research would be needed to answer the question of whether such an impression would result from the stimulus of a bright meteor seen close.

Please note that statement by Hynek again. He is suggesting that the Chiles and Whitted sighting can be explained as a meteor if there is a psychological reason to believe that the artifacts of the sighting—the ion trail, for example—could create the impression of lighted windows. That is, of course, if Massey was mistaken about the timing of the event.

The case, in 1948, was listed as an unexplained sighting. The Project Blue Book files master index, however, lists a solution for the case. It claims that Chiles and Whitted saw a "fireball"—that is, an extremely bright meteor that fooled them.

How did this change come about? How did we go from an unexplained sighting of a cigar-shaped craft to the belief that the two pilots had misidentified a bright meteor? In the late 1940s, an answer had been proposed, but then rejected. The evidence from the file seemed to suggest that a meteor was not responsible. Now, in the late 1990s, a solution has been offered, and apparently accepted.

The case file provides us with an explanation for that. On July 13, 1961, Dr. Donald E. Menzel wrote to Major William T. Coleman at the Pentagon, discussing UFO sightings and a book that Menzel was writing. Menzel noted, "One further question that we have. Our study of the famous Chiles case indicates that the UFO was merely a meteor. Apparently this was a considered solution in the early days. We wonder why it was abandoned."

Of course, he is referring to Hynek's suggestion that had not gained much support at Project Sign (forerunner to Project Blue Book) in 1948. By way of contrast to Menzel's argument for the meteor theory is Dr. James McDonald's counterargument, which was based on his review of the newspaper files and his own personal interviews with Chiles and Whitted conducted sometime later. McDonald wrote, "Both pilots reiterated to me, quite recently, that each saw square ports or windows along the side of the fuselage-shaped object from the rear of which a cherry-red wake emerged, extending back 50–100 feet aft of the object. To term this a 'meteor' is not even *qualitatively* reasonable. One can reject testimony; but reason forbids calling the object a meteor."

And, we can take this one step further. As mentioned, it is well known that meteors can appear to fly parallel to the ground. They can fall straight. They come in a variety of colors that can fool people. In his statement, Chiles explained that they lost sight of the object as it "pulled up sharply" and disappeared into a cloud. That description alone should be sufficient to eliminate a meteor from consideration as the explanation.

So we're back to where we started. Two airline pilots saw something flash through the sky at them. Both talked of a double row of square windows, a cigar shape, and a red flame from the rear. A passenger on the plane saw a streak of light, but no details.

An hour earlier a man at Robins Air Force Base saw a cigar-shaped craft flash overhead. He saw no windows, but his position on the ground and his viewing angle of the craft might have precluded his observing those details. His general description matched that given by the pilots. If the cases are linked, then the meteor answer is lost because of the timing of the two events.

If the cases are separated, then it might be conceivable that Chiles and Whitted saw a meteor. But there seem to be no indications that someone confronted with a bright light streaking past would "manufacture" a double row of windows and a cigar shape. No one has conducted experiments to learn if this is something the mind does when confronted with the sudden appearance of a "streak of light."

Furthermore, an examination of the case file reveals no persuasive evidence to suggest that a meteor is, in fact, responsible for the sighting. If we take the sighting at face value as Sneider, one of the Air Force investigators on the case, suggested, then contrary to the Air Force opinion, there is no viable solution for the sighting. It should have stayed labeled as unknown or unidentified.

If we do not separate the cases and we accept Massey's timing of his sighting, then the meteor explanation fails completely. We must remember that Massey was standing fire guard for an aircraft that took off shortly after the sighting. In other words, there was a written record to corroborate his timing of the event, which, apparently, no one bothered to check in 1948. We are, therefore, left with two sightings of a single object that has no solid explanation.

We'll come back to the original point. There is no solution for this case. That does not mean that Chiles and Whitted saw a craft built on another planet. As mentioned throughout this work, eyewitness testimony, by itself, is never going to be sufficient to prove that theory. However, given Chiles and Whitted's description of the object, their credibility, and the fact that both men had been pilots during the Second World War, accumulating hundreds, if not thousands, of flying hours, it is reasonable to believe they reported accurately what they saw. Those are the facts. Everything else is speculation.

It should be noted that no one at the Air Force investigation ever researched the question about the psychological aspect of seeing the windows on the ion trail of a meteor. It provided the Air Force officers with a convenient explanation, so no research was done. Later there would be other cases in which witnesses claimed to have seen windows and in which the Air Force offered the same explanation. But the question was not answered. Do people, when confronted by the ion trail of a meteor, sometimes "invent" square windows?

Utah and Nevada
April 18, 1962

The Air Force, as it had done in so many other cases, overlooked the obvious in their attempts to explain away the Utah and Nevada sightings. Maybe that's not quite fair. Maybe they didn't overlook the obvious but just ignored it. If they had paid too much attention to the facts, if they had actually done a "real" investigation, they would have been stuck with another inexplicable sighting. This way they could explain it to their satisfaction, and that seems to be all they wanted.

In fact, the Air Force files about the case are confusing. They have broken the reports apart, suggesting that the Utah sightings happened one day and the Nevada events happened on another. But when studying the file carefully, it is revealed that the events took place about 16 minutes apart. There is good reason to connect the events, and when that is done, the simple bolide explanations are eliminated.

According to the late Frank Edwards (a former radio newscaster and writer about UFOs), the Air Force, and some of the witnesses, the sighting began when an object was sighted over

Oneida, New York, on April 18, 1962. Before the event was over, people in several states would report it, it would be tracked on radar, it would cause power outages in Nephi and Eureka, Utah, and it would then disappear in a bright red explosion that illuminated the skies around Las Vegas, Nevada.

According to a story that appeared in the *Las Vegas Sun,* a spokesman for the North American Defense Command, Lieutenant Colonel Herbert Rolph, told reporters that the object was a glowing ball of red seen over New York and heading to the west. It was at high altitude, made no noise, and disappeared in seconds.

Over the Midwest, radar operators picked up the object and continued to track it. According to the article, the Air Defense Command alerted a number of bases, including Nellis in Las Vegas. Apparently fighters were scrambled from Nellis and from Luke Air Force Base near Phoenix.

Near Nephi, Utah, the glowing red object raced overhead. According to witnesses there, the city lights dimmed. When the object was gone, there was a rumbling like that of jet engines. Edwards believed the rumbling might have been the fighters that had been scrambled to intercept the UFO.

Among the first to report the object near Nephi was Sheriff Raymond Jackson. According to what he told me, he was on Main Street and "heard kind of a roar." He glanced up in time to see a yellow-white flame going west, heard a series of loud detonations, and then the lights in the town went out. Jackson said, "All the lights went out temporarily." He specifically noticed the lights in the doctor's office close to where he was standing.

Maurice Memmott and Dan Johnson were south of town when the object flew over, according to a story published in the *Nephi Times-News.* Memmott told me that he no longer remembers much about the incident. He saw only a bright streak in the sky that lighted the ground like the sun on a bright afternoon. He also told me that he believes that what he saw was a meteor.

Dan Johnson, on the other hand, remembered the events vividly. He told me, "The two of us [Memmott and Johnson] were out in the fields . . . there were no lights so we were in total darkness . . . It was a very bright light." He said that it came from the southeast and passed directly overhead. He thought that it had landed somewhere close, no more than 5 or 6 miles away.

Johnson said that within days of the event he spoke to several men whom he believed were military, though none were in uniform. The men had both Memmott and Johnson take them to the spot where they had watched the object. He believed they were soldiers from the army's Dugway Proving Ground nearby.

Sergeant E. C. Sherwood, of the Utah State Highway Patrol, looked up in time to see the ball of fire. It was a bright light that was mostly blue, and it seemed to explode right over him, throwing off a cloud of white sparks. He thought, originally, that it was something that had gone astray from New Mexico's White Sands Proving Grounds.

Sherwood's wife heard the detonations and ran outside. All she saw was a bright light. She told me that she did see other neighbors outside, all looking up into the night sky.

Others in Nephi also reported the explosions or roar. Some of them explained that it was a long series, as many as twenty or thirty detonations strung together. Some of their descriptions ran from rocket engine to artillery shell.

From Nephi, the object traveled to the northwest, toward Eureka, about 30 miles away. The direction of flight would become an important clue as we try to determine what was seen that night.

Near Eureka, the object flew over Bob Robinson and his friend Floyd Evans. According to Robinson, he was traveling south of Eureka when they slowed to a stop. Both men climbed out of the pickup truck. Robinson saw the light in the southeast and pointed it out. Evans told Robinson that he thought it was a jet aircraft.

The object approached rapidly and seemed to pass directly overhead, only about 500 feet high. Robinson told me it was a flaming object, and he believed that he could see a series of square windows hidden in the glow of it.

Robinson said that he was frightened by the craft and dived under the truck for protection. The engine of the truck, which had been left running, began to sputter and run roughly. The headlights dimmed as the object got close, but the engine didn't quit completely and the lights didn't go out completely.

Robinson thought that the object slowed as it approached, as if taking a good look at the truck. It then sped up and disappeared to the west. As it disappeared, the truck's engine began to run smoothly, and the lights brightened. Robinson told me that he thought the light was in sight for about 2 minutes or so.

When Robinson returned home, his wife, Betty, said that he looked as white as a ghost. He was so excited about the event that it was hard for her to understand what he was saying.

But he wasn't alone. Betty had seen the light, too. She'd heard the roar as the object flew over and had seen the light from it. It was so bright that the interior of the house had been brightly illuminated with a strobe effect.

Also in Eureka was Police Chief Joseph Bernini, who was at a city council meeting when they all heard the roar. Bernini described the sound as that of an artillery shell. He also saw the light but didn't see any object associated with it. He hadn't ventured outside, however.

As the object flew over Eureka, the streetlights all went out. Bernini said that the streetlights were on photoelectric cells, and the bright light had caused those cells to go out. According to him, no one else reported any power failure, and he didn't notice anything in the council room.

Bernini's wife and son also saw the light, but his son, David, also saw the object. Those who did see the object confirmed the direction of flight. According to them, it was moving from the southeast to the northwest.

It was also near Eureka that the object was reported to have landed near a power plant, shutting down part of the power grid. One witness, who wished to remain anonymous, told me that he had seen the oval-shaped, glowing object on the ground and watched as it lifted off, resuming its flight to the west. In seconds it was gone, but the man also heard the rumbling of what he thought of as jet engines.

Reports that would complicate the investigation came in from farther west. Near Reno, Nevada, the flight crew of a small commercial airliner reported that the light had passed beneath their aircraft, which was flying at 11,000 feet. They made a report to Stead Air Force Base near Reno.

Others in Reno, such as Dwight Dyer, the controllers in the Reno Airport control tower, and witnesses in Elko, Nevada, and Las Vegas saw a bright flash. Homer Raycraft, of Reno, said that he saw a "big fireball traveling due east." He reported that it disappeared behind a mountain range, and then there was a big flash.

That is an interesting point. In Utah all the witnesses had described an object that had been flying generally to the west. Now, suddenly, over western Nevada, the object is observed flying in the opposite direction.

That was confirmed by a number of different sources. The *Los Angeles Times* reported that the object was seen over Reno and traveling east. It was also reported that the object was seen in Las Vegas.

That flash could have come from the explosion witnessed by thousands in the Las Vegas area and reported in the *Las Vegas Sun*. The Clark County Sheriff's Office was swamped with telephone calls about the explosion. Witnesses said the object was traveling northeast of Las Vegas until the final explosion, which came from the direction of Mesquite, Nevada, on the stateline with Utah.

I was able to locate former sheriff's lieutenant Walter Butt, who had led the search and rescue unit, and who had driven into the Spring Mountain area near Mesquite to search for wreckage. Butt told me they had searched through the night; when the sun rose, they expanded the search to include aircraft. He said they hadn't found anything of importance, except some ashes that could easily have been the remains of a hunter's campfire from weeks earlier. When no one reported a downed or missing aircraft, Butt and the other deputies suspended their search operations.

Another witness in Las Vegas was Frank Maggio, who had at one time worked for the *Las Vegas Sun*. He told me that he couldn't remember much about the incident. He described the object as a "tremendous flaming sword." He thought there was a series of explosions that broke up the trail across the sky. He seemed to remember that it had vanished to the northeast of Las Vegas, in the direction of Mesquite.

The next step would be to review the Air Force files on the

case. According to the project record card (ATIC Form 329), the case was a "Radar sighting. Speed of object varied. Initial observation at 060, no elevation. Disappearance at 105 [degrees] az 10,000 feet altitude. Heading tentatively NE, however disappeared instantly to S. Observed by search and height radars. No visual."

The project card and the master index of the sightings showed that the case was first labeled as "unidentified." Later someone changed the analysis to "insufficient data for a scientific analysis." The question that must be asked is, What piece of information was lacking so that they couldn't make a scientific investigation? It seems they had everything they needed to make their investigation. What they didn't have was a solution to the sighting.

According to the Air Force, then, there was no visual sighting. However, had anyone at the base bothered to look at the morning newspaper they would have seen that someone saw the object. It should be noted that the radar sightings tend to corroborate the visual sightings. The radars displayed an object to the northeast—that is, in the Mesquite area. The search by the sheriff's department to the northeast of Las Vegas and near Mesquite tells us that the sightings are linked.

In that file there was no mention of the Utah end of the case. The master index had no listing for Utah on April 18, but it did list a meteor on April 19. The project record card claimed that "Obj came in over Cuba and apparently landed in rough terrain West of Eureka, Utah. Bright enough to trip photo electric cell which controlled city street lights."

The card also noted that there were "multiple reports. Attempted recovery by Col Friend [chief of Project Blue Book at the time] and Dr. Hynek." They determined that the sighting was the result of an astronomical phenomenon, probably a meteor.

Contained in the Blue Book files was a long investigation conducted by Douglas M. Couch, who was the chief of the criminal investigations section at Hill Air Force Base. He had interrogated Captain Herman Gordon Shields, a C-119 pilot who had seen the object from his aircraft. According to Shields, something had illuminated the cockpit from above. He thought it might have been a landing light from another aircraft.

Shields entered a slight turn and saw that the illumination

kept increasing until he could see things on the ground. It was almost as bright as daylight. He noticed that colors were distinguishable.

As the light began to fade, he saw an object to the left, lower than the aircraft. It was a long, cylindrically shaped, slender object, not unlike a cigarette, that was very bright, with an intense white color. The rear, or the last half, was yellowish. He could see no tail, trail, or exhaust. Shields believed that it was in sight for only a second or two.

The Air Force file also contained other reports about the object. One of them ran to seven single-spaced pages on legal-sized paper. Many of the witnesses mentioned had reported only a ball of fire and a series of detonations after the object was gone. Some said they had seen a trail of gray smoke.

In another report, a man in Silver City, Utah, claimed that the object was a glowing ball of light about the size of a soccer ball. He confirmed Shields's color description, saying that the object had a yellowish tint, but he also said he had seen a bright yellow flame coming from the rear. He said, "As the object passed over Robinson [Utah], it slowed down in [the] air, and after, [a] gasping sound was heard, the object spurted ahead again. After this procedure was repeated three or four times, the object turned bluish color and then burned out or went dark. After the object began to slow down it began to wobble or 'fishtail' in its path."

When Couch completed his investigation, he wrote, "Preliminary analysis indicates that each of the observers interviewed were logical, mature persons, and that each person was convinced that he had observed some tangible object, not identifiable as a balloon or conventional type aircraft . . . With the completion of this initial report, no explanation has been developed for the brilliant illumination of the area, the object itself, or the explosions in the wake of the object."

Although Couch, in his report, didn't believe that a meteor could explain the sighting, at Blue Book headquarters, Colonel Friend and Hynek disagreed. Friend, in a letter to the headquarters of the Office of Information for the Secretary of the Air Force (SAFOI), wrote, "The number of reports generated by the 18 April 1962 sighting, and the fact that Air Force investigation came to a negative conclusion regarding the UFO, they indicated it couldn't have been a meteor . . . prompted further investigation by FTD [Foreign Technology Division]. . . . This investigation was completed in one full day and it concluded the object was a bolide."

Friend rejected Couch's conclusion that it couldn't be a meteor, deciding that it was. His conclusion was confirmed by Dr. Robert Kadesch, an associate professor of physics at the University of Utah. Quoted in several area newspapers, he said, simply, "[It] . . . probably was a bolide."

When I interviewed Kadesch, he said that he believed the object had exploded in the sky some 60 or 70 miles above the ground. The flash was so bright that people as far east as Kansas had seen it.

Kadesch was not impressed with the descriptions of the object given by the witnesses, nor was he impressed with the fact that most had estimated it as being little more than a thousand feet high. He said it was difficult, if not impossible, for people to judge the size and distance of an object, especially if they didn't know what they were seeing. This is, of course, exactly right.

Although he hadn't seen the object himself, he said that both his wife and son had. He still believed that it was a meteor. When I asked about the flight crews who claimed it was below their aircraft, he said, "That information is too fragmentary. It could be the curvature of the earth made them believe that."

Another fact that is important is that the Air Force did scramble fighters in an attempt to intercept the object. Although a letter in the files claimed that there was no intercept, other information proved there was. Documents available in the file show that fighters were scrambled from two Air Force bases. Of course, if they didn't catch the object, then technically it wasn't intercepted.

So, do we have two separate events on two separate days, as indicated by the Air Force files, or do we have a single event that took place on a single day? If we take a look at the Air Force files, we begin to be able to put the sequence of events together. For example, we see that the sightings in Utah took place about 15 minutes after the hour, reported at 8:15 P.M., Mountain Standard Time. The events near Reno and Las Vegas took place about

7:16 P.M. However, both Reno and Las Vegas are on Pacific Standard Time. In other words, the sightings took place about the same when the hour is subtracted to compensate for the difference in time zones.

The radar case from Nellis, if we read the file, takes place on April 18, and the Utah case, on April 19. What we see by examining the case is that one is based on local time and the other is based on Greenwich Mean Time, or "Zulu" time. If we eliminate the differences created by that we find that the events are not separated by a day as suggested, but by 16 minutes. In other words, the Nellis case takes place within minutes of that in Utah.

There are other interesting points in the Air Force file. A spokesman for the 28th Air Division at Stead Air Force Base admitted that power had been knocked out in Eureka and that fighters had been scrambled from Nellis as a result of the radar sightings.

Then, on September 21, 1962, about half a year after the events, Major C. R. Hart of the Public Relations office responded to a letter sent by a New York resident. Hart wrote, "The official records of the Air Force list the 18 April 1962 Nevada sighting to which you refer as 'unidentified, insufficient data.' There is an additional note to the effect that 'the reported track is characteristic of that registered by a U-2 or a high altitude balloon but there is insufficient data reported to fully support that evaluation. The phenomenon reported was not intercepted or fired upon."

Not intercepted? Maybe he was suggesting that the fighters had been unable to catch the object. Maybe the radar vectors had failed the pilots so that they never caught the object. That way Hart could be correct—the object wasn't intercepted—without lying outright to the man. Clearly fighters were scrambled. It was the sort of word games the Air Force would play throughout their investigation.

And what about the explanation—the reported track was like that of a U-2 or a balloon? Well, which was it? And how could the track of a balloon, drifting with the vagaries of the wind, look like the flight path of an aircraft under intelligent control? Clearly they were grasping at straws here, because it was neither a balloon nor a U-2.

So, what do we have here?

We have a report of an object that was seen to begin its journey over Oneida, New York, and complete it near Las Vegas, Nevada, when it apparently exploded. It was seen by thousands during the journey. In Utah it landed and took off near Eureka. It was close enough to the ground that the witnesses got a good look at it. It affected the lights in a number of small towns; tales of photoelectric cells do not explain the power blackouts in Nephi, as demonstrated by the lights of the doctor's offices and pickup trucks. It continued its journey until it reached Reno, Nevada, after it apparently had made a long, looping turn so that it was now headed to the southeast rather than the northwest. It flew on toward Las Vegas, where it was tracked on radar until it vanished from the scopes to the northeast near the small town of Mesquite.

I might point out that we do have a case for the scientific community here because we have dozens of independent witnesses and physical evidence in the form of the radar tracks as reported by various Air Force installations. We also have a craft that interacted with the environment, given the reports of its electromagnetic effects. We have the multiple chains of evidence that the scientific community demands.

I might also point out that we have documentation in the form of the Air Force records available on microfilm from the National Archives. Using those records, we can demonstrate that something unusual happened, but more importantly, we can demonstrate that the Air Force and the government have been less than candid about what they found when they investigated. We can show by the contradictory documentation that the Air Force was neither telling all it knew nor accurately telling what it knew. This is just one more of the chains of evidence about the reality of the situation.

What we do know is that something extraordinary happened on the night of April 18, 1962, and the government and Air Force were aware of it. We have seen the series of explanations that ignored the facts, and the separating of the cases as if that somehow rendered them less inexplicable.

But we also have some of the same elements that were seen

during the Chiles and Whitted case a decade and a half earlier—a bright streak of light that appeared to have square windows on it and a cigar shape. We have the same sorts of testimony as that supplied earlier, but we also have more information. These cases are linked by those descriptions. Maybe we're beginning to understand the working of the human mind. We have witnesses telling us of artifacts on those streaks of light. Can we draw any conclusions about it?

Not yet. But these aren't the only such cases. Within a couple of years, there would be another case, with similar elements. To some, it provides the final proof, but to others, it merely deepens the mystery.

Tennessee and Indiana
March 3, 1968

There is a third series of reports that impact on the current discussion. It is a series that matches, to some extent, the description of the craft given by Chiles and Whitted in 1948 and by Bob Robinson in 1962. Because these new sightings had a ready-made explanation, it has been applied as proof that Chiles and Whitted saw a similar natural phenomenon, allowing us to disregard their detailed descriptions.

On March 3, 1968, over parts of Tennessee, Indiana, Pennsylvania, and Ohio, thousands watched as a procession of fiery debris with brilliant golden tails fell to the ground. Many, if not most, of the witnesses watched as two distinct objects fell. As the object broke apart toward the end of the flight, some witnesses saw more than two pieces of the flaming debris. The North American Defense Command, according to some sources, identified the debris as part of the Soviet-launched Zond-IV mission, which failed with spectacular results.

In the Blue Book files there are a number of memos for the record that confuse the issue. On one, dated March 4, it was noted, "Talked to Sgt Farrel at SPADATS. He stated that the only object that came down late the third of March and early on the 4th came down at 0120Z on the 4th in the Pacific and would not have been over the United States."

In another memo for the record, this one dated March 5, it was noted, "Lt. Marano spoke with Captain Shea, SAFOIP at 1300 hours regarding release of information on the UFO report of 3 March. Captain Shea informed Lt Marano that the whole question on the release of the information on this sighting was becoming more and more complicated. He said that NORAD is reluctant to say that this is a piece of Zond-4. NORAD won't buy the fact that it is positively ZOND-4. Kitnchee [sic] from NORAD doesn't want to say this. Lt Barlett had said, 'We are quite certain that this is a piece of debris from the USSR launch ZOND-4 which is the most recent launch. It, the debris, was about 16 minutes ahead of the launch. We have no visuals, but are putting ground tracers on it. Al Waters, from SAO, had reports Louisville, Kentucky.' Shead [sic] said he would say that to DOD. He says they are having problems with NASA and Kitchnee. Lt Marano gave Capt Shea the following short brief description that could be used in place of the previous release given to Shea earlier today."

Shea had apparently written a press release about the incident, explaining it as "a satellite decay." He was then going to take the release down to DOD "and see if they would buy it."

From Indiana, a young man wrote that he had been at his cousin's house, waiting for his family's return, when he saw "some kind of fire-colored object fly across the valley." He wrote to Project Blue Book telling them that "It was at about tree-top level and was seen very very clearly and was just a few yards away. All of the observers [his cousin, aunt, and uncle, who were outside, also saw the object] saw a long jet-airplane-looking vehicle without any wings. It was on fire both in front and behind. All observers also saw many windows in the UFO." He noted that the object flew from horizon to horizon and that it had been in sight for a short period of time at about 9:45 P.M.

In Tennessee, several people, including the mayor of Nashville, were talking when one of them saw something in the distance and pointed it out to the others. As the object approached, they saw an orange-colored flame firing from the rear. All thought the object was a fat cigar, "the size of one of our largest airplane fuselages, or larger. . . . It appeared to have rather square windows along the side that was facing us. I remember the urge to count windows, but other details flashed in view and my curiosity made me 'jump to other observations.' "

In a report to the Air Force, the woman also suggested that she thought the fuselage had been constructed of flat metal riveted together, and she believed it to be about 200 feet long. After the object passed over, she and her companions discussed what they had just witnessed. Later she wrote to the Air Force, providing a drawing of the UFO for the investigators.

At about the same time, a group of six near Shoals, Indiana, saw a huge cigar-shaped craft with a flaming tail and many brightly lighted windows flash overhead. The people thought the object was at treetop level and believed it to be between 150 and 200 feet long. One of those who reported the sighting to the Air Force even suggested that it wasn't a meteor because "meteors don't have windows and don't turn corners." In fact, none of the observers in the group believed it to be a meteor, and all agreed to the general facts of their observations.

In memos for the record, the Air Force officers detailed other reports they received. From Athens, Ohio, ". . . [the witness] was driving west, around Albany, near Athens, Ohio when they saw an object in the northern sky going West to East at 25 deg elevation. Looked like a satellite re-entry, two to three minutes, glowing red almost white. Didn't attach much importance to the object . . ."

From Centerville, Ohio, it was reported that ". . . [a witness] saw an unidentified object at 945 pm, for three minutes, saw a cluster of starlike objects which disappeared in the southwest . . . At first thought they were shooting stars, howevery [sic] they were too long, it was like the trail was burning. Seemed like six or eight objects together."

A witness near Madison, Ohio, reported that four objects, all yellowish-orange, with tails that were orangish-yellow, had flown over at about 10:00 P.M. eastern standard time. The general course was to the northeast, and the objects were brighter than Venus.

These weren't the only reports received by the Air Force. In fact, Air Force officers received nearly eighty UFO reports that night. The descriptions offered were sometimes radically different. For example, there was the report made by a Columbus, Ohio, schoolteacher with four academic degrees, including a Ph.D. She was out walking her dog when she saw three objects fly overhead, flying in some kind of formation. Using her binoculars, she studied the objects, suggesting they looked like inverted saucers. She thought they were about 1500 feet above the ground.

But hers wasn't the only sighting in Ohio. An industrial executive who worked for General Motors and who lived in Dayton was returning from Cincinnati when he saw three bright objects in what he thought of as a triangular formation. The objects were going very fast, there was no sound, and they left a trail. "The brightness was not consistent, it seemed that the two on the side were more consistent, appeared like a flame and was sparking." Because of their speed and lack of noise, the executive believed that the three objects were under intelligent control. Because of their flight dynamics and the lack of noise associated with them, the executive believed that the objects were not military jets.

Also from Dayton came another report of the three bright "meteor like objects" that flew almost to the ground before they "seemed to burn out." There were sparks behind the objects.

There were many other reports from around Ohio, all mentioning that there were three objects, that they were yellowish, and that they looked like balls of fire. The times, which were all estimates, ranged from 9:30 P.M. to 10:00 P.M. The discrepancies in the times were probably because they were just estimates.

A man and wife in Kentucky reported that they saw an object traveling to the northeast. There was no real detail to the memo for the record, but the sighting might be important because of the mention of a single object rather than three.

From Lexington, Kentucky, came a report of two objects that were described as high-intensity lights traveling with other objects that were not as bright. In another report, a string of lights was seen at 9:46 P.M.

If we study the reports sent to the Air Force, we find some interesting things. About twenty of the sightings reported a lack of sound. In seventeen of them, the witnesses believed the objects were flying in formation. In thirteen of them, the witnesses believed the objects were closer than 20 miles away. Interestingly, in twelve of the reports, the witnesses thought it was some kind of meteor or the reentry of some earth-launched spacecraft.

At the distant end of the spectrum, there were reports that the craft was saucer or cigar shaped, that its outline was fuzzy, that there were windows or lights on the craft suggesting windows, and that there was some sound associated with it. The school-teacher reported that her dog had been frightened by the object and that she was extremely tired after it passed, but that the reaction disappeared about two hours later.

If we assume that the observers in Tennessee and Indiana saw the same objects that were sighted in Ohio, and we check the time carefully, we learn that the reentry of a Soviet booster of the Zond-IV occurred about the same time. Is it possible that the Zond-IV is responsible for the series of sightings, including those of a cigar-shaped craft that is quite similar to that reported by Chiles and Whitted almost twenty years earlier and the one Bob Robinson reported about five years before?

First, it should be noted that there is no doubt that the Zond-IV reentered about the same time the sightings took place. There is no doubt that many of the witnesses were able to correctly identify the objects they watched as parts of a reentry. Others thought that it was a meteor, which is exactly what the fiery reentry would have looked like. It is also clear, and may be important, that the object was breaking up as it traveled from southwest to northeast. Some of the objects would burn out quickly. That would explain the discrepancies in the number of objects reported as the object moved across the United States.

There is a problem with those assumptions, however. Some witnesses in Tennessee and Indiana saw a single object. Their descriptions do mirror those of Chiles and Whitted in 1947 and later those by Robinson in 1962. But the witnesses in Ohio saw *three* objects. Philip Klass wrote in *UFOs Explained*, ". . . there are a total of nine observers in Tennessee and Indiana who reported a saucer/cigar-shaped object with illuminated windows and only two in Ohio who reported a squadron of three smaller objects in flight formation, and so one might well decide there was only one giant UFO with numerous windows. *But in reality the two lone witnesses in Ohio were far more accurate observers* [emphasis in original]."

If we separate the sightings, then we have two events, not a single case. And, if there are two events, then the Zond-IV reentry is inadequate to explain everything. In fact, the witnesses in Tennessee and Indiana might have seen exactly what they reported, and if that is the case, then a link to explaining Chiles and Whitted's sighting as a natural phenomenon is broken. There is no reason to assume that Chiles and Whitted saw a meteor, nor is there sufficient reason to believe that the witnesses in Tennessee and Indiana saw Zond-IV.

The connection was the similarity of the drawing made by Chiles and Whitted, one of the observers in Tennessee, and another made by the young man in Indiana. If all of them saw Zond-IV, then that would be suggestive of a psychological aberration that would induce the hallucination of windows on bright streaks of light. But once again, we have the same problem that Hynek had two decades before: There is no solid scientific evidence to support the conclusion.

Analysis of the Data

When we look at these cases, separated by decades, we can draw a few conclusions. We can note, for example, that each of the witnesses reported a cigar-shaped craft that contained square windows. The observations were of relatively short duration—that of Chiles and Whitted, about ten seconds; those of Robinson, about a minute or so.

The Air Force, the Condon Committee, the skeptical community, and Donald Menzel have all decided that these cases can be explained by meteors or Zond-IV's reentry, which they considered to be the same thing. They caution us to not clutter the situation with irrelevant material because that can confuse us easily. They eliminate the information that is contradictory to their points of view and then claim they have solved the case. But let's look at that.

First, the meteor explanation does make some sense if we can identify a psychological phenomenon that will account for the development of a specific shape and artifacts on that shape. In other words, is there something about the human mind that will create square windows on what is essentially a streak of colored light?

The question could become moot, however, if we determine that the Massey sighting is related to that of Chiles and Whitted. It becomes moot if the timing of the Massey sighting has been reported accurately. In other words, if Massey saw the same thing that Chiles and Whitted did, then the meteor explanation is eliminated.

We can also examine Chiles and Whitted's description of the event and their belief that the object, as it passed them, climbed and disappeared climbing. We know that meteors can appear to have a nearly flat trajectory and can appear to travel nearly horizontally. Some astronomers have even suggested that meteors can appear to climb under the proper circumstances. However, both Chiles and Whitted had seen meteors in the past, and there is no reason to suspect they would be fooled in this case, even if it was an exceptionally bright meteor.

Hynek reported that if we accept Chiles and Whitted's report at face value, then the meteor explanation is eliminated. He didn't seem to be satisfied with that as an explanation and noted as much.

So, with this case, we have, basically, a sighting by two men sitting next to one another in the cockpit of an aircraft. Both describe, essentially, the same thing, including the double row of square windows. If Massey is part of the equation, then a meteor does not answer the questions. If Massey is not a part, then the meteor explanation, though still somewhat extreme, does seem to make a little more sense.

With the Utah and Nevada sightings of 1962, such answers don't seem to explain the sighting. We don't have as many descriptions of a cigar-shaped object with windows, but we do have a few. More importantly, we have a number of reports of the object interacting with the environment.

The streetlights in Eureka went out as the object passed over. The police chief, among others, said that the lights were on photoelectric cells and the sudden brightness of the object fooled the cells, causing the lights to go out. That doesn't explain, however, the other reports of light and power outages in the area.

We also have the data, from a single witness, suggesting the object landed and then took off, and the belief, by many people, that it came down west of the Nephi-Eureka area, in the rough, mountainous terrain. Both Friend and Hynek tried to locate the meteor but failed to do so. It must be noted that neither tried very hard to find it, and the lack of positive results in that respect means very little.

When we look at the Nevada end of the sightings, we find that the object was flying in the opposite direction, there were multiple witnesses, and there were the radar tracks. Meteors, according to the Air Force, don't register on radar, though the ion trails will. Those sorts of trails should be easily identifiable to experienced radar operators.

So if we combine the sightings, we have literally hundreds of witnesses, power outages, and radar sightings. Airline crews and Air Force flight crews reported the object being below them. Astronomer Robert Kadesch said that was an optical illusion and he believed the sightings could be explained as a bolide.

But there is a major problem with the bolide answer. The object, according to the witnesses, made a hundred-and-eighty-degree turn. A bolide couldn't do that. So now we must postulate two bolides that appeared sixteen minutes apart. There is nothing in the astronomical records to suggest this answer is accurate.

Finally, we have the sightings from March 3, 1968. There seem to be two distinct events. One involves the reentry of the Zond-IV. The other does not. The Air Force, the Condon Committee, and the debunkers have linked the events, assuming that the explanation for some is the explanation for all. In fact, they have used this to suggest that Chiles and Whitted saw a bolide because the descriptions by some of the witnesses match the drawings made by Chiles and Whitted.

The problem is that the sightings should not be linked. Those who suggested they had seen a single object are lumped in with those who claim to have seen multiple objects. It seems here that the events should be severed rather than linked.

Why do we argue that here, when we argued to link those

first cases—Chiles and Whitted and Massey, in addition to the Utah and Nevada sightings? The answer is, simply, the descriptions by the witnesses. All the documentation suggests that the Zond-IV reentry involved at least two pieces of debris. During its fall to the ground, it fragmented further, meaning there were more than two pieces. Klass even commented about it, writing that those who reported the "formation" were more accurate than those who reported a single, cigar-shaped craft. In other words, the reentry of the Zond-IV does not match the description given by those who spoke of a single object. Therefore, I believe, it is logical to separate the sightings. If that is done, than Zond-IV is not an adequate explanation.

It also leaves us with the question of whether the human mind will create square windows on a streak of light. Is there a psychological explanation for this? The Condon Committee, when discussing the problem, brought up questions of perception, contamination, confabulation, and optical illusion. They cited examples of these problems, but nothing that actually related to the cases in question.

So, if we are making a scientific analysis of this small part of the UFO phenomenon, we can design an experiment and conduct scientific research to find the answer. In other words, we do not have to rely on the opinions of experts who have an agenda. We can learn the answers for ourselves by performing the proper research. So, let's do just that.

Review of the Literature

To begin any scientific research project, we should review the available literature. That is, we use the various scientific databases to determine if the question has been asked and answered by others in the past. Today's environment makes this task easier because of computer access to scientific journals from all disciplines. The review of the literature provides us with clues about what we might expect to find as we continue our investigation.

The question is one of perception, illusion, priming, and conformity. When presented with a nonspecific stimulus such as an ill-defined light, a number of different cognitive processes are brought into play, according to various researchers. Each of these processes can be affected by various factors, including confabulation. Is there a psychological phenomenon in which those presented with an unrecognizable stimulus will perceive artifacts when no such artifacts exist? Does the human mind create those artifacts to bring the stimulus into line with their experiences and perceptions from the past? These are questions that have plagued scientists for many years.

H. Wallach, author of *On Perception*, wrote, "The farther natural science has developed the greater has been the discrepancy between the picture of the world which it has presented us and the world we experience through our senses."

Wallach continued in this vein when he wrote, "All sorts of physical processes cause qualitative experiences in perception as, for instance, colors, tones, noises, the sensations of cold, warm, and hot."

Because we are examining the human perception of the artifacts in the "real" world around us, we are susceptible to illusion, according to Wallach. L. Kaufman writes in his book, *Perception*, "Illusions . . . occur in daily life."

What has fascinated psychologists for decades are these illusions, according to Kaufman. H. Kender defines illusion as "A false perception, one that fails to correspond with the actual stimuli," in his book *Basic Psychology*.

"Most of the illusions studied by psychologists are visual phenomena, such as the perception that one line is longer than another line even though the two lines are of equal length," writes Kaufman.

It should be noted that according to Stanley Coren and Joan Girgus, authors of *Seeing Is Deceiving: The Psychology of Visual Illusions*, the defining characteristic of these illusions is that they are surprising. If there is an explanation for a specific phenomenon that might be illusional to those who do not understand it, then it is not a real illusion. In other words, if we understand the illusion, even if we are fooled by it, then it is not considered a "real" illusion.

These sorts of studies have provided information about the processing of information by the human brain and the retrieval of memory. C. Krumshansl, in his 1982 article, "Abrupt Changes in Visual Stimulation Enhance Processing of Form and Location Information," suggested that the ease of identification of a brief stimulus may depend on the rate at which it is processed. Interestingly, and according to an article by L. Stelmach, identification accuracy is expected to be easier during the earlier portion of a display than during the later portion of it.

J. Foley suggested that "Pattern vision is conceived of as a process in a network of interconnected units (mechanisms)." Foley, quite obviously, was searching for patterns and how those patterns were recognized by the brain.

However, there has been little written about human responses to a nonspecific visual stimulus such as a colored streak of light. Most of the experimental work has been conducted concerning nonspecific words and the process of human memory. Hermann Ebbinghaus, for example, used nonsense syllables to study the process of learning and memory. He sought material that he believed would be unfamiliar to him and therefore would be free of associations. He wanted to create words that had no meaning in and of themselves. This is, in one sense, a nonspecific source. His problem, however, was to learn these words so he could study the process of memory, and not identify them as anything specific.

When looking at something like a nonspecific light source, priming seems to be of importance. According to R. Ratcliff and G. McKoon, "Priming in object decision is a particularly important piece of the implicit memory framework because, unlike most other implicit priming effects, it shows memory for novel information in that the objects have never been seen by participants before the experiment."

Light sources that are nonspecific have been around since the beginning of human history. In the last half century many of these have been related to the UFO phenomenon. Hynek termed those seen at night "nocturnal lights." These could be as simple as discharges of swamp gas, Venus seen under unusual conditions, other astronomical phenomena, or lights that are seen and reported but that seem to have no known cause.

Michael Persinger wrote, "From a behavioral perspective, the report of UFOs can be considered contemporary responses to persistent environmental stimuli." He noted that "a substantial number of UFO reports (UFORs) may reflect as yet unspecified stimuli."

Persinger also wrote, "Indeed, some of them may be correlated as well with the unusual perception of routine objects." That is, people misidentify meteors, airplanes, clouds, or weather balloons when these are seen under unusual circumstances. Air Force investigations into the UFO phenomenon seem to bear this out.

Persinger also offered an explanation of some of the UFO sighting reports made. He wrote, "One hypothesis suggests that more than 50% of the variance in these stimuli are associated with tectonic strain within the earth's crust." This means, quite simply, that the stress of movement in the earth's crust, given the proper geological formation, can result in a display of light.

Persinger further defined this when he wrote, "At the farthest distance, when the observer is outside the local field disruptions associated with the luminosity, the primary experience, would be of an odd shape of light with unusual kinetics. As the observer approached it, physical features of the luminous condition would become obvious. Symmetric lines or apparent internal structure could be discerned."

Persinger concluded, "Specific details will be loaded by the verbal label paired with the event (or its context) at the time of the stimulation. Whereas the words 'spaceship' or 'flying saucer' would evoke a variety of images conditioned to that label, words such as god, devil, ghost, or angel would also evoke their appropriate associations."

Persinger, in his work, is suggesting two things of relevance here. One is that these luminous displays, also known as "earthquake lights," can result in a UFO report. The spinning of the luminous display would result in a flattened disk that could be mistaken for an alien spaceship. Second, the label applied by the witness could influence the identification of the light source by that witness.

Impacting on this is the work of J. Campbell, A. Tesser, and P. Fairey, who wrote, "People examine the stimulus until they reach a response decision; high attention indicates that the decision was not a quick and easy one."

They also suggest, "Although there has been virtually no research examining attention to the stimulus, two important theorists have discussed its role in the influence process. S. Asch speculated that group pressure, self-doubt, and extremity of the norm would increase attention to the stimulus."

Also important is the work of Robert L. Goldstone, who suggested, "Much of the recent work in reasoning and judgment concerns the use of heuristics to make decisions. Heuristics that usually yield reasonable accurate judgments also result in systematic biases under some circumstances."

A confirmation bias is a tendency for people to seek or use confirmatory, rather than disconfirmatory, evidence, according to a variety of authors.

Because there is no specific shape behind the light sources, the interpretation of them is open to speculation. Often the physiology of the human body can create the illusion of motion where there is none. When the human eye is trained on a point of bright light such as the planet Venus, especially at night, erratic motion in the muscles and optic nerve in the eye create the illusion that Venus is darting around the night sky. This is known as autokinesis, which is defined as "the apparent motion of an object due to the small, involuntary movements of one's eyes."

Of course, the current discussion is about points of lights, or nonspecific sources of lights. There have been no cases in the literature in which a nonspecific light source has been endowed with various perceived mechanical features such as those described by Chiles and Whitted. It seems that when confronted with a nonspecific light source, witnesses report that sort of light. In other words, they do not report a UFO sighting.

One consideration that must be explored is that of priming. As noted earlier, the work of Ratcliff and McKoon is of importance here. Their studies of bias in the priming of object decisions provides some insight into the effects of priming. Ratcliff and McKoon noted, "Because the amount of information stored in human memory is so large, a successful model of memory requires mechanisms that allow fast and efficient search and access."

In understanding at least some of the sightings, especially

those from the Midwest in 1968, the theory of conformity is important. According to S. McKelvey and N. Kerr, "There is ample evidence that groups of friends conform to shared standards in daily life."

This work is relevant when it is remembered that Chiles was the airplane captain and Whitted was the copilot. Chiles was in a position of authority over the copilot, and that specific relationship may have affected the situation as well as their perceptions.

In summary, there is little in the way of experimental work about nonspecific light sources and witnesses' perceptions of them. The work that has been done has focused on other aspects of the sightings. Persinger was testing his hypothesis that "earthquake lights" were responsible for some reports.

Although there is controversy about the nature of UFOs, there is no question that a body of reports exists. An understanding of the workings of the human mind, the nature of perception, and response to stimuli can provide some answers. Although not all UFO sighting reports can be identified here, some questions will be answered. This could relieve the anxiety expressed by some of those who see strange lights in the sky.

The Experiment

To determine if a nonspecific stimulus, such as a streak of light that is reminiscent of a bolide or the reentry of the Zond-IV, results in a very specific response, the participants were shown one of two short videotapes. One tape contained a streak of light reminiscent of a meteor that closely matches the flight descriptions provided by witnesses to UFO-related phenomena. The tape also mirrored the flight characteristics of a bolide.

A second group saw a tape that contained a streak of light with a cigar-shaped object with square windows and an exhaust embedded in the light. The object seen conformed to the descriptions provided by the witnesses in the Chiles-Whitted UFO sighting of July 1948, the Las Vegas/Utah sightings of April 1962, and some of the March 3, 1968, sightings in the Midwest.

The participants were randomly placed in one of four groups. The four groups were those who saw only the streak of light, those who saw the object embedded in the light, those who were primed with UFO material and shown the streak of light, and those who were primed with UFO material and shown the cigar-shaped object.

Each of the participants was given a questionnaire modeled after the document used by the Air Force to gather UFO-related sighting reports. The purpose was to determine what the participant believed he or she saw and how long the light was in sight. After the completion of the questionnaire, an interview was conducted in a manner consistent with Air Force investigations of similar events. The responses from the questionnaires were summarized and tabulated.

As mentioned, the questionnaire was based on Air Force Form 117, which was used to gather data about UFO sightings, but modified for this study. It was used to assess the cognitive responses of the participants. It was designed to determine if the participant saw any sort of shape behind the streak of light, the form that shape took, and the length of time the streak of light was in sight. It was noted on the form if the participant had been primed or not, and if the participant was shown only the streak of light or the light with the object.

The participants were exposed to one of two short videotapes. Each tape was of a dark sky that contained stars and little motion. Three minutes and twenty-five seconds into the tape, a small point of light appeared. It grew steadily and then streaked by the viewer to disappear to the left of the screen. It was in sight for three seconds. The tape continued for another three minutes.

On one version of the tape, the streak of light mimicked the actions of a bolide. It was basically nothing other than a brightly colored streak of light. The second version contained a cigar-shaped object buried behind the light. A row of square windows was visible, and there was an exhaust trail. A bright glow surrounded the object. The actual shape of the object and the artifacts that accompanied it were in view for only two seconds.

This study is unique in one aspect: The body of evidence that exists concerning nonspecific light sources and detailed investigation is related to balls of light rather than streaks. Not only has Persinger studied the "earthquake" light phenomenon, providing a scientific base for it but the Air Force has also collected thousands of UFO sighting reports, many of which were little more than lights seen at night.

A study of reports that relate to nocturnal lights and witness statements can be made. By comparing the original statements, sometimes made within hours of the initial report, with investigative forms filled out sometimes months later, a pattern might be discovered. Does confabulation influence those reports, and how? This section of the study will be carried out using those statements. The results will be summarized and displayed in tables contained in the text.

This study is designed to learn if there is a psychological phenomenon that causes witnesses of unusual lights in the night sky to attribute mechanical aspects to them where none should exist. It will provide data on the perception of light seen in the night sky and the reaction to that light. It will suggest whether perception can be colored by priming with UFO-related material. A study of the Air Force case files can provide some insight into confabulation.

The Results

What we learned from the experiment was that people do not normally create, in their minds, square windows on a streak of light. Some do perceive a shape where none exists, especially those who have had the idea of spaceships and UFOs implanted before they participated in the experiment. Priming, then, does contribute to the description of the phenomenon. There was nothing extraordinary about that finding.

One of the questions that concerned me was the affects of conformity. In psychological experiments, it was shown that subjects could be made to accept the dictates of a majority even when that majority was obviously wrong. Some subjects resisted the effects of conformity but not all were successful at it. It should be noted that those numbers were relatively small, suggesting that conformity is an important factor in situations where there is a majority view.

In the Chiles and Whitted case we find a circumstance that

is important to understanding the sighting. Chiles was the captain—that is, the pilot in command. Whitted was his subordinate. Even though this was a civilian situation, we would be remiss if we overlooked that fact. Whitted wouldn't want to be in a situation in which he was contradicting the man who was, in essence, his boss.

Does this mean that Whitted could have been led to the belief that he was seeing something that wasn't there? Remember, Chiles had "primed" the situation by suggesting that what they were about to see was one of the army's new jet aircraft. That simple statement by Chiles set the tone for the observations they were about to make.

They expected to see a jet aircraft but instead saw a cigar-shaped object that bore little resemblance to any of the aircraft flying in 1948. They saw a double row of square windows, a long flame shooting from the rear, but no wings, no tail assembly, and nothing that resembled a jet or aircraft cockpit. Though "primed" by Chiles's comment, they seem to have observed something other than a jet. They did, however, see some sort of craft.

It is true that in the later sighting that night, Massey saw no windows, though the rest of his description seemed to match that of Chiles and Whitted. It could be that Massey, standing on the ground and looking up, was in no position to see windows, just as someone standing on the ground and looking up at a jet airliner flying over won't be able to see windows.

The passenger McKelvie didn't report anything other than a streak of light, but he was looking out the side of the aircraft—not the front, as were Chiles and Whitted—and didn't have a chance to see much of anything on the craft. Both Chiles and Whitted reported that the craft was climbing as it passed them, which might account for what McKelvie said.

The important point here, however, is that the experiment didn't produce any evidence that would suggest that Chiles and Whitted had misperceived the stimulus. There is no evidence that the human mind, even when confronted with an unidentified light source, will create the impression of lighted square windows on a cigar shape. In and of itself, this would mean that the Air Force and Condon explanation—that Chiles and Whitted had seen a bolide—is disproved. There is no psychological reason for them to have created these artifacts in their mind if they had not been present during the sighting.

The same can be said for the Utah and Nevada sightings. Although there were few reports of the windows besides that given by Bob Robinson, there were other reports of the cigar-shaped craft. Once again, those reporting the craft but no windows were not necessarily in a position to see windows if they did exist on the craft. The descriptions of the craft, as well as its passing, all generally agree. Discrepancies can be easily dismissed as differences in the perceptions of the witnesses, the angle at which they viewed the craft, and their positions on the ground.

What is critical about this series of sightings is the number of witnesses, the interaction with the environment, and the reaction of the authorities. The Air Force scrambled fighters to intercept the object over the southwestern United States. Had it been a bolide, as later concluded by the Air Force, they wouldn't have had the time to scramble the fighters.

If we break this case and the evidence into its components, we have four separate chains of evidence. First, again, are the witness reports from widely scattered locations, by individuals who did not know one another, and who were of various educational and social backgrounds. We find a consistency in the description of the object.

Granted, some details do match those reported during the passing of a bolide. The roar, or string of detonations, is a well-known phenomenon often associated with bolides. In most cases of bolides or other bright meteors, there are reports of a string of explosions. The fact that these were reported in this case, however, does not rule out other explanations. It is an interesting and entirely relevant fact here.

The dimming of the streetlights in central Utah is evidence of an interaction with the environment and is, therefore, the second independent chain of evidence. There are two possible explanations. One is that the brightness of the meteor was sufficient to trip the photoelectric cells that controlled the streetlights. The lights went out because of the brightness of the meteor. Again, this is a phenomenon that has been reported in the past.

However, there were additional witnesses who reported that the passing of the object caused lights on their vehicles to dim and the motors to sputter. This is a well-known phenomenon, as studied earlier, associated with close approaches of UFOs. It is called an EM Effect. The theory is that electromagnetic radiation from the craft suppresses the electrical fields of the cars, stopping the engines and dimming the lights.

There are also reports from the highway patrol sergeant who claimed that the lights in Nephi were dimmed by the passing of the object. These were not lights controlled by a photoelectric cell, so the solution for this must be found elsewhere. In other words, the brightness of the object is irrelevant, and the meteor explanation, for this particular aspect of this case, is eliminated.

Further, that explanation is eliminated when the reversal of course is plugged into the formula. Clearly a meteor, no matter how bright, will not change course. While minor "course corrections" can be explained by the misperceptions of the witnesses, this 180-degree loop as reported by the witnesses, first near Reno and later near Las Vegas, cannot be explained by a meteor. Couple that to the radar reports, and the meteor explanation is eliminated.

The radar reports constitute the third independent chain of evidence. Clearly, and according to the records, the object was seen on at least two separate radars and two different types of radar. There is nothing in the files to suggest that the object was not real or solid. There is nothing in the files to indicate that the radar sighting was of a natural phenomenon, a malfunction, or operator error or misidentification. Instead, fighter aircraft were scrambled, which is a positive reaction to data received on the radarscopes. These radar reports provide a government record and a source of proper documentation for the event.

That documentation, available through government resources and Freedom of Information Act requests to all who wish to review it, constitutes the fourth independent chain of evidence. It also reveals the misinformation and distortion of these events provided to the public. When a citizen asked about the fighters that were scrambled, he was told that the object had not been intercepted. If everything is as the Air Force reported, as Condon reported, and as the government would have us believe, why would they conspire to conceal the data? Why not just tell the truth? Fighters had been scrambled but had failed to intercept, or locate and then identify, the object.

And once again, we are stuck with the sightings in which the witnesses claimed to have seen a row of square windows on the side of the cigar-shaped craft. This description matches that given some fifteen years earlier during the Chiles and Whitted case. And again, our psychological experiment provides no evidence that a subject, when confronted by a bright streak of light, will confabulate windows.

Finally we reach the Zond-IV reentry, which to many proved that Chiles and Whitted had seen a bolide, that those in Utah and Nevada had seen a bolide, and that this explanation eliminates a body of UFO reports.

But as we review the Air Force file on this case, a file that runs to more than three hundred pages and is composed of statements taken within days of the event, we find some interesting problems. First, we can see that the object reported is not a bolide but the claimed reentry of the Zond-IV space vehicle. We can ask, with justification, if the burning of a meteor as it falls through the atmosphere is the same as the reentry of a spacecraft.

The answer is no. The composition of meteors is fairly well established and limited to only a few elements. Meteors are not manufactured craft. They are shaped like rocks, which means that there is no shape to them other than a random conglomeration of material.

Spacecraft are made of many different components made of many different materials. Some of those components will resist air friction and heating better than others. Some will flame and burn out quickly. Others will not.

What has been introduced to our discussion is a variable that could make enough difference that we cannot deduce, from the evidence, that those seeing the reentry of a space vehicle will be fooled in the same way as those watching a meteor. There are enough differences that haven't been reviewed that they could skew the results. Solid conclusions can't be drawn about them.

Second, the Zond-IV was breaking up as it fell. There are

cases in which meteors are seen to break apart at the end of their flight. The most spectacular meteor I ever saw was at dusk, over Cheyenne, Wyoming. It was blue-green and broke into four sections before it disappeared from sight. I recognized it immediately as a meteor even though it seemed to be much lower and brighter than other meteors I had seen.

The point is that the breakup of the meteor, the "sparking" that was reported by some witnesses, might be enough of a change to create an illusion of windows. There is no evidence for this, but it must be considered as we review the material. And if that is so, then there was an aspect to the sighting that was unique to this case and therefore cannot be generalized to the whole population of such sightings. In other, more mundane, words, it means that the Zond-IV reentry does not apply to either the Chiles and Whitted sighting or the Utah and Nevada sightings.

The Condon Committee, in discussions of the Zond-IV reentry and the Chiles and Whitted case, presents arguments about psychological perception, illusion, autokinesis, recognition, and conception. While interesting, most of the discussion is irrelevant to these cases. There is nothing to link the phenomenon of autokinesis to a confabulation of square windows on a cigar-shaped craft. Autokinesis is the phenomenon behind our seeing a point of light dance around in an erratic fashion, as described earlier.

If we are being scientific in our research, we must also note that our experiment may not be generalized to the population that witnessed the cigar-shaped craft in the real world. A better experiment, had the equipment and the money been available, would have been to program a flight simulator with the streak of light that matched the general description provided by the pilots Chiles and Whitted. In this way the conditions faced by Chiles and Whitted would have been more accurately duplicated. They would have had no warning that they would see something unusual. The crew in the simulator would have been surprised in the same fashion as Chiles and Whitted.

Our experiment more closely represents the situation during the Zond-IV reentry. Those participating in the experiment knew they would see something, just not what it would be. Their descriptions of what they saw were accurate without creating impressions of artifacts that were not present. In other words, no one saw the square windows unless they were shown the tape with the object that had square windows.

What we can conclude from this study is that there is no apparent psychological reason for any of these witnesses to have seen square windows unless those windows were present during the sighting. There is no reason to believe that a bolide or the reentry of a Soviet craft could be responsible for the sightings of Chiles and Whitted, those in Utah and Nevada, and those in the Midwest of a definite craft with square windows.

It must be noted here that the reports from the Midwest, which seemed to coincide with the reentry of the Zond-IV, were of a single craft. None of the witnesses who reported seeing windows reported more than a single craft. Those who reported the Zond-IV reported two or more objects during its entire flight path. This is a discrepancy that must be noted because it confounds our results.

It is quite true that people will report a bright meteor as a UFO when that meteor differs from the normal by a wide margin. However, those who report the meteors do not normally attribute artifacts to them that will suggest a cigar-shaped craft with a long exhaust flame and square windows.

There is another point here that must be made. We must remember that the evidence suggests that the Air Force officers conducting the investigation, especially after 1953, were searching for solutions even if those solutions were invalid or invented. They were slapping labels on cases regardless of the facts. This has been demonstrated time and again.

What this means to us is that solutions appended to these specific cases are not valid. To Air Force investigators, to some in the scientific community, and to the skeptics, these sightings have been identified as natural phenomena. Our research and experimentation suggests that the labels as applied here have no validity. The cases demand better, objective, scientific research before we apply any explanations.

At the moment, based on the evidence at hand—and that is *all* the evidence—there is no solid explanation for these sightings. We can conclude, if we want to make the leap, that they demonstrate a technology far beyond our own, and thereby suggest extraterrestrial visitation. Without some sort of physical debris from the craft or the bodies of the alien flight crew, there will always be some room for doubt. However, these cases seem to provide strong evidence that visitation is taking place, and they demand further investigation.

7

The Hoaxer Spoils the Evidence

Any scientific field is subject to the possibility of hoax. Hoaxes have dotted the landscape in all sorts of arenas from the beginning of the age of scientific enlightenment. They have been motivated by all sorts of reasoning, not the least of which is monetary. However, many have been perpetrated for no other reason than to make someone else look bad or to propel someone into the spotlight. The UFO field has had more than its share of hoaxes, many of which persist until today.

Depending on how we want to define the UFO phenomenon and its beginning, we can find hoaxes related to UFOs that are more than a century old. In the spring of 1897 there were reports of an airship that appeared over a great many regions of the United States. In most of the cases the airship looked as if it was some kind of balloon or blimp that carried its crew aloft. While some researchers argue that there was a core of solid and inexplicable reports buried in this mountain of nonsense, some of the admitted hoaxes are perpetuated today by investigators who refuse to look at the evidence, or who have their own agenda.

The first of the abduction reports took place during the Great Airship sightings of 1897. Those reports varied from modern abductions in a number of ways. First, most often, the pilots of the airship were human scientists who were on the verge of a great new scientific discovery. In only a few of the cases were nonhumans reported; in those few cases, they predicted the current UFO trends.

For example, Alexander Hamilton, a rancher in Kansas, was the first to report a tale of cattle mutilation and an extraterrestrial visitor. Today, ranchers and researchers claim that an unknown agency, probably extraterrestrial, is killing and mutilating cattle around the world. According to these researchers, no one can explain how it is being done. It is a modern mystery that, according to the mutologists (those who study mutilations), has no simple solution.

In April 1897, Hamilton reported that one of his cows had been stolen from a closed corral late at night. The entire account of the aerial cattle rustling was published in the *Yates Center Farmer's Advocate* on April 23. Hamilton and a number of his friends signed an affidavit attesting to the truthfulness of the story. According to that document:

> Last Monday night [April 19] about half past ten we were awakened by a noise among the cattle. I arose thinking perhaps my bulldog was performing some pranks, but upon going to the door, saw to my utter amazement, an airship slowly descending over my cow lot about 40 rods from the house.
>
> Calling Gid Heslip, my tenant, and my son, Wall, we seized some axes and ran to the corral. Meanwhile the ship had been gently descending until it was not more than 30 feet about the ground and we came up to within 50 yards of it . . . It was occupied by six of the strangest beings I ever saw. There were two men, a woman and three children. They were jabbering together but we could not understand . . .
>
> When about 30 feet above us, it seemed to pause, and hover directly over a three-year-old heifer which was bawling and jumping, apparently fast in the fence. Going to her, we found a cable about half an inch in thickness . . . fastened in a slip knot around her neck, one end passing up to the vessel . . . We tried to get it off but could not, so we cut the wire loose, and stood in amazement to see the ship, cow and all rise slowly and sail off . . .
>
> . . . Link Thomas, who lives in Coffee Country about three

or four miles west of LeRoy, had found the hide, legs, and head in his field that day. He, thinking someone had butchered a stolen beast and thrown the hide away, had brought it to town for identification but was greatly mystified in not being able to find a track of any kind on the soft ground . . .

The affidavit was signed by a number of men who claimed they had known Hamilton for years and "that for truth and veracity we have never heard his word questioned and that we do verily believe his statement to be true and correct."

During the mid-1960s, the Hamilton tale surfaced again and was repeated in a number of magazine articles and UFO books about the history of the UFO phenomenon. Each time, the statement of Hamilton's friends was mentioned without question. Here was a tale that deviated from the airship stories in a number of ways, suggested an extraterrestrial explanation for the event, and involved the rustling of a cow. It proved the strangeness of some of the airship tales and suggested to those who wanted to believe that something otherworldly was happening.

Jerry Clark, who had reported the case seriously a number of times, did some additional investigation on his own in the 1970s. He learned that one of the Hamilton's daughters still lived in Kansas, and he interviewed her about the story. Although she hadn't been born until after the event, she had heard her father talk about it on many occasions. She said that Hamilton belonged to a local liars club, as did all the men who sighed the affidavit attesting to Hamilton's truthfulness.

Even worse for the true believers was a published letter found by Eddie Bullard. In the May 7, 1897, edition of the *Atchison County Mail*, Hamilton wrote in the letter that he had fabricated the tale. There simply is no reason for it to continue to circulate.

The story was a joke, invented by Hamilton, and told at the time the airship was reported flying across the country. There was not a word of truth in it. Hamilton would have been delighted to learn that his joke had fooled another generation seventy years later.

The airship craze of 1897 also provided the first of the UFO crash retrieval stories to gain widespread publicity. According to many newspapers of the time, and later to dozens of UFO writers, the airship was seen over Aurora, Texas, early on the morning of April 17, 1897. It swooped low over the town, buzzed the town square, and continued on to the north. There it slammed into a windmill on the farm of Judge Proctor and exploded. The badly burned body of the dead pilot was recovered. T. J. Weems, a Signal Corps officer, said that the pilot, obviously not human, was probably from Mars.

In the wreckage, searchers found several documents covered with strange writing. Some of these were somehow translated, telling the investigator that the airship weighed several tons and was made of aluminum. By noon that day, April 17, the debris had been collected, and later in the afternoon, the Martian was given a Christian burial.

It probably isn't necessary to point out that here we have all the elements of the modern UFO crash retrieval, including the mystery writing, the disappearance of the debris, and the recovery of an alien body. It wasn't covered up by the American government; it was disposed of by the local residents in their desire to provide the alien occupant with a proper burial. None of the debris has survived until today, so that no analysis of it can be performed.

The truth of the Aurora case, however, is that it is another hoax, just like the Alexander Hamilton cow-napping. H. E. Hayden, a stringer for the *Dallas Morning News*, reported the Aurora crash to the newspaper. They printed it, just as they had earlier printed several airship stories. Hayden apparently saw an opportunity to put his hometown back on the map. He missed by more than seventy years.

The fact it was a hoax has been demonstrated time and again. T. J. Weems, the Signal Corps officer, was, in fact, the local blacksmith. In the early 1970s I interviewed people who were living in Aurora in 1897, and they claimed they knew nothing about the event. Members of the Wise County, Texas, historical society told me they wished the story was true, but there was just no reason to accept it.

Many of the airship tales recounted in articles and books have been proven to be hoaxes. In Iowa, telegraphers, apparently with nothing better to do, would report that the airship was over their city, heading on to the next. Soon, telegraphers in the next city would report that, yes, it had flown over. Newspapers picked up the stories and ran with them. Researchers, looking for old airship stories, would discover them sixty or seventy years later and report them as if they were the truth.

If we are looking for something more modern, we have only to look at the very beginning of the "flying disk" craze of late June 1947. Almost at the moment that Kenneth Arnold claimed to have seen his nine crescent-shaped objects flying near Mt. Rainier, Washington, others began telling stories that were not true.

It was on July 31, 1947, that the intelligence office at Hamilton Army Air Field was alerted to the fact that two harbor patrolmen had found what they believed was metal from a flying saucer. Within an hour, two officers—Lieutenant Frank Brown and Captain William Davidson—left California for Tacoma, Washington. There they met with Kenneth Arnold, who, at the insistence of Ray Palmer, was investigating the case.

The story being told was that the two harbor patrolmen, later identified as Fred L. Crisman and Harold Dahl, had been working in Puget Sound when they had seen a flight of six doughnut-shaped objects. They photographed them and noticed that one seemed to be in trouble. The others might have been trying to help. It rocked from side to side, and eventually it dumped something that fell to the beach and onto Crisman and Dahl's boat. It injured a boy and killed a dog.

The two Army Air Force officers listened to the story and decided from the beginning it was a hoax. The photographs had disappeared, and the metal turned out to be worthless slag. The harbor patrolmen were, in fact, men who "patrolled" the sound looking for lumber to salvage. The officers made quick plans to return to California as soon as possible.

The only reason the case remained in the UFO literature was that on their way back to California, the officers' aircraft crashed, killing both men. Suddenly rumors began to fly that the officers had been killed because of the metal samples they carried. They had been killed to stop them from reporting what had been found.

The reality was that it was an aircraft accident that had nothing to do with the UFO investigation.

Ed Ruppelt, onetime commander of Project Blue Book, labeled the case as the dirtiest hoax in UFO history because it had, indirectly, cost the lives of the two officers as well as those of the aircrew. But the story, although rejected as a hoax, is revitalized periodically by those who see conspiracy everywhere. The facts are twisted to suggest something sinister, but no evidence is ever offered that a conspiracy took place. That is the key: lack of evidence.

But there is another side to this coin. The debunkers of the UFO phenomenon, knowing of the long and twisted history of hoaxes, quickly apply that label when they have no other explanation. Lonnie Zamora didn't really see an object land in the New Mexico desert; he was participating in a hoax. The Johnson family in Delphos, Kansas, didn't have something strange land on their farm; they invented a hoax for monetary gain. The Trents didn't photograph a strange object over their farm; they were engaging in a hoax.

We have seen that there is a lack of evidence to support these allegations. But the point is that the debunkers, when they have no other solution, offer the hoax explanation, even if the facts don't support that sort of a conclusion.

Of the debunkers, Harvard astronomer and late scientist Donald H. Menzel, who was rabidly anti-UFO, was the worst of the lot. He wrote books decrying the belief in flying saucers, apparently worked with the Air Force as a part-time consultant to Project Blue Book, and argued with other scientists about the reality and nature of UFOs. He wasn't above making up an explanation when there were no facts to fit the case.

Take, for example, the photographs of the lights seen over Lubbock, Texas, taken by Carl Hart, Jr. at the end of the summer in 1951. For a couple of days, reports had been in the Lubbock newspaper about strange lights flashing through the sky. Hart, soon to be a freshman at Texas Tech, was in his bedroom, looking up into the night sky, when a formation of lights flew over. Knowing that they sometimes returned, he grabbed his camera and waited. In the next hour or so, he managed to take five pictures of two formations of the lights.

The Air Force investigated, advising Hart of his rights under the Fourth Amendment to the Constitution. The editors of the Lubbock newspaper told Hart that if he was pulling a hoax, he would be sorry. Even with the threats of legal action, Hart said that he had not faked the pictures. In fact, in an interview I conducted with Hart more than forty years later, he said, "I don't know what I photographed."

The Air Force determined that the Lubbock Lights were the result of birds reflecting the bright light from the recently installed sodium vapor street lamps. It made no difference to them that there were no birds with the proper coloring flying in V-formations in Lubbock at the time. (I checked with the local fish and game people on the campus of Texas Tech to learn that). It means that the Air Force explanation is wrong, but they didn't care because the case was off the books.

It also means that there is no good explanation for the pictures taken by Hart. Donald Menzel, in a June 1952 article in *Look*, claimed the lights were not birds but reflections of the city's lights—that is, "mirages caused by an atmospheric condition known as a temperature inversion."

In his own laboratory, Menzel was able to chemically reproduce to his own satisfaction what he insisted were the Lubbock Lights. His photograph did not look like the ones taken by Hart, and they had no motion. They were static. Again, a solution had been offered, and for the time being, Menzel was happy with the results.

But as time passed, Menzel became disenchanted with that explanation. In his 1977 book, *The UFO Enigma* (written with Ernest H. Taves), he devoted less than a paragraph to the Lubbock Lights. "We believe that some of the Lubbock photographs may have been hoaxes." Left with no convincing alternative explanation, Menzel, without justification, called Hart a liar.

Menzel, who was quite fond of the temperature inversion explanation, wasn't reluctant to apply it to fellow scientists. Charles B. Moore, who would gain later fame as one of the few surviving members of the New York University balloon project code-named Mogul, also had a UFO sighting that was solved by Menzel.

In April 1949, Moore, living in New Mexico and launching balloons, for General Mills, spotted an object that was "ellipsoid . . . white in color except for a light yellow on one side as though it were in shadow." Moore knew that it wasn't a balloon and watched it, with the technicians, for about a minute.

The Air Force was unable to identify the sighting, and it is carried as an unidentified in the Project Blue Book files. Menzel, however, did what the Air Force had failed to do: He identified the object. According to him, the object was a mirage, an atmospheric reflection of the true balloon, making it appear as if there were two objects in the sky—the balloon launched by Moore and his group, and a second object, flying along at high altitude and at great speed. Menzel was so sure of this that he reported it to Moore.

Moore, however, is an atmospheric physicist. He is as qualified as Menzel to discuss the dynamics of the atmosphere. When interviewed on El Paso radio station KTSM, Moore said that the weather conditions had not been right for the creation of mirages. Since Moore was on the scene, and since his training qualified him to make judgments about the conditions of the atmosphere at the time of the sighting, his observations are more important than Menzel's wild speculations.

When Moore spoke to Menzel, the Harvard professor would not listen to what Moore had to say. Menzel had found what to him was a satisfactory solution, and he didn't want to discuss it seriously. Menzel *knew* there were no such things as flying saucers and the explanation to Moore's sighting must lie elsewhere. This is not particularly good science.

I said earlier that I believed Menzel was a consultant to Project Blue Book, although this seems not to be acknowledged. We can deduce this from a number of facts, including the fact that galley proofs of his anti-UFO books are often appended to case files. In other words, the "scientific" explanations offered by Menzel in his books and magazine articles are in many of the Air Force case files. It provides the Air Force with a plausible explanation for a sighting if those who are reviewing the files are not familiar with UFOs. It makes it look as if a legitimate investigation has taken place.

There is an even better bit of evidence. In 1969 a symposium on UFOs was sponsored by the American Association for the Advancement of Science. One of those invited to present a paper was Menzel. In the course of it, he castigated the late Dr. James McDonald, a professor of atmospheric sciences at the University of Arizona. Menzel wrote, "He accuses me of glossing 'over the reported rocking of the DC-3.' Nonsense! There was no mention of such 'rocking' in the official report."

Menzel is referring to the 1948 sighting by Chiles and Whitted in which they saw a bright light come at them, flash past, and then disappear. Both men reported seeing a double row of windows, a cigar shape behind the glow, and a red flame from the rear. Menzel and the Air Force, believed the men had seen a bright meteor. Others, such as McDonald, thought they had seen a ship from another world.

The point, however, is the disputed claim of rocking motion. Menzel is both right and wrong in his claim. There is a mention of the rocking in the official file, which I have read, but it is in the newspaper clippings that accompany it. In none of the statements given by either Chiles or Whitted is there a mention of the rocking motion. What this means is that Menzel had read the file and McDonald had not. And, since this was 1969, within days of the announced closing of Project Blue Book, Menzel wouldn't have had access to the files, as we do today, unless he was working with the Air Force on their so-called investigation. This association, which was never made public, explains much of the negative spin put on UFO sightings and those who reported them.

The point here, however, is to note that much of what Menzel said, much of what the Air Force investigators said, about UFOs, was not borne out by evidence. In other words, Menzel wasn't above massaging the information if it suited his purposes. That has been demonstrated time and again as we review the UFO situation. There is much about the UFO phenomenon that we do not know, and it was under the influence of such learned men as Dr. Menzel that we have not progressed farther and faster than we have.

In science we are not supposed to massage the information or add to it things that have not been observed. We are not supposed to invent answers to questions simply because the facts are difficult to explain.

Yes, there have been hoaxes in the UFO field. About ninety percent of the UFO photographs have been taken by teenaged boys, and about ninety-nine percent of those are hoaxes. That does not mean we can label a photograph a hoax simply because we can find no other explanation for it. It does not mean that we can call any case a hoax just because there is no easy way to solve it.

But we must also be aware that having no solution to a case does not lead us directly to the extraterrestrial hypothesis. Some of the reports do suggest manufactured crafts that are operating outside the realm of our technology and that suggest alien visitation. But the observational evidence presented does not provide the proof that we all desire. It is a strong indication, but in the end, we must be fair and admit that it is not definitive.

Other areas can take us toward that definitive proof. But we must be aware that there have been hoaxes, some of which fooled even the most skeptical of the UFO researchers. And sometimes the hoaxes have taken on a life of their own, proved to be hoaxes, and been rejected. We must search each case carefully, aware that there are many clever people in the world; even if we don't find evidence of a hoax, it might be there.

8

Conclusions

The most obvious conclusion, after examining the evidence presented here, is that there is no evidence that conclusively proves that UFOs represent alien visitation. Read that again carefully to fully understand. There is no evidence that is conclusive. There is, however, a great deal of evidence that is suggestive of that conclusion. At this time, that is about the best we could hope for.

So let's take a look at what we've learned. First is the eyewitness testimony. We have learned that human memory is poor and can't always be trusted. If there is a written record, that helps, but when relying only on memory, it must be corroborated by additional information or testimony. When several people tell the same story, when they have had no opportunity to compare those stories, then those memories can be judged as reliable.

That's what makes the Oregon sightings of July 1947 and those in Levelland some ten years later so important—multiple witnesses telling the tales to governmental officials, sometimes within minutes of the sightings. Corroborated testimony tends to rule out a hoax.

In Levelland there was an additional, and important, piece of evidence. Witnesses, unknown to one another, were reporting the same sort of interaction with the environment. The UFO—whatever it was—stalled car engines and dimmed headlights. Radios were filled with static and then silenced. Had only one witness reported the odd effects, they could be dismissed, but there were several such reports. Given the location, number of reports, and short period of time in which they were made, hoax can be eliminated in the Levelland case.

While there were no measurements made during investigation of these cases, there were reports made and written within hours of the sightings. And while there are only the observations of the witnesses, about a dozen of them reported that there was electrical interference. The reports of these observations are consistent.

Mark Rodeghier, scientific director of the J. Allen Hynek Center for UFO Studies, produced an analysis of 441 instances in which the UFO suppressed electrical systems including car engines and headlights. The phenomenon, then, was not unique to the Levelland cases but something that was reported over many years. Rodeghier wrote, "It is unlikely that a natural phenomenon would suddenly begin occurring with some frequency after 1953 [the first year that we have reports of vehicle interference], when many vehicles had been on the road for dozens of years before that date."

He also noted that a natural phenomenon would probably not occur in unpopulated areas. That is, there should be a statistically significant number of the sightings and experiences in heavily populated areas if this was some sort of natural occurrence, but such doesn't seem to be the case. According to Rodeghier, there was no reason for the majority of the cases to take place at night. He thought that the presence of humanoids in several of the cases made it difficult to explain the cases as a natural phenomenon, if we accept those cases at face value.

Finally he wrote, "While a spinning plasma might appear metallic to an individual under certain conditions, it is unlikely that so many witnesses have been unable to determine the true appearance of the phenomenon."

Rodeghier wrote that there was an undiscovered natural phenomenon that did explain a few of the cases. These were piezo-electrical displays that were first discussed by Dr. Michael Persinger. But even the discovery of that phenomenon argued for the reality of the cases in which cars were stalled and electrical systems suppressed.

Of course, it should be mentioned that this in no way proves that some UFO sightings represent visitation by alien creatures. It merely suggests that something unusual, undefined by science, has been occurring. It suggests a real phenomenon that warrants further study so that we can unravel the problem and define it.

These sorts of reports, such as Levelland, where the UFO interacted with the environment, are made up solely of witness observations. In most cases, those witnesses were selected at random by fate. Few scientifically trained witnesses were available, and the preconceptions and education of the witnesses certainly colored their thoughts and their reports of what happened to them.

Photographic evidence, whether in the form of motion picture footage or still photos, provided another level of evidence. Eliminating those that are obvious hoaxes, those that are admitted hoaxes, and arbitrarily all those taken in the last twenty years, there is still a significant number of good pictures that offer us a form of physical evidence.

The two pictures that have undergone the most scrutiny and study present us with evidence that something real and unexplainable is happening. Although explanations have been offered, those explanations seem to be more in line with the wishful thinking of debunkers than with critical scientific thought.

Both the Montana movie and the Utah movie show bright objects in a nearly cloudless sky. Both show the objects as points of light with little detail visible. Both are short segments. And explanations have been offered for both, but those explanations are not adequate.

Unfortunately for us, neither movie does much more than complicate the situation. While it can be said that balloons, rockets, and natural phenomena are not represented on the film, there are those who would suggest that aircraft in one and birds in the other are suitable explanations.

I don't believe that either explanation is accurate. It smacks too much of trying to force a mundane answer. But it must also be pointed out that neither film provides us with the conclusive evidence that we are being visited by aliens. There is simply not the sort of evidence on the film to support that conclusion. In other words, the films by themselves are inconclusive. Interesting but inconclusive.

Stills have been offered. Two of the best were taken in McMinnville, Oregon, in 1950. During this study, I found it curious that the Air Force hadn't made more of an effort to investigate the claim, Instead, they ignored these pictures, apparently hoping that the problem would just go away.

Nearly everyone who has studied the pictures and the circumstances surrounding their creation has suggested this was a good case. The Condon Committee, not noted for their candor, failed to find a good explanation for them. As noted earlier, William K. Hartmann, the chief investigator on the photographic cases, wrote, "Two inferences appear to be justified: 1) It is difficult to see any prior motivation for a fabrication of such a story, although after the fact, the witnesses did profit to the extent of a trip to New York; 2) it is unexpected that in this distinctly rural atmosphere, in 1950, one would encounter a fabrication involving sophisticated trick photography (e.g. a carefully retouched print). The witnesses also appear unaffected by the incident, receiving only occasional inquiries."

Phil Klass and others suggested that light shadows proved that the pictures were taken in the morning rather than the evening, proving them to be a hoax. But that argument is weak. The story told by the Trents is consistent with the evidence available and has been since it first popped into the public arena. Calling the case a hoax based on poor evidence doesn't make it a hoax. It taints the case and taints the phenomena, but that doesn't make the explanation real.

Again we are presented with the fact that good physical evidence, while interesting and suggestive, is certainly not conclusive. There seems to be no solid alternative explanation, but that does not equate with proof of alien visitation.

The same can be said for the radar sightings. There are some very interesting cases, when examined in an objective light, that suggest something unusual was observed. The Washington National sightings of 1952 have not been adequately explained, regardless of Air Force attempts to label them as temperature inversions. There were dozens of visual sightings, there were attempted intercepts, and there was a reaction to the presence of the interceptors by the UFOs, which argue for the reality of the sightings.

Qualified observers, familiar with their equipment, their surroundings, and the weather-related phenomena that could confound and confuse, were on the scene. A military expert familiar with radar was on hand. None of these people would be fooled for hours by temperature inversions that are supposed to answer all the questions. And one expert on the scene is worth five who investigate ten years later.

Edward Ruppelt's claim that the temperature inversion explanation came about through a misunderstanding is revealing. The failure of others to corroborate and substantiate it is also important.

The Minot Air Force Base sightings are not as impressive or as spectacular as the Washington Nationals. Only two radar sets were involved, and the information about one of them is little more than a reference in the case file. But there were a large number of witnesses, all of whom should have been familiar with the military aircraft that have been offered as an explanation for some of the visual sightings.

In the end, the Air Force proposed a multiple-event answer that sounded scientific and well thought out but held little of scientific value. It was an explanation slapped on a case to provide an answer that would be acceptable to the high-ranking brass, and that is just what the Blue Book staff wanted to accomplish.

By themselves, the radar cases do not provide a definitive answer. They give us clues and provide a mechanical corroboration for the visual sightings, suggesting that something was seen in the air. If the radar operators were qualified and trained, it adds a new dimension to the UFO phenomenon, but it does not provide the positive proof that we are being visited by aliens from other solar systems.

All these sorts of physical evidence—the car interference cases, the photographic cases, and the radar cases—provide us with some information about alien visitation. It all suggests that something is going on, but we need more. That is where the landing trace cases become important. One of the best is the landing near Socorro, New Mexico.

Here the alien craft interacted with the environment, leaving traces of itself. This was not something that was illusionary. It can't be written off as a weather phenomenon. It was a solid object that left landing gear prints that could be analyzed long after the craft was gone.

Klass believes he has solved this case. It was a hoax probably engineered by the former mayor of Socorro with the cooperation of Lonnie Zamora. It was done to create a tourist attraction in Socorro, according to Klass's analysis.

There are, of course, problems with that explanation. First is the two new witnesses discovered in the course of this investigation. Neither of the men lived in New Mexico, neither had any ties to Zamora or the mayor, and neither of the men gained a thing from their telling of the tale. What they did do was eliminate the possibility of a hoax by Zamora and the mayor.

Donald Menzel had a different idea, suggesting that teenagers who hated Zamora because he gave them speeding tickets had designed the sighting to embarrass him. They used fireworks, balloons, and a coordination accomplished through two-way radio in a plot that would have been complicated for Jim Phelps and his *Mission: Impossible* team. Of course there was no evidence offered for this implausible scenario, and no one other than Menzel ever seriously considered it.

So the question becomes, If it wasn't a hoax, then what could it have been? Several UFO researchers, such as Russ Estes, have suggested some sort of experimental craft that had strayed from the White Sands Missile Range. That certainly is a possibility, but there has never been any documentation discovered to support the claim. Researchers have looked, and one Air Force officer told me that he thought he had found the proof, but the timing was wrong.

The Delphos UFO ring turns on the testimony of a single teenaged boy. He was the one who saw the craft hovering just above the ground where the ring was found. His testimony ties the ring to the UFO. Others—his parents and one other man—

saw the craft in the sky, but only young Ronald Johnson saw it on the ground.

Again Klass offered the theory that it was a hoax for monetary gain. But that explanation doesn't work when it is remembered that no cash rewards were being offered for UFO sightings when the Johnsons began to claim they had seen the saucer. Durel Johnson seemed to have become obsessed with the money and how much others were making on his sighting, but that does not provide the motive for the sighting.

Klass himself admits, "In this respect the Delphos case is not 100 percent explained." He realized the weakness of his argument, even overlooking the analysis that has been performed on the various soil samples. They suggested something unusual.

But, again, they don't prove the case. The analysis of the samples provides clues and deepens the mystery, but there is not the sort of evidence that proves some UFOs are alien spacecraft. It suggests something other than natural phenomena, but it just doesn't have the persuasive influence that the body of an alien creature or the craft itself would have.

Yes, there is a case in which a bit of material was seen to come from a craft that exploded near Ubatuba, Brazil, in 1957. The metal was picked up from the beach and sent on to a newspaper columnist. Though he and APRO Brazilian representative Dr. Olavo Fontes tried to identify the source, they were unable to do so.

Fontes did have the metal tested by Brazilian authorities, who suggested that it was magnesium of a purity unobtainable by technology current at the time—that is, in 1957. Fontes sent the test results and samples of the metal to APRO Headquarters in Tucson, Arizona. They offered to allow the Air Force to test it, but somehow the Air Force technicians managed to destroy the sample without results. They asked for more, but APRO declined.

During the Condon Committee study, the samples were loaned to the scientists for nondestructive analysis. Their tests, according to the report, did not confirm the Brazilian tests. They also learned that magnesium of equal purity was available from Dow Chemical research scientists at the time. To them, both these points weakened the value of the sample, but it could not be conclusively stated that the sample proved an extraterrestrial origin.

Additional tests were conducted. Scientists such as Dr. Walter Walker suggested that the metal samples were either extraterrestrial or part of a hoax. To him and others there were no other possible explanations. Unfortunately, from a scientific point of view, we can't specify which is the proper answer.

Remember, the metal was found by an unidentified witness. There is no eyewitness testimony, other than the letter received, to prove that the metal came from a large flying craft. The first link in the chain of evidence is broken; because of that we are left with an enigma. We do not have the proof that we need, though we have an indication that it exists.

All we have been able to accomplish in this work is an answer to the question, Where is the physical evidence? We have demonstrated that physical evidence does exist. The interpretation of the evidence is where we begin to run into problems, at least from a scientific point of view.

For some, pictures such as those taken in McMinnville and California are enough. They see no conclusive evidence of a hoax, and the shape of the craft in the photographs suggests something that was manufactured on some other planet.

For some, radar cases such as the Washington Nationals and the first Bentwaters case are enough. There are tracks of objects that suggest technology that outflies ours. The fact that the objects were seen on radar, that intercepts were attempted, and that pilots saw the objects in the sky is enough. The men involved in the sightings were competent. They were well trained. There is no reason to believe that they had suddenly lost their abilities to recognize the mundane.

For some researchers the two movies are enough. They study those films and believe that jet aircraft or seagulls soaring on thermals do not explain the images. The shape of the objects is enough to suggest something otherworldly. To them it is the proof they seek.

For some the landing trace cases are enough. The UFOs interacted with the environment, leaving impressions in the soil or burned areas. There are more than five thousand reported landing traces. To be honest, we must point out that in the majority of the cases, the landing spots were found and assumed to be from a UFO, but there was no direct observation of any UFO activity.

But there are cases such as that at Socorro and Delphos where the object was seen close to or on the ground. Because the craft resembled nothing that we have, or had, the conclusion that it was extraterrestrial has been drawn. But again, we are left with few witnesses and evidence that does not prove the case conclusively.

All of these reports represent physical evidence of some kind. The physical evidence exists. What has been lacking is a solid, independent scientific study of that evidence. What has been lacking is a study in which the conclusions weren't drawn before the first word of testimony was gathered, before the first exhibit was examined, or the first day of investigation had begun.

The skeptics and the debunkers hold up the Robertson Panel, sponsored by the CIA in 1953. Here five scientists spent five days reviewing the best of the Project Blue Book cases. They had access to everything in the Blue Book files, and they had access to the best of the evidence. After five days they determined that UFOs posed no threat to national security and that the evidence didn't support the extraterrestrial hypothesis.

The Condon Committee study was held at the University of Colorado. They studied UFOs for eighteen months. At the end of that time, they determined that UFOs posed no threat to national security and that there was no evidence UFOs were extraterrestrial in origin.

But the Robertson Panel was composed of scientists who were rabidly anti-UFO. They made jokes about the evidence, rejecting much of it out of hand. On a Friday night, Robertson said he would write the draft of the final report. He arrived the next morning with the document in hand. Not only that, it had already been reviewed by one of the panel members and the Air Force Directorate of Intelligence. In 1953, with no FAX machines, computers, or on-line services, it seems impossible to believe he could have written the document late on a Friday night and arrived for the sessions the next day with it already reviewed. It suggests that the document was created before that Friday night. It suggests that the conclusions had been written before the meetings began the Monday preceding.

Another of the so-called scientific studies was completed, under Air Force contracts with the Battelle Memorial Institute, in the mid-1950s. Dr. Bruce Maccabee, after studying the report provided to the Air Force, wrote, "Still another case they avoided explaining may be one of the most credible on record. The summary in SR 14 [Special Report #14] does not do the case justice . . . Case X [which took place on May 24, 1949] describes a sighting by two aeronautical engineers who worked at the Ames Research Laboratory and three other people. Each engineer had the opportunity to observe a 'flying saucer' through binoculars for a period exceeding 60 seconds. The drawings produced by these witnesses were extremely detailed. The intelligence information on this case is missing from the Project Blue Book section of the microfilm record at the National Archives. However, Maccabee has found the original interviews, etc. in the Office of Special Investigations section of the microfilm record and has published the information along with some supplementary weather data."

Air Force writers had suggested, "It can never be absolutely proven that 'flying saucers' do not exist. This would be true if the data obtained were to include complete scientific measurements of the attributes of each sighting, as well as complete and detailed descriptions of the objects sighted. It might be possible to demonstrate the existence of 'flying saucers' with data of this type, IF they were to exist."

So now we see the problem they had—explain the sightings with "incomplete" data, or so they would have us believe. But, as Maccabee pointed out, Case X had the very attributes the Air Force suggested didn't exist. There were qualified witnesses—that is, two aeronautical engineers who had ample opportunity to observe the craft through binoculars. This wasn't a case like the Chiles-Whitted sighting in which the object flashed by. This was a case where minutes passed as the observation continued, enabling the witnesses to take notes.

In fact, what we see from this report is that there is TOO much information to allow investigators to find a plausible explanation. They have all the information they could desire from the location and exact time, to the descriptions of the craft including detailed drawings provided by aeronautical engineers. No natural phenomenon is going to explain it. Nor will it be eliminated as a misidentification of military or civilian aircraft. It will remain unknown.

In order to eliminate it, then, it is combined with other cases in which there is no good, plausible explanation. All the information is correlated, and an attempt is made to produce a single type of flying saucer. The assumption seems to be that if flying saucers were real, then we would be able to take the cases of the unknowns and combine them to produce a composite "model" of a flying saucer in much the same way that police artists can produce a composite sketch of a single criminal.

However, more than one type of craft could be involved. Take, for example, an aircraft carrier from our modern navy. It's floating in the Mediterranean Sea and launching a variety of aircraft to survey the surrounding territory. We know that such ships carry two or three different types of jet fighters, as well as a variety of reconnaissance aircraft, tankers, and even helicopters.

Now, let's say that we have a number of people who have seen those various aircraft over a period of a couple of months. We interview them, study the weather, length of sightings, and locations of each of them. From that we attempt to build a model of the aircraft on the carrier, assuming a single type.

Given that we have a craft with swept wings and a narrow fuselage, a huge craft with two engines, another with no wings but a rotor overhead, with different configurations for the lighting, we would be unable to manufacture a single model. Should we then conclude that no sightings had been made? Should we conclude that, with better information, we would have been able to answer the questions? No. We have more than one type, and by combining information that shouldn't be combined, we have destroyed our database.

Of course, by combining that information we can suggest that there is no commonality among the sightings. We can deduce that each of the witnesses is mistaken in some critical observation. We can suggest that this proves there is nothing to the sightings of these very common (to us), aircraft. And each of these conclusions would be wrong, though to a hurried and noncritical reader of our work, we have demonstrated a "flaw" in the sighting reports. We can now reject them.

The Condon Committee was even more of a setup than the Robertson Panel or the Battelle study. Dr. Michael Swords has spent the last several years studying the history of the Condon Committee and confirms the view that the Air Force used Condon to end the UFO investigation with a bogus study. But Condon was a willing participant in the deception. According to a letter discovered by Swords and written by Lieutenant Colonel Robert Hippler to Condon, the plan was laid out in no uncertain terms. Hippler told Condon that no one knew of any extraterrestrial visitation and, therefore, there "has been no visitation."

Hippler also pointed out that Condon "must consider" the cost of the investigations of UFOs and to "determine if the taxpayer should support this" for the next ten years. Hippler warned that it would be another decade before another independent study could be mounted that might end the Air Force UFO project.

Condon understood what Hippler was trying to tell him. Three days later, in Corning, New York, Condon gave a lecture to scientists, including members of the Corning Section of the American Chemical Society and the Corning Glass Works Chapter of Sigma XI. He told them, "It is my inclination right now to recommend that the government get out of this business. My attitude right now is that there is nothing in it. But I am not supposed to reach a conclusion for another year."

Robert Low responded to Hippler's letter a day or so after Condon's Corning talk, telling him that they, the committee, were very happy they now knew what they were supposed to do. Low wrote, ". . . you indicate what you believe the Air Force wants of us, and I am very glad to have your opinion." Low pointed out that Hippler had answered the questions about the study "quite directly."

What this means, quite simply, is that the conclusions of the Condon Committee mean nothing. It was not a scientific study because they knew what the answer was before they began. Then, when evidence appeared that suggested that something real might

it will be identified. The more information provided, the better the report.

We are told by the skeptics that there are no UFO sightings in which there aren't ambiguous conclusions. They suggest that all the "good" cases have been tainted by some element. The Trent photographs were taken in the morning. Money and tourism might have induced the Socorro mayor into inventing a tale to bring in money, or Durel Johnson had been swayed by the prospect of money for his sighting. They suggest that we discount the evidence because there is nothing about UFOs that doesn't have the taint of hoax, misidentification, delusion, or illusion— at least according to the skeptics.

But is that fair? Isn't it somewhat like the young man who kills his parents and then asks for mercy because he is an orphan? Skeptics create the controversy around the cases, often with little more than speculation and innuendo, and then complain because no case is without that controversy.

So where are we? Can we draw any conclusion?

We have seen, over the last fifty years, a real attempt to keep solid information about alien visitation out of the hands of the general public. We have seen the Air Force and the government lie about their involvement in UFO research as documented time and again by newly released letters, reports, and correspondence. We have seen the flawed scientific studies of UFOs. We have seen studies sponsored by the Air Force concluding precisely what the Air Force wanted them to conclude. We have seen the mishandling of the scientific method and the gathering of information. What we have seen is either incompetence or active attempts to misinform. It doesn't matter which, because the solution is the same: We need an independent and proper scientific investigation.

The evidence is out there. Lots of good evidence gathered over fifty years. It might not prove that UFOs are extraterrestrial in origin, but there is certainly enough there that the scientific community should take notice. There is the physical evidence demanded by science and journalism, there are good reports from dozens of people who have no reason to invent their stories, and there are photographs and movies. Everything we need to conduct a proper scientific investigation is available.

This work was created with my personal bias in mind. I believe that we have been visited by aliens. Not often, but we have been visited. The evidence, to me, is quite persuasive.

But the real point to be made is that it has not been reviewed in a proper scientific arena. It has not had the objective review that it demands. Instead, we are stuck with the personal biases and the Air Force–sponsored studies. We need to move beyond that if we are ever going to fully understand what is happening.

Bibliography

Air Defense Command Briefing, Jan 1953, Project Blue Book Files.

ARNOLD, Kenneth and PALMER, Ray. *The Coming of the Saucers*. Amherst, Wis.: Legend Press, 1952.

ASCH, S. *Social Psychology*. New York: Prentice-Hall, 1952.

ASIMOV, Isaac. *Is Anyone There?* New York: Ace Books, 1967.

ATIC UFO Briefing, April 1952, Project Blue Book Files.

"The Aurora, Texas, Case," *The APRO Bulletin* (May/June 1973): 1, 3–4.

BAKER, Raymond D. *Historical Highlights of Andrews AFB 1942–1989*. Andrews AFB, Maryland: 1776th Air Base Wing, 1990.

BAXTER, John and ATKINS, Thomas. *The Fire Came By*. Garden City, N.Y.: Doubleday, 1976.

BERLITZ, Charles and MOORE, William L. *The Roswell Incident*. New York: Berkley, 1988.

"Big Fire in the Sky: A Burning Meteor," *New York Herald Tribune* (December 10, 1965).

BINDER, Otto. *What We Really Know About Flying Saucers*. Greenwich, Conn.: Fawcett Gold Medal, 1967.

———. *Flying Saucers Are Watching Us*. New York: Tower, 1968.

———. "The Secret Warehouse of UFO Proof." *UFO Report*. (Winter 1974): 16–19, 50, 52.

BLOECHER, Ted. *Report on the UFO Wave of 1947*. Washington, D.C.: Author, 1967.

BLUM, Howard, *Out There: The Government's Secret Quest for Extraterrestrials*. New York: Simon and Schuster, 1991.

BLUM, Ralph with BLUM, Judy. *Beyond Earth: Man's Contact with UFOs*. New York: Bantam Books, 1974.

BONTEMPTO, Pat. "Incident at Heligoland." *UFO Universe* (Spring 1989): 18–22.

BOWEN, Charles (ed). *The Humanoids*. Chicago: Henry Regnery, 1969.

"Brilliant Red Explosion Flares in Las Vegas Sky," *Las Vegas Sun* (April 19, 1962), p. 1.

BROOKSMITH, Peter. *UFO The Complete Sightings*. New York: Barnes & Noble Books, 1995.

BROWN, Eunice H. *White Sands History*. White Sands, N.M.: Public Affairs Office, 1959.

BRYANT, C. *Close Encounters of the Fourth Kind*. New York: Albert A. Knopf, 1995.

BUCKLE, Eileen. "Aurora Spaceman—R.I.P.?" *Flying Saucer Review* (July/ August 1973): 7–9.

CAHN, J.P. "Flying Saucer Swindlers." *True*. (August 1956).

———. "The Flying Saucers and the Mysterious Little Men," *True* (September 1952).

CAMPBELL, J. and FAIREY, P. "Informational and Normative Routes to Conformity: The Effect of Faction Size as a Function of Norm Extremity and Attention to the Stimulus." *Journal of Personality and Social Psychology*. Vol. 57, No. 3 (1989): 457–468.

CAMPBELL, J., TESSER, A. and FAIREY, P. "Conformity and Attention to the Stimulus: Some Temporal and Contextual Dynamics." *Journal of Personality and Social Psychology*. Vol. 51, No. 2 (1986): 315–324.

CANADEO, Anne. *UFO's The Fact or Fiction Files*. New York: Walker, 1990.

CATOE, Lynn E. *UFOs and Related Subjects: An Annotated Bibliography*. Washington, D.C.: Government Printing Office, 1969.

CHARITON, Wallace O. *The Great Texas Airship Mystery*. Plano, Tex.: Wordware, 1991.

CHAVARRIA, Hector. "El Caso Puebla." *OVNI*: 10–14.

CLARK, Jerome, "Airships: Part I." *International UFO Reporter* (January/February 1991): 4–23.

———. "Airships: Part II." *International UFO Reporter* (March/April 1991): 20–23.

———. "The Great Unidentified Airship Scare." *Official UFO* (November 1976).

———. *High Strangeness: UFOs from 1960 through 1979.* Detroit: Omnigraphics, Inc., 1995.

———. "Crashed Saucers—Another View." *Saga's UFO Annual 1981* (1981).

———. *UFO's in the 1980s.* Detroit: Apogee, 1990.

COHEN, Daniel. *Encyclopedia of the Strange.* New York: Avon, 1987.

———. *The Great Airship Mystery: A UFO of the 1890s.* New York: Dodd, Mead, 1981.

———. *UFOs—The Third Wave.* New York: Evans, 1988.

Committee on Science and Astronautics, report, 1961.

COOPER, Milton Willam. *Behold a Pale Horse.* Sedona, Ariz.: Light Technology, 1991.

COREN, S. and GIRGUS, J. *Seeing Is Deceiving: The Psychology of Visual Illusions.* Hillsdale, N. J.: Lawrence Erlbaum Association, 1978.

CREIGHTON, Gordon. "Close Encounters of an Unthinkable and Inadmissible Kind." *Flying Saucer Review* (July/August 1979).

———. "Further Evidence of 'Retrievals.' " *Flying Saucer Review* (Jan 1980).

———. "Continuing Evidence of Retrievals of the Third Kind." *Flying Saucer Review* (January/February 1982).

———. "Top U.S. Scientist Admits Crashed UFOs." *Flying Saucer Review* (October 1985).

DAVIDSON, Leon (ed). *Flying Saucers: An Analysis of Air Force Project Blue Book Special Report No. 14.* Clarksburg, Va.: Saucerian Press, 1971.

DAVIES, John K. *Cosmic Impact.* New York: St. Martin's, 1986.

"DoD News Releases And Facts Sheets," 1952–1968.

EBERHART, George. *The Roswell Report: A Historical Perspective.* Chicago: CUFOS, 1991.

EDITORS OF LOOK. "Flying Saucers." *Look* (1966).

EDWARDS, Frank. *Flying Saucers—Here and Now!* New York: Bantam, 1968.

————. *Flying Saucers—Serious Business.* New York: Bantam, 1966.

————. *Strange World.* New York: Bantam, 1964.

Eighth Air Force Staff Directory, Texas: June 1947.

ENDRES, Terry and PACKARD, Pat. "The Pflock Report in Perspective." *UFO Update Newsletter.* Vol. 1, No. 5 (Fall 1994): 1–6.

ESTES, Russ (producer). "Faces of the Visitors." Crystal Sky Productions, 1997.

————. "Quality of the Messenger." Crystal Sky Productions, 1993.

————. "Roswell Remembers." Crystal Sky Productions, 1995.

"Experts Say a Meteor Caused Flash of Fire," *Deseret News* (April 19, 1962), p. 1.

Fact Sheet, "Office of Naval Research 1952 Greenland Cosmic Ray Scientific Expedition," October 16, 1952.

FAWCETT, Lawrence and GREENWOOD, Barry J. *Clear Intent: The Government Cover-up of the UFO Experience.* Englewood Cliffs, N.J.: Prentice-Hall, 1984.

Final Report, "Project Twinkle," Project Blue Book Files, Nov. 1951.

FINNEY, Ben R. and JONES, Eric M. *Interstellar Migration and the Human Experience,* Berkeley, Calif.: University of California Press, 1985.

"Fireball Explodes in Utah," *Nevada State Journal* (April 19, 1962), p. 1.

First Status Report, Project STORK (Preliminary to Special Report No. 14), April 1952.

"Flying Saucers Again." *Newsweek* (April 17, 1950), p. 29.

"Flying Saucers Are Real." *Flying Saucer Review* (January/February 1956): 2–5.

FOLEY, J. "Human Luminance Pattern-Vision Mechanics: Masking Experiments Require a New Model." *Journal of the Optical Society of America.* Vol. 11, No. 6: 1710–1717.

FORD, Brian. *German Secret Weapons: Blueprint for Mars.* New York: Ballantine, 1969.

FOSTER, Tad. Unpublished articles for Condon Committee Casebook. 1969.

FOWLER, Raymond E. *Casebook of a UFO Investigator.* Englewood Cliffs, N.J.: Prentice-Hall, 1981.

————. "What about Crashed UFOs?" *Official UFO* (April 1976): 55–57.

——. *The Watchers*. New York: Bantam Books, 1990.

FULLER, John G. *The Interrupted Journey*. New York: Dial, 1966.

——. *Incident at Exeter*. New York: G.P. Putnam's Sons, 1966.

——. *Aliens in the Sky*. New York: Berkley Books, 1969.

GILLMOR, Daniel S. (ed). *Scientific Study of Unidentified Flying Objects*. New York: Bantam Books, 1969.

GOLDSMITH, Donald. *Nemesis*. New York: Berkley Books, 1985.

——. *The Quest for Extraterrestrial Life*. Mill Valley, Calif.: University Science Books, 1980.

GOLDSTONE, R. "Feature Distribution and Biased Estimation of Visual Displays." *Journal of Experimental Psychology: Human Perception and Performance*. Vol. 19, No. 3: 564–579.

GOOD, Timothy. *Above Top Secret*. New York: Morrow, 1988.

——. *The UFO Report*. New York: Avon Books, 1989.

——. *Alien Contact*. New York: Morrow, 1993.

GRIBBIN, John. "Cosmic Disaster Shock." *New Scientist* (Mar 6, 1980): 750–52.

"Guidance for Dealing with Space Objects Which Have Returned to Earth," Department of State Airgram, July 26, 1973.

HALL, Richard. "Crashed Discs—Maybe," *International UFO Reporter*. Vol. 10, No. 4 (July/August 1985).

——. *Uninvited Guests*. Santa Fe. N. Mex.: Aurora Press, 1988.

HANRAHAN, James Stephen. *History of Research in Space Biology and Biodynamics at the Air Force Missile Development Center 1946–1958*. Alamogordo, N. Mex.: Office of Information Services, 1959.

——. *Contributions of Balloon Operations to Research and Development at the Air Force Missile Development Center 1947–1958*. Alamogordo, N. Mex.: Office of Information Services, 1959.

HAUGLAND, Vern. "AF Denies Recovering Portions of 'Saucers.'" *Albuquerque New Mexican* (March 23, 1954).

HAZARD, Catherine. "Did the Air Force Hush Up a Flying Saucer Crash?" *Woman's World* (February 27, 1990): 10.

HEGT, William H. Noordhoek. "News of Spitzbergen UFO Revealed." *APRG Reporter* (February 1957): 6.

HENRY, James P. and MOSELY, John D. "Results of the Project Mercury Ballistic and Orbital Chimpanzee Flights," NASA SP-39, NASA (1963).

HIPPLER, Lt. Col. Robert H. "Letter to Edward U. Condon," January 16, 1967.

"History of the Eighth Air Force, Fort Worth, Texas" (microfilm). Air Force Archives, Maxwell Air Force Base, Ala.

"History of the 509th Bomb Group, Roswell, New Mexico" (microfilm). Air Force Archives, Maxwell Air Force Base, Ala.

HOGG, Ian V. and KING, J.B. *German and Allied Secret Weapons of World War II*, London: Chartwell, 1974.

HYNEK, J. Allen. *The Hynek UFO Report*. New York: Barnes & Noble Books, 1977.

———. *The UFO Experience: A Scientific Inquiry*. Chicago: Henry Regnery, 1975.

HYNEK, J. Allen and VALLEE, Jacques. *The Edge of Reality*. Chicago: Henry Regnery, 1972.

JACOBS, David M. *The UFO Controversy in America*. New York: Signet, 1975.

JUNG, Carl G. *Flying Saucers: A Modern Myth of Things Seen in the Sky*. New York: Harcourt, Brace, 1959.

KAUFMAN, L. *Perception*. New York: Oxford University Press, 1979.

KEEL, John. *Strange Creatures from Space and Time*. New York: Fawcett, 1970.

———. *UFOs: Operation Trojan Horse*. New York: G.P. Putnam's Sons, 1970.

KENDER, H. *Basic Psychology*. New York: Appleton-Century-Crofts, 1968.

KEYHOE, Donald E. *Aliens from Space*. New York: Signet, 1974.

———. *Flying Saucers from Outer Space*. Tandem, 1969.

KLASS, Philip J. *UFOs Explained*. New York: Random House, 1974.

———. "Crash of the Crashed Saucer Claim," *Skeptical Enquirer*. Vol. 10, No. 3 (Spring 1986).

———. *The Public Deceived*. Buffalo, N.Y.: Prometheus Books, 1983.

KNAACK, Marcelle. *Encyclopedia of U.S. Air Force Aircraft and Missile Systems*. Washington, D.C.: Office of Air Force History, 1988.

KRUMSHANSL, C. "Abrupt Changes in Visual Stimulation Enhance Processing of Form and Location Information." *Perception & Psychophysics*. Vol. 32 (1982): 511–523.

Library of Congress Legislative Reference Service. "Facts about UFOs." May 1966.

LOFTUS, R. *Eye-Witness Testimony.* Cambridge, Mass.: Harvard University Press, 1979.

LORE, Gordon and DENEAULT, Harold H. *Mysteries of the Skies: UFOs in Perspective.* Englewood Cliffs, N.J.: Prentice-Hall, 1968.

LORENZEN, Coral and Jim. *Flying Saucers: The Startling Evidence of the Invasion from Outer Space.* New York: Signet, 1966.

———. *Flying Saucer Occupants,* New York: Signet, 1967.

———. *Encounters with UFO Occupants.* New York: Berkley Medallion Books, 1976.

———. *Abducted!* New York: Berkley Medallion Books, 1977.

LOW, Dr. Robert J. "Letter to Lt. Col. Robert Hippler," January 27, 1967.

MACCABEE, Bruce. "Hiding the Hardware." *International UFO Reporter* (September/October 1991): 4.

———. "What the Admiral Knew." *International UFO Reporter* (November/December 1986).

———. "The Arnold Phenomenon: Part I, II, and III." *International UFO Reporter* (January/February 1995–May/June 1995).

MACK, John E. *Abduction.* New York: Charles Scribner's Sons, 1994.

"McClellan Sub-Committee Hearings," March 1958.

"McCormack Sub-Committee Briefing," August 1958.

MCDONALD, James E. "Science in Default." In *UFOs: A Scientific Debate,* ed. Carl Sagan and Thornton Page. New York: W. W. Norton and Co., 1972: 52-122.

MCDONOUGH, Thomas R. *The Search for Extraterrestrial Intelligence.* New York: Wiley & Sons, 1987.

MCKELVEY, S. and KERR, N. "Differences in Conformity Among Friends and Strangers." *Psychological Reports.* Vol. 62 (1988): 371–378.

MENZEL, Donald H. and BOYD, Lyle G. *The World of Flying Saucers.* Garden City, N.Y.: Doubleday, 1963.

MENZEL, Donald H. and TAVES, Ernest H. *The UFO Enigma.* Garden City, New York: Doubleday, 1977.

"Meteor Lands in Utah, Lights Western Sky," *Los Angeles Times* (April 19, 1962).

MICHEL, Aime. *The Truth about Flying Saucers.* New York: Pyramid, 1967.

MILGRAM, S. "Behavioral Study of Obedience." *Journal of Abnormal Social Psychology.* Vol. 1: 371-378.

MOORE, Charles B. "The New York University Balloon Flights During Early June, 1947." Author, 1995.

MUELLER, Robert. *Air Force Bases: Volume 1, Active Air Force Bases within the United States of America on 17 September 1982.* Washington, D.C.: Office of Air Force History, 1989.

National Security Agency. Presidential Documents. Washington, D.C.: Executive Order 12356, 1982.

NICAP. *The UFO Evidence.* Washington, D.C.: NICAP, 1964.

OBERG, James. "UFO Update: UFO Buffs May Be Unwitting Pawns in an Elaborate Government Charade." *Omni.* Vol. 15, No. 11 (September 1993): 75.

OLIVE, Dick. "Most UFO's Explainable, Says Scientist." *Elmira (NY) Star-Gazette* (January 26, 1967), p. 19.

PAPAGIANNIS, Michael D. (ed) *The Search for Extraterrestrial Life: Recent Developments.* Boston: Kluwer Academic Publishers, 1985.

PEEBLES, Curtis. *The Moby Dick Project.* Washington, D.C.: Smithsonian Institution Press, 1991.

———. *Watch the Skies.* New York: Berkley Books, 1995.

PEGUES, Etta. *Aurora, Texas: The Town that Might Have Been.* Newark, Tex.: Author, 1975.

PERSINGER, Michael. "Geophysical Variables and Human Behavior: XVIII. Expected Characteristics and Local Distributions of Close UFO Reports." *Perceptual and Motor Skills.* Vol. 58 (1984): 951–959.

———. "Geophysical Variables and Behavior: IX. Expected Clinical Consequences of Close Proximity to UFO Related Luminosities." *Perceptual and Motor Skills.* Vol. 58 (1983): 259–265.

PFLOCK, Karl. *Roswell in Perspective.* Mt. Rainier, Md: FUFOR, 1994.

———. "In Defense of Roswell Reality." *HUFON Report* (Feb. 1995): 5–7.

———. "Roswell, A Cautionary Tale: Facts and Fantasies, Lessons and Legacies." In Walter H. Andrus, Jr. (ed). *MUFON 1995 International UFO Symposium Proceedings.* Sequin, Tex.: MUFON, 1990: 154–68.

———. "Roswell, The Air Force, and Us." *International UFO Reporter* (November/December 1994): 3–5, 24.

Press Conference—General Samford, Project Blue Book Files, 1952.

"Project Blue Book" (microfilm). National Archives, Washington, D.C. Rolls 1–92, 1997.

RANDLE, Kevin D. *Conspiracy of Silence*. New York: Avon Books, 1997.

———. "The Flight of the Great Airship. *True's Flying Saucers and UFOs Quarterly* (Spring 1977).

———. "Mysterious Clues Left Behind by UFOs." *Saga's UFO Annual* (Summer 1972).

———. *A History of UFO Crashes*. New York: Avon, 1995.

———. *The October Scenario*. Iowa City, Iowa: Middle Coast Publishing, 1988.

———. "The Pentagon's Secret Air War Against UFOs." *Saga* (March 1976).

———. *Project Blue Book—Exposed*. New York: Marlowe & Co., 1997.

———. *The Randle Report*. New York: M. Evans & Co., 1997.

———. *The UFO Casebook*. New York: Warner, 1989.

RANDLE, Kevin D. and CORNETT, Robert Charles. "Project Blue Book Cover-up: Pentagon Suppressed UFO Data." *UFO Report*. Vol. 2, No. 5 (Fall 1975).

RANDLE, Kevin D. and SCHMITT, Donald R. *The Truth about the UFO Crash at Roswell*. New York: Avon Books, 1994.

———. *UFO Crash at Roswell*. New York, N.Y.: Avon, 1991.

RANDLES, Jenny. *The UFO Conspiracy*. New York: Javelin, 1987.

RATCLIFF, R. and MCKOON, G. "Bias in the Priming of Object Decisions." *Journal of Experimental Psychology: Learning, Memory and Cognition*. Vol. 21, No. 3 (1995): 754–767.

"Rocket and Missile Firings," White Sands Proving Grounds, Jan–Jul 1947.

RODEGHIER, Mark. "Roswell, 1989." *International UFO Reporter* (September/October 1989): 4.

———. *UFO Reports Involving Vehicle Interference*. Chicago: CUFOS, 1981.

RODEGHIER, Mark and CHESNEY, Mark. "The Air Force Report on Roswell: An Absence of Evidence." *International UFO Reporter* (September/October 1994).

RUPPELT, Edward J. *The Report on Unidentified Flying Objects*. New York: Ace, 1956.

RUSSELL, Eric. "Phantom Balloons Over North America." *Modern Aviation* (February 1953).

SAGAN, Carl and PAGE, Thornton (eds). *UFO's: A Scientific Debate.* New York: Norton, 1974.

SANDRESON, Ivan T. "Meteorite-like Object Made a Turn in Cleveland, O. Area," *Omaha World-Herald* (December 15, 1965).

———. "Something Landed in Pennsylvania." *Fate* (March 1966).

———. *Uninvited Visitors.* New York: Cowles, 1967.

———. *Invisible Residents.* New York: World Publishing, 1970.

SAUNDERS, David and HARKINS, R. Roger. *UFOs? Yes!* New York: New American Library, 1968.

SCHAFFNER, Ron. "Roswell: A Federal Case?" *UFO Brigantia* (Summer 1989).

SCULLY, Frank. "Scully's Scrapbook." *Variety* (October 12, 1949): 61.

———. *Behind the Flying Saucers.* New York: Henry Holt, 1950.

SHEAFFER, Robert. *The UFO Verdict.* Buffalo, N.Y.: Prometheus, 1981.

SMITH, Scott. "Q & A: Len Stringfield." *UFO.* Vol. 6, No. 1 (1991): 20–24.

"The Space Men at Wright-Patterson." *UFO Update.*

Special Report No. 14, Project Blue Book, 1955.

SPENCER, John. *The UFO Encyclopedia.* New York: Avon, 1993.

SPENCER, John and EVANS, Hilary. *Phenomenon.* New York: Avon, 1988.

Status Reports, "Grudge—Blue Book, Nos. 1–12."

STEIGER, Brad. *Strangers from the Skies.* New York: Award, 1966.

———. *Project Blue Book.* New York: Ballantine, 1976.

STEIGER, Brad and STEIGER, Sherry Hanson. *The Rainbow Conspiracy.* New York: Pinnacle, 1994.

STEMLACH, L. "Does Rate of Processing Determine Ease of Target Detection?" *Journal of Experimental Human Performance.* Vol. 10, No. 1 (1984): 108–118.

STONE, Clifford E. *UFOs: Let the Evidence Speak for Itself.* Calif: Author, 1991.

———. "The U.S. Air Force's Real, Official Investigation of UFO's." Private report: Author, 1993.

STORY, Ronald D. *The Encyclopedia of UFOs.* Garden City, N.Y. Doubleday, 1980.

STRINGFIELD, Leonard H. *Situation Red: The UFO Siege!* Garden City, N.Y.: Doubleday, 1977.

——. *UFO Crash/Retrieval Syndrome: Status Report II.* Sequin, Tex.: MUFON, 1980.

——. *UFO Crash/Retrieval: Amassing the Evidence: Status Report III.* Cincinnati, Ohio: Author, 1982.

——. *UFO Crash/Retrievals: The Inner Sanctum: Status Report VI.* Cincinnati, Ohio: Author, 1991.

——. "Roswell & the X-15: UFO Basics." *MUFON UFO Journal.* No. 259 (November 1989): 3–7.

STURROCK, P.A. "UFOs—A Scientific Debate," *Science.* Vol. 180 (1973): 593.

SULLIVAN, Walter. *We Are Not Alone.* New York: Signet, 1966.

SWORDS, Michael D. (ed). *Journal of UFO Studies, New Series, Vol. 4.* Chicago: CUFOS, 1993.

Tech Bulletin, "Army Ordnance Deaprtment Guided Missile Program." Jan 1948.

Technical Report, "Unidentified Aerial Objects, Project SIGN." Feb. 1949.

Technical Report, "Unidentified Flying Objects, Project GRUDGE." August 1949.

"Two Dubuquers Spot Flying Saucer." *Dubuque Telegraph-Herald* (Iowa), (April 29, 1964).

U.S. Congress, House Committee on Armed Forces. *Unidentified Flying Objects.* Hearings, 89th Congress, 2nd Session, April 5, 1966. Washington, D.C.: U.S. Government Printing Office, 1968.

U.S. Congress Committee on Science and Astronautics. *Symposium on Unidentified Flying Objects.* July 29, 1968, Hearings, Washington, D.C.: U.S. Government Printing Office, 1968.

VALLEE, Jacques. *Anatomy of a Phenomenon.* New York: Ace, 1966.

——. *Challenge to Science.* New York: Ace, 1966.

——. *Dimensions.* New York: Ballantine, 1989.

——. *Revelations.* New York: Ballantine, 1991.

"Visitors From Venus." *Time* (January 9, 1950): 49.

WALLACH, H. *On Perception.* New York: Quadrangle, 1976.

WHEELER, David R. *The Lubbock Lights.* New York: Award Books, 1977.

WHITING, Fred. *The Roswell Events.* Mt. Rainier, Md.: FUFOR, 1993.

WILKINS, Harold T. *Flying Saucers on the Attack.* New York: Citadel, 1954.

——. *Flying Saucers Uncensored.* New York: Pyramid, 1967.

WISE, David and ROSS, Thomas B. *The Invisible Government.* New York: Vintage Books, 1964.

ZEIDMAN, Jennie. "I Remember Blue Book." *International UFO Reporter* (March/April 1991): 7.

Index

A

Abduction reports, 199–200
Air Force study, critique of, 218–19
Airship stories, 201–203
Alabama/Georgia sightings, 158–66
  experimental evidence and,
  191–93
Almirante Saldanha, 106
Alvarez, Luis, 93–94
Asch, S., 188
Autokinesis, 188

B

Baker, Robert M.L., Jr., 74–75
  on Montana movie, 84–85, 88, 89–90
  on Tremonton movie, 91, 94–95, 97
Barauna, Almiro, 106–8
Bentwaters (England), UFO sightings at,
  51–60
Biot, Jean-Baptiste, investigation of mete-
  orite fall by, 3–5
Bolides, 166, 173, 183
Boyd, Lyle (L.G.), 111
  on Tremonton movie, 94, 96

C

Campbell, J., 187–88
Case for the UFO, The (Jessup), 7
Chiles, Clarence S., 158–60, 163–66,
  180, 181, 188, 189
Chop, Al, 44–46, 51, 94
Clark, Jerry, 110, 111, 201
Condon Committee, 37–40, 49, 55, 58,
  71, 85, 105–106, 118, 120, 123,
  196
  critique of, 220–21
Conformity, UFO sightings and, 184,
  189, 191–92
Considine, Bob, 81, 83
Coren, Stanley, 185
Crash retrieval stories, 202
Czyzewski, Francis K., 7

D

Delphos (Kansas), UFO landing at,
  145–56, 214–15, 217
Diaries, as documentation, 13
Direct physical evidence of UFOs,
  128–57